AN AROMA OF LIFE

Generations of Yemenis following Jesus

DANIEL AL-YAMINI

An Aroma of Life

Publisher Information
YCA Press

For more information or to contact the author, please email info@danielalyamini.com

ISBN 979-8-9934937-1-8 (softcover)
ISBN 979-8-9934937-0-1 (hardcover)
ISBN 979-8-9934937-2-5 (eBook)
ISBN 979-8-9934937-3-2 (audio)

Cover design: Alexander Perelman
Cover photo credit: YCA Press
Artwork used by permission: YCA Press
Map of Yemen adapted from an original design by Amira Ann.
Modified and © Daniel al-Yamini, 2025.
Editorial team: Rachel Pieh Jones and Amy Sinnott
Interior design: Ben Wolf, Inc.
Publishing services provided by BelieversBookServices.com

First printing: 2025

Printed in the United States of America

I dedicate this book first and foremost to the Yemeni people, who have loved me as family. Secondly, to my parents, who lead Godly lives by example; to my lovely wife, who has always embodied faithfulness; and to my children, of whom I am immensely proud of. Finally, I dedicate this book to those with whom I have bled. I will always choose to be in the foxhole and trenches with you—you know who you are.

CONTENTS

PART III
LISTENING

Map of Yemen

Map of Yemen

SAUDI ARABIA

OMAN

Rub' Al Khālī Desert

AL-MAHRĀH

Hawf

Al-Ghaydah

Sayḥūt

Socotra

Ḥadībū

Ather

Qalansiyah

Darsa

Samha

'Abd al-Kūrī

ARABIAN SEA

Najrān

Al-Ukhdūd (archeological site)

Al- Jawf

Qabr Hūd

As-Som

Tarīm

Sayūn

Wādī Hadramawt

Ash-Shihr

Ar-Rayyān Airport

Al-Mukallā

Burūm

Shibām

Al-Qatn

Wādī Do'an

HADRAMAWT

As-Sfaal

Mayfa'ah

Bir 'Alī

Wādī Ḥajar

Ma'rib

Habbān

Shabwah

GULF OF ADEN

Mudiyyah

Lawdar

Shaqrā

Al-Bayḍā'

Zinjibār

ABYAN

Ṣa'dah

Amrān

Hajjah

Al-Maḥwīt

Ṣan'ā

Dhāmār

Yarīm

Zafār

Ad-Dāli'ah

Ibb

Lawdar

Aden

Lahjī

At-Turba

Raymah

Jiblā

Ta'izz

Al-Mukhāh

Kamarān

Al-Ḥudaydah

Al-Khawkha

TIHĀMAH

Bab al-Mandab

RED SEA

ERITREA

DJIBOUTI

ETHIOPIA

FOREWORD

An Aroma of Life: Generations of Yemenis Following Jesus is the book we've been waiting for, a long overdue spotlight on a vital chapter in global missions. It highlights one of the last geographical frontiers for the gospel and reveals how the message of Christ is reaching "the ends of the earth."

Yemen often appears in the global headlines as a breeding ground for terrorism, or as the site of one of the world's worst humanitarian crises, marked by war, religious extremism, and poverty. Yet there's another story unfolding—one of spiritual awakening, courage, and hope.

Operation World—originally authored by Patrick Johnstone, a renowned expert who has tracked global Christian demographics for over sixty years—confirms that Yemen is among the countries with the smallest known Christian presence in the world, estimated at less than 0.1% of its nearly forty million people. According to historians, Yemen is the land of the ancient South Arabian kingdom of Sheba, mentioned in the Bible (1 Kings 10:1-13; 2 Chronicles 9:1-12).

Jesus also mentioned Yemen, as *"the ends of the earth"* (Mt. 12:42; Lk. 11:31), speaking about how the Queen of Sheba, three thousand years before, traveled a long way to find the truth about King Solomon and his God.

For Jesus, it was clear. "This gospel of the kingdom will be proclaimed throughout the whole world as a testimony to all nations, and then the end will come" (Mt 24:14). He sent his followers around the world with the words: "You will receive power when the Holy Spirit has come upon you; and you will be my witnesses in Jerusalem ... and to the ends of the earth" (Acts 1:8).

This book is a powerful account of what that looks like in Yemen.

Within these pages, you'll meet modern-day truth seekers—spiritual descendants of the ancient Queen of Sheba—who are encountering Christ in profound ways. You'll learn of the many struggles, sacrifices, and breakthroughs that have brought the gospel to every province of Yemen, this last frontier ("the ends of the earth"). You will also see how the message of Christ was multiplied among the local people and is now spreading throughout the entire country of Yemen through local ambassadors of Christ. Just recently, Yemeni Christian leaders inside the country confirmed to me that now the gospel has reached every corner of Yemen with at least one known disciple of Christ in every governorate —a remarkable testament to the quiet but unstoppable movement of God.

As someone who has known Yemen deeply since the early 1990s— through frequent travel, long-term residence, and historical research—I consider this book a historic breakthrough. I am not aware of any other work that presents such a comprehensive and authentic account of the spiritual development of Yemen to date. I can verify the reported stories and accounts as both a Yemen insider and an academic historian.

Daniel al-Yamini has not only researched the facts thoroughly—he has lived this story wholeheartedly on the ground with Yemenis for over two decades. No one else would be better equipped or more insightful to write such a book. *An Aroma of Life: Generations of Yemenis following Jesus* is also the fruit of a collective effort by local Christians. It stands as a voice for the Yemeni Church—particularly the Yemeni Christian Alliance (YCA), the best advocate for the nationwide Yemeni Church—which recently became a full member of the World Evangelical Alliance.

In a land of war, tribal divisions, and political fragmentations, the body of Christ has emerged as a powerful witness for unity and a peace-promoting factor—reaching across frontlines, religious ideologies, and people groups.

Undoubtedly, *An Aroma of Life: Generations of Yemenis Following Jesus* is the work of a learned scholar and is well worth reading. Let it encourage you. Let it challenge you. Let it show you what God is doing in Yemen—in one of the most unlikely places, under the most unbearable conditions, and despite all other headlines.

May God fulfill His ancient promise through Yemen:

"… all those from Sheba will come. They shall bring gold and frankincense, and shall bring good news, the praises of the LORD" (Isaiah 60:6).

Thank you, my dear friend, for writing this wonderful book.

Matthias Schwab
Director of Middle East Development

PROLOGUE

One night the Lord spoke to Paul in a vision: "Do not be afraid; keep on speaking, do not be silent. For I am with you and no one is going to attack and harm you, because I have many people in this city."
Acts 18:9-10

God has always had people in Yemen. At times they have been afraid, attacked, and harmed. But at more times, they have continued speaking. And at all times, the Lord has been with them.

Bartholomew, one of Jesus's twelve apostles, was the first bearer of the news of the Kingdom of God to Yemen in the first century AD. Or did he bring the good news to India? Ancient Byzantine writers often called Ethiopia and Yemen "India,"[1] for reasons that are not entirely clear. And was his name Nathaniel? Bartholomew is a last name meaning "son of Tolmai." According to Coptic and Anglican Christian historians, the Bartholomew in lists of Jesus's twelve disciples in

---

1. Philip Mayerson, "A Confusion of Indias: Asian India and African India in the Byzantine Sources," *Journal of the American Oriental Society* 113, no. 2 (1993): 169–74.

Matthew, Mark, and Luke becomes Nathaniel in the list in the Gospel of John, rendering his full name Nathaniel bar Tolmai.[2]

Early Islamic sources also reference this apostolic figure. In Ibn Hishām's 9th-century Sīrah, he is referred to as "Ibn Thalmai,"[3] and it is said that he was sent to the land of al-Ḥijāz. These accounts are echoed by later Muslim historians such as Ibn Khaldūn[4] and al-Maqrīzī[5]. Remarkably, the same name appears in ancient Arabic Gospel manuscripts housed in the Vatican[6] and Leiden University Libraries[7]—specifically in poetic or rhymed prose version of the Four Gospels—Bartholomew is referred to as "Ibn Thalmai," underscoring this tradition across both Islamic and Arab Christian sources.

What most traditions do agree on is that Bartholomew at least passed through Yemen on a roundabout journey to Armenia where he was skinned alive and crucified upside down. Or, where he was flayed to death and then beheaded. In any event, he died. He is depicted in Michelangelo's Sistine Chapel painting *The Last Judgment* holding his own skin.

Other traditions propose that in 305 AD, Theognosta, an enslaved woman, brought the story of Jesus to Yemen.[8] She was reading a book when she was kidnapped from Rome, and delivered to the King of Yemen as a gift. Her name means "she who has known God" and she worked many healings and miracles. When the king himself fell ill after returning from a war, she made the sign of the cross over him. Immediately, he was healed and converted to Christianity.

While Theognasta's story highlights one early introduction of the gospel, other sources trace the spread of Christianity within Yemen to a Socotri Yemeni named Theophilus—nicknamed the "Indian," who

---

2. Justus Anglican, "Biography," August 24, n.d., http://justus.anglican.org/resources/bio/234.html.

3. Ibn Hishām, *al-Sīrah al-Nabawiyyah*, ed. al-Saqqā et al., vol. 4, p. 1027.

4. Ibn Khaldūn, *Tārīkh Ibn Khaldūn*, vol. 2, p. 150.

5. al-Maqrīzī, *Kitāb al-Khiṭaṭ wa al-Āthār*, vol. 2, p. 483.

6. *The Four Gospels in Arabic (al-Injīl al-Sharīf)*, Vat. ar. 18, Bibliotheca Apostolica Vaticana.

7. *The Four Gospels in Rhymed Arabic Prose*, Or. 3101, Leiden University Libraries.

8. Andrea Sterk, "Mission from Below: Captive Women and Conversion on the East Roman Frontiers," *Church History* 79, no. 1 (2010): 1–39.

played a key role in spreading the gospel to the islanders of what then was called Divus during the reign of Constantius II (337-61).[9] His mission led to the founding of a church in the Himyari capital of Tapharon (Zafār), located just ten kilometers southeast of Yarim, providing clear evidence of early Christian influence in the heart of Yemen.[10]

"Nestorian chronicles attribute the conversion of Najrān's inhabitants to the activities of a Najrānī merchant named Ḥannān or Ḥayyān, who had come into contact with Nestorians in Ḥīra in the time of Yazdagir I (AD 399-420). On his return he converted his family and formed a house-church."[11]

Medieval Muslim authors present yet another source of pre-Islamic Christianity in Yemen. One account comes from Wahb ibn Munabbih (d/c/AH 110-116)[12] who wrote that Bedouins captured a wandering Syrian ascetic named Fīmiyyūn and sold him in the city of Najrān. The holy man was known for his devotion to prayer and his gift of healing. The area boasted thriving sectors of palm trees, and a few records note that the people considered them sacred and maybe even worshipped the trees. "One night his master discovered him engaged in his prayers with the house filled with light, and was impressed by this evidence of his holiness."[13] Fīmiyyūn's saintly behavior impressed his Yemeni master, who inquired about his faith. Fīmiyyūn taught him Christianity, destroyed one of the sacred palm trees in Najrān, and his master became a Christian. Following his example, many other people in the region also converted. Fīmiyyūn's influence appears to have been substantial. Another story "derived from Muhammad ibn Ka'b al-Quraẓi (d.AH 119/20) and confirmed to Ibn Isḥaq by a Najrānī, attributes the initial

9. J. Spencer Trimingham, *Christianity Among the Arabs in Pre-Islamic Times* (London: Longman, 1979), 291-292.

10. Ibid.

11. *The Arabic Nestorian Chronicle of Seert*, Patr. Or. IV, 330–331, as quoted in J. Spencer Trimingham, *Christianity Among the Arabs in Pre-Islamic Times* (London: Longman, 1979), 294.

12. Trimingham, *Christianity Among the Arabs in Pre-Islamic Times*, 294.

13. Ibid.

conversion to the miracle-working of a Najrānī, ʿAbdallāh ibn Thāmir, converted by Fīmiyyūn."[14]

Najrān sits on the border of what is now Saudi Arabia and Yemen. Originally, Najrān was an independent principality. Then, it became part of Yemen. In 1934 it was annexed by Saudi Arabia. But in ancient times, nation-states did not yet exist, and governance was in the hands of kings, religious rulers, and tribal leaders. Who brought Christianity to Yemen is not as important as the reality that, though not significant in population size, Christians lived in relative peace in southern Arabia for hundreds of years, especially flourishing in Najrān.[15]

Najrān was a semi-fertile valley with a steady source of water from streams flowing down the surrounding mountains. It was also the meeting point of two trade routes, a northward route from Hijaz to the Mediterranean, and a northeasterly route crossing the desert to Wādi Dawāsir, Yamāma, Bahrain to Iraq.[16] Picture caravans of camels and traders, bearing frankincense and myrrh along these ancient spice routes from Yemen to India (the real India) and China, or toward Europe.[17] This is the foundation of the Incense Road. More than three thousand tons of incense moved along this road every year in the time of Jesus's birth.

Frankincense in Yemen, *luban* in Arabic and colloquially known as Yemeni chewing gum, comes from the Boswellia sacra tree found in Yemen, Oman, and Somalia. The resin flows like translucent amber tears from narrow incisions made by harvesters.[18] The resin hardens along the papery tree trunks and is pried off. Emirati journalist Reem al-Kamali

---

14. Ibid.
15. Ibid.
16. Ibid.
17. Elise Vernon Pearlstine, "A Brief History of Frankincense," *Lapham's Quarterly*, June 2022, https://www.laphamsquarterly.org/roundtable/brief-history-frankincense.
18. Paul Hayman, "Resins of Yemen – Frankincense, Myrrh and ... Dragon's Blood!," *Herbal Dimensions*, August 2023, https://www.herbaldimensions.com/blogs/news/resins-of-yemen.

tells the story shared by Yemenis, Omanis, and Somalis of a mythical legend regarding the origins of the Boswellia tree.[19]

Once upon a time, a young *jinn*[20] girl fell in love with a human boy. This kind of love was unacceptable, and she was punished by the jinn counsel. She would be transformed into something else, something of her own choosing. The young jinn wept at the prospect of losing her love and the looming punishment, and finally, she chose to become a tree. Immediately, she was turned into a tree, but even then her weeping did not stop. Her tears turned into musky resin as they seeped through her bark. Humans came and gathered these tears and cried for her lost love. They burned the resin, turning it into pure smoke that could heal their ailments, and soothe their own broken hearts. This is one legend of frankincense.

Christians have another story about incense, an eternal story of saints and prayer. Revelation 8:3-4 says, "And another angel came and stood at the altar with a golden censer, and he was given much incense to offer with the prayers of all the saints on the golden altar before the throne, and the smoke of the incense, with the prayers of the saints, rose before God from the hand of the angel." A letter from the Syrian Orthodox Church praised the Christians in Yemen and compared them to the incense of frankincense, much like these saintly prayers in the *Injil*[21], "Oh beautiful beloved of God; news of your true faith emanates across our land like the sweet fragrance of choice and precious perfumes. Your delightful aroma, as from a pleasing censer of incense, lingers and clings to our souls. I rejoice to hear of your endurance..."[22]

Frankincense was considered a luxury good. The emperor Nero burned an entire year's supply when his wife died. Or maybe it was his concubine. Earlier, Caesar Augustus had sent ten thousand troops to

---

19. Reem Al-Kamali, "Frankincense, the Story of a Tree That Continues to Weep for Love," *Al Arabiya*, May 2017, https://english.alarabiya.net/views/news/middle-east/2017/05/26/Frankincense-the-story-of-a-tree-that-continues-to-weep-for-love.
20. Abdul Meshiah, "The Church of Najran of Present-Day Saudi Arabia," *Shuhada-Najran*, https://shuhada-najran.com/english/.
21. The gospels
22. Meshiah, "The Church of Najran."

Yemen in search of frankincense. They failed in their quest, crushed beneath the harsh environment.

To protect the tree from thieves, harvesters developed enduring myths. It is possible that massive, fiery red snakes protected the Boswellia trees and leaped from the branches to attack outsiders. It is possible the trees only grew in areas rife with deadly contagious diseases. It is possible to imagine the mythical phoenix used branches of the frankincense tree to build its nest and burst into flame to protect the tree from invaders. It is possible the Queen of Sheba, often claimed to have come from Yemen, bore her great caravan of spices, gold, and precious stones to King Solomon through this region. It is likely the wise men who carried perfumed gifts to Jesus in the *Injil* followed the northern incense route.

By 500 AD, whether through an enslaved Roman woman working miracles, a Socotri evangelist, or through a saintly ascetic Syrian devoted to prayer, thousands of Najrāni Yemenis were devoted Christians. In 513 they were sufficiently numerous that they requested a bishop from Emperor Anastasius and were sent a man named Silvanus to lead the Christian community.[23]

Najrān also boasted a sizable Jewish population before Islam became the dominant religion, including a powerful Jewish king, Zur'ah Yusuf ibn Tuban As'ad Abi Karib, who became known as King Dhū Nuwās. Over time, regional politics embroiled Najrān in a wider conflict between Byzantium and Abyssinia. Both these empires were persecuting Jews within their regions and Dhū Nuwās retaliated by attacking Christians in Najrān.

The violence began in 521 AD with the king ordering the murder of merchants as they traveled along the Incense Road. He then destroyed the church in 523 that had been built by indigenous Christians in Zafār. Islamic historical sources, including the works of prominent Islamic exegetes, al-Ṭabarī, Ibn Kathīr, and al-Qurṭubī, describe the presence of a thriving Christian community in Najrān during this period, detailing their interactions with the Himyarite kingdom and the events that led to their persecution. The king decimated the Christian community of the

---

23. Trimingham, *Christianity Among the Arabs in Pre-Islamic Times*, 296.

coastal tribe of Ash'ar, and sent his general Sharaḥīl Dhū Yaz'an to attack Christians in the Yemeni port city, Mokha. This wave of violence escalated quickly and culminated in the Najrān massacre.[24]

At the center of this persecution stood a remarkable figure of faith and leadership: al-Ḥārith bin Ka'b bin 'Amar bin 'Ula bin Jald bin Mālik (Maḏḥij).[25] "The leader of the Christian community in Najrān at the time...was a respected ruler, a warrior who fought and won seven battles, a renowned poet, a believer from youth, an elder who was revered as a wise teacher, and the patriarch of a large tribe that even today bears his name."[26]

Al-Ḥārith's legacy was forged not only in life, but also in martyrdom. That same year, Dhū Nuwās and thousands of Himyarite troops laid siege to Najrān for six months. Against the Christian patriarch, Al-Harith's wise counsel, city leaders acquiesced to what was a false truce. As soon as Dhū Nuwās entered the city, he demanded all Christians deny Jesus or die. Islamic scholars, including Ibn Kathīr, have noted that this period saw the persecution of monotheists in the region. Some interpretations of Surah Al-Buruj (85:1-7) suggest that it may allude to these events, describing a group of believers thrown into trenches of fire for their faith. The Christians' corporate refusal launched a week of bloody brutality. Dhū Nuwās ordered al-Ḥārith beheaded. As the ninety-five-year-old man bowed his head for the sword's blade, other Christians with their hands tied behind their backs, cried out, "Peace to you with a holy kiss!" Al-Ḥārith responded, "May you, his holy disciples receive peace from the merciful Christ, Amen."

Hundreds were herded into the church, locked inside, and burned to death, including women and children who willingly walked into the church, choosing to die alongside their brethren. Others were marched into ditches that had been dug to hold their bodies, and were stabbed, beheaded, and burned. The testimonies of Islamic historians recount how events led to widespread upheaval and eventually triggered Abyssinian military intervention in Yemen. Three of the victims were a

---

24. Ibid., 298.
25. Meshiah, "The Church of Najran."
26. Ibid.

grandmother named Ruhm along with her daughter and granddaughter. As she died, Ruhm prayed, "See to the oppression of your servants and sustain your true religion in this town until the end."

The testimony of Najrāni Christians continued even in death. Three women who refused to spit on a cross and to say Jesus was just a man were dragged behind wild camels in the desert until they died. The brother of one of the women, then not a follower of Jesus, searched for her body for kilometers. Upon finding the three bodies, he gave the women a respectful burial. Years later, he was baptized as a Christian in Iraq. The persecution was so severe that even the remains of their bishop, who had passed away two years before the massacre, were cast into the fire when the church was burned.[27] About the martyrs, Dhū Nuwās said, "I wonder at a people like this, seeing how they take upon themselves torture with joy."

Ultimately, 4,252 people were slaughtered and 1,297 children from Christian families were sold into slavery. Other Islamic accounts, such as that of Ibn Isḥāq, report that as many as twenty thousand Christians were killed.[28]

News of the massacre reached the Christian Ethiopian king Kālēb Ellā Aṣbeḥā of the Aksumite Empire, who invaded and fought against Dhū Nuwās in 525.[29] Upon defeating him, Kaleb initially appointed Sumyafaʼ Ashwaʼ (Esimiphaios) as viceroy, but after a period of unrest, one of his generals, Abraha al-Ashram, seized power in 530 and declared himself ruler of Ḥimyar and Sabaʼ, and, eventually, of Ḥadramawt (Yemen).[30] Abraha ruled independently, expanding Christian influence in the region. According to al-Ṭabarī and Ibn Isḥāq, Abraha constructed a magnificent cathedral in Ṣanʿāʼ, known as *al-Qulīs*, richly adorned with mosaics and marble, with the intention of diverting pilgrimage away from the Kaaba in Mecca.[31] Christianity became the religion of

---

27. Trimingham, *Christianity Among the Arabs in Pre-Islamic Times*, 298.

28. Ibn Isḥāq, *The Life of Muhammad*, trans. Alfred Guillaume (Oxford: Oxford University Press, 1955), 17.

29. Derek Cooper, *Introduction to World Christian History* (Westmont: InterVarsity Press, 2016).

30. Trimingham, *Christianity Among the Arabs in Pre-Islamic Times*, 300.

31. al-Ṭabarī, *The History of al-Ṭabarī: The Sāsānids, the Byzantines, the Lakhmids, and*

southern Arabia for the next forty years.[32] Abraha intended to march all the way to Mecca but was defeated by an army led by the future prophet of Islam's grandfather, an event mentioned later in the Quran, in Surah Al Fīl 105:1-5. These ongoing battles between East and West, Byzantium and Abyssinia, with Yemen caught in the middle, weakened the religious fervor of the tribespeople and ultimately destroyed the Christian leadership infrastructure of churches, bishops, convents, and monasteries.

Forty-seven years later and 922 kilometers to the north, Mohammad was born in Mecca, the land of Najd and Hejaz (modern day Saudi Arabia). By 630 AD, Islam was rapidly becoming the regional religious powerhouse. In the seventh century, Islam poured south from Saudi Arabia, into Yemen in the form of marauding armies and peaceful traders. The remaining Najrāni Christians made a treaty with the Muslim caliphs and agreed to pay *jizya*, a tax on non-Muslims granting them protection, oversight, and the right to survive as second-class citizens. They appear to be the only group in South Arabia to form such a treaty, and though the community continued to be Christian for at least another two hundred years, eventually they were subsumed into Islam.[33]

More recently, in 1885, Scottish missionary Ion Keith-Falconer arrived in Aden, Yemen. He died of fever at the age of thirty and was buried there.[34] He was succeeded by John Cameron Young, who took leadership of the Scottish Mission. Together with his Danish friend, Pastor Olaf Johannes Hoyer from the Danish Church Mission in Arabia, they worked to establish a Christian community in Yemen.[35] Their work was deemed largely unsuccessful due to a lack of converts,

Yemen, trans. C. E. Bosworth, vol. 5 (Albany: State University of New York Press, 1999), 934–936; Ibn Ishāq, *The Life of Muhammad*, trans. Alfred Guillaume (Oxford: Oxford University Press, 1955), 21.

32. Christoph Baumer, *The Church of the East: An Illustrated History of Assyrian Christianity* (London: I. B. Tauris, 2006), 142.

33. Trimingham, *Christianity Among the Arabs in Pre-Islamic Times*, 307, n. 59.

34. Robert Sinker and I. G. N. Keith-Falconer, *Memorials of the Hon. Ion Keith-Falconer: Late Lord Almoner's Professor of Arabic in the University of Cambridge, and Missionary to the Mohammedans of Southern Arabia* (Cambridge: Deighton, Bell & Co., 1903).

35. https://www.myjacobfamily.com/favershamjacobs/olafhoyer.htm

but their respectful attitude toward Islam, cooperation with the government, and partnerships with Yemeni religious leaders provided a powerful example for others to follow.

Despite the lack of numerical success and a tragic history, a Christian remnant remains. Christians who are proudly Yemeni, who love their nation and harken back to their Christian roots, nearly two thousand years ago. They are as resilient as the ancient Najrānis, and their ambition is to know Christ and the power of his resurrection and the fellowship of sharing in his sufferings, becoming like him in his death, and so, somehow, to attain the resurrection of the dead.[36]

To appreciate the obstacles, rich heritage, and vision of the church in modern-day Yemen, it is vital to understand these deep roots Judaism and Christianity have in pre-Islamic southern Arabia. From the beginning, the story of the church in Yemen has been messy, violent, beautiful, and unstoppable.

The resilient church in Yemen began with Bartholomew's preaching and persevered through the Najrān massacre. Before being martyred, the patriarch al-Ḥārith said, "I am persuaded that, as a vine pruned at the correct time gives a good yield of fruit, God will multiply the Christian population in this city and in the whole of Himyar. Before God, I tell you: This church, which has been burned down by you, will be raised up."[37] His prediction rings true down through the centuries.

The Yemeni Church al-Ḥārith was referring to is made up of entire families from every major Yemeni tribe and continues to joyfully endure as a community, the Body of Christ. The Yemeni Church was raised up once again, not in buildings but as the vibrant people of God, following the Word of God, filled with the Spirit of God, for the glory of God.

---

36. Philippians 3:10-11, NIV
37. Meshiah, "The Church of Najran."

Today, a common Yemeni belief is that to be Yemeni is to be Muslim. But there has always been a remnant of disciples of Christ in Yemen. To be Yemeni is also to be Christian. Yemeni followers of Jesus have not converted to a foreign faith but have returned to the faith of their forefathers. This book tells the story of these Yemeni disciples of Christ still living in Yemen as they continue to bear faithful witness to Jesus and seek peace with all those they live among. They are a people who have learned the power of the perfect love that casts out fear.

This is not a book exhaustively detailing the strengths and weaknesses of a missions method or of an indigenous-led church. It is in no way prescriptive and contains only the smallest sliver of stories covering decades of desolations and consolations.

This is one perspective on a small but mighty work of God. You could line up my enemies and detractors and hear innumerable other versions, each likely containing some truth! One of the greatest gifts St. Augustine gave the church amidst all his theological writings is his book *Confessions,* in which we read about his struggles and through which he becomes one of us—a flawed human saved by grace and walking by faith. This is not my *Confessions,* but know that it is written by one of us, a flawed human saved by grace and walking by faith.

❧ I ❧
LEARNING
THE WAY IN THE WILDERNESS

Thus says the Lord,
    who makes a way in the sea,
    a path in the mighty waters,
who brings forth chariot and horse,
    army and warrior;
they lie down, they cannot rise,
    they are extinguished, quenched like a wick:
"Remember not the former things,
    nor consider the things of old.
Behold, I am doing a new thing;
    now it springs forth, do you not perceive it?
I will make a way in the wilderness
    and rivers in the desert."

Isaiah 43: 16-19

MIRACLES IN FLORIDA

I grew up on the Florida panhandle, in a fishing town, overrun by tourists in the summer but too small for its own high school. Native Americans lived here since at least 700 AD. Prehistoric mounds dating from 1100 suggest the culture emerged from Weeden Island cultures, known for their sacred and secular pottery. In 1566 a Spanish map labeled the area as "forty deaths a day." Rumors of the region being a pirate hotspot persisted, though with scant evidence.

I didn't care about that history. It was the 1980s, and I had a serious wart problem. At that time, I didn't care if we had the most pristine beaches and the most beautiful emerald water in the region. I was too focused on my warty hands to be thankful for the white beach sand gold that I grew up with. My warts might sound trivial compared to God's beautiful creation but they were a big deal to a kid in Florida. I'm not talking about one or two warts. I'm talking about more than thirty, more than forty sometimes.

Dozens of stubborn, cauliflower-like growths protruded from the skin of my hands. Counting them was an unhelpful habit that only discouraged me by their apparent miraculous multiplication. They covered both hands, like miniature jagged volcanoes. They snagged on my clothing when I got dressed, made it hard to hold a pencil at school, and turned bright red if aggravated. They were embarrassing. I hated when someone wanted to shake my hand and tried to get out of any situation requiring handshaking. I didn't like to wave at people. No way was I going to clap along to any songs at church.

I prayed for healing, head bowed, warty hands folded together like a good American Christian, and God didn't remove them.

I grew up embracing the truth of Hebrews 13:8, "Jesus Christ is the same yesterday and today and forever." I believed the God who parted the Red Sea, the God who dwelled within us by the Spirit, was also the God of the present. The same God who provided the people with manna from heaven and water from a rock was the one who would provide for me. The God who caused the walls of Jericho to fall was the protector who would stand by me throughout my life. I have believed in this God of miracles for as long as I can remember. So why didn't God heal my warts the first time I asked? Or the second time? Third time?

Where was my miracle?

Miracles can be complex. What I perceive as a frustratingly long wait, another might see as a miraculous cure when it finally comes, and you might see as serendipitous timing. Your miraculous financial windfall could appear to me as mere statistical probability. As humans, we may be skeptical of each other's miracles, but this should not lead to discouragement. Instead, we should rejoice in and be inspired by each other's miracles, allowing them to strengthen our faith.

What matters is that God is involved in the routine cares and concerns of humanity, and miracles are how some of us choose to describe that involvement. You are welcome to choose another term, but I can think of no other way to describe God's movement in my life, in the history of Yemeni Christians, or in the story of how the two became intertwined.

Miracles are also tricky because an accompanying assumption is that after a miracle occurs, life improves, peace is achieved, and health is restored. But miracles are no guarantor of future ease and happiness. In John 11, Jesus's friend Lazarus dies. Jesus goes to Lazarus's grave where he weeps and prays, and miraculously, raises Lazarus from the dead! But Lazarus did not live forever. Eventually, he died again. The miracle was temporary and one-time only. The five thousand men, along with women and children, who ate loaf after loaf of miraculously multiplied bread, were hungry again the very next morning.

In scripture, when God miraculously intervened in someone's life, it was to get their attention and to make a massive ask or entrust them with a weighty responsibility. Bushes burned without being consumed and fish swallowed men whole, then spit them up unharmed. Jewish maidens became queens. These prophets were then told to lead a nation out of slavery, preach mercy to their worst enemies, and risk their lives to save their people.

I have not seen men raised from the dead or bushes on fire without being burned to ash. But I have seen God work in ways I can only describe as miraculous, and they get my attention.

The first miracle I remember involved my warts and a girl I later married. Another involved millions of dollars. But according to my mother, one of the earliest miracles to bless my family occurred at the grocery store when I was too young to remember.

My parents, immigrants who came to the United States seeking a better life, and my older sister and I settled in Florida when I was a toddler. My mother's brother had hired my father to work for his architecture firm. They were strangers in the foreign country of the United States, and money was tight. A deal had gone poorly, affecting the company's financial standing, and they lost everything.

My mother managed a high-end clothing boutique and had organized a group sale. My mother is a gracious hostess, and she planned to serve drinks and snacks while the women shopped. It would be embarrassing to not be able to offer at least something small.

She went to the grocery store with two one-dollar bills in her pocket. The supermarket was new and holding a sale; two Cokes for a dollar. She hoped the other dollar would be enough for a bag of chips. Though eventually my father would have steady work, at this moment, those two one-dollar bills were all the cash we could spare.

My mother knew she needed to make a profit, and that to earn money, she needed to spend money on the snacks. She also knew how to listen to the still, quiet voice in her spirit. As she walked through the grocery store aisles, the voice spoke to her.

"Fill up your cart."

She looked around to see if anyone else had heard.

I don't have any money.

"Fill up your cart."

She obeyed and placed chips, produce, juice, milk, meat, and cereal into the cart. The more the food piled up, the more nervous she felt, and slightly ridiculous. What was the cashier going to say after ringing up this full cart and she handed over two dollars? Would she have to put it all back or could she leave the items at the counter and slink out of the store in silent shame, hoping no one would notice?

"Do you trust me?"

"Yes Lord," she responded, and the peace of God flooded her.

The cashier rang up each item and my mother reached into her pocket for the bills.

Suddenly, an announcement came over the intercom, "Customer number fifty-seven" (or maybe she was customer one hundred and twelve or six, it didn't matter, she was the magic number). "Your groceries are free!"

"What?" my mother said.

"You're the winner!" the cashier said. "Free groceries."

"Oh Jesús! Alabado sea el Señor! Aleluya!" She nearly grabbed the cashier's face to kiss his cheeks. She danced to where her heap of groceries sat on the conveyor belt and began to bag them, singing loudly in Spanish, and crying tears of joy.

My mom called my father, so he could come home from work to celebrate their miracle, and later she went to the Christian radio station to tell people what happened.

My parents raised me in this expectant faith-filled environment, and I don't remember ever doubting that God was real, or that God cared about and speaks to humans. Spiritual life in my family wasn't a ritualized liturgy on Sunday morning or empty routine, but a living, breathing faith that made room for miracles. More importantly, our spirituality made room for a vibrant relationship with God unhindered by cultural, geographic, or linguistic barriers.

When I was in elementary school, my family crossed another border when my father accepted two jobs which moved our family to the Canary Islands. Our church in Florida sent him and my mother as missionaries to help lead a church in the islands. A wealthy businessman also hired my father to work as an architect in his firm. At that time, it was unusual for professional work to be recognized as ministry, but in his life the two were naturally integrated.

J. Christy Wilson coined the term "tentmaking," which became broadly popularized among Christians through his 1979 book *Today's Tentmakers*. The concept is based on Acts 18, which shows Priscilla, Aquila, and Paul combining their professional skills as tentmakers with their ministry. In 1989 the Lausanne Conference in Manilla, Philippines, developed a statement on tentmaking affirming that Christians working in professions were equally involved in kingdom labor as they proclaimed Jesus cross-culturally and witnessed with their whole lives, including in the workplace. Christians have always worked in secular jobs, but until the modern tentmaking movement, "missions" was often separated as something for those specifically called to it.

A positive outcome of tentmaking is that it reinforced the idea that every Christian in every place is called to love every person and to serve their neighbor, to share the reason for the hope they have in Jesus. A negative development has been a shift into "platform" work in which the Christian promotes a professional veneer but is not trained for the work they propose to do or does not actually engage in it.

My father's architectural work in the USA and in the Canary Islands was not a platform, a cover, or an excuse. Like Priscilla and Aquila, he worked diligently to fund our lives and his ministry. In the 1980s this kind of bivocational ministry was not widely talked about in the American church, though globally, Christians have been living and serving this way since the beginning.

I was too busy living a preteen dream of adventure and wealth to think about issues like tentmaking. Thanks to my father's job, I was able to have a British private education at Wingate School. Not that we were rich, but we had come a long way from my mother dancing in stores over free groceries. My father's employer was the wealthy one. He invited my family to extravagant parties, let us splash around in his luxurious pool surrounded by tropical plants, and had a Porsche and a Rolls Royce that he let me climb into.

The Canary Islands are an autonomous community of Spain. The archipelago of seven main islands is one hundred kilometers west of the Moroccan coast. We lived on Tenerife, the largest island. Volcanoes, mountains, endless beaches, forests, and a year-round moderate climate made it the ideal location for hiking, camping, and exploring. My parents balanced their time between work, church, and family. My mother and father simply and powerfully loved Jesus, loved people, and worked hard. It was a dream childhood.

It can be easy to assume that children raised in one religious environment are automatically members of that faith. But by the time I was old enough to develop a childlike understanding of faith, my parents did not assume I was a Christian because they were—as though by genetic inheritance or family commitment. To be a member of our family was not to be a Christian by default. My parents taught me the Bible and prayed I would put my faith in Jesus. I naturally loved what they loved but have a clear memory of realizing I needed my own experience with God.

My mother taught Sunday school in the Canary Islands, and one day she told the story of Zacchaeus from Luke 19. She talked about what it meant that Zacchaeus was a sinner. How his response of joyfully welcoming Jesus, generously blessing the poor, and making restitution for what he had gained through illicit means demonstrated great faith.

Though I was young, I felt an overwhelming sense of sin. Like Zacchaeus, I was sometimes greedy, hoarded gain for myself, didn't want to give to others, looked to my own interest. It was simple, childlike faith, and I cast myself on Jesus, the one who noticed those who longed to see him, even from between the branches of trees, the one who loved sinners and ate with them in their homes. I claimed Jesus as my Savior.

After seven years in the Canary Islands, my family moved back to the United States. I didn't have any trouble adjusting to American middle school life. Soccer and tennis provided immediate communities, and the quality of Wingate's education placed me at an advanced level in the classroom.

I did have one problem. The warts had not gone away, and I was growing more and more self-conscious.

One afternoon I sat under a billowing white tent on the lawn outside our Florida church. Music streamed from speakers and families shuffled into folding chairs around me. A traveling preacher had set up a tent revival and I was the obedient son of faithfully attending parents. Meaning, I had no choice. To keep things interesting at church, sometimes I hid under the stage or removed hood ornaments from expensive Cadillacs in the parking lot. I trusted Christ but clearly needed ongoing sanctification.

I don't remember what the preacher looked like or what his message entailed. I can't recall the sound of his voice or what song was playing. All I know is that he stood up there, Florida sweat soaking through his collared shirt, and he said,

"God has given me the anointing to heal warts."

No way. Is this guy for real? Who has such a specific healing gift, and for warts?

"If anyone would like prayer to heal warts, come to the front."

I had prayed about these warts. My parents had prayed. The church had prayed. I had faith but I also had questions, what I like to think of as a healthy skepticism.

What have you got to lose?

I wasn't counting on being healed and did not have faith that could move mountains of warts. Still, the little voice was right. What did I have to lose?

I walked to the front, with a surprising number of others plagued by warts, though none with as massive an infestation as mine. The pastor prayed an undramatic, thirty-second prayer asking God to take away the warts in the name of Jesus. He said "amen" and I walked back to my folding chair with my warty hands, disappointed. It was all very anti-climactic.

At the time, I was dating my sister's best friend, Lydia. She also had an infestation of warts on her hands. After the service, I told her about the man who had prayed for me. Nothing had happened to my warts. I'd felt no zap from heaven, no tingling sensation, no urge to run and sink my hand into the nearest body of water for cleansing. Still, I figured there was no harm in praying again, together.

"Do you think it will work?" Lydia asked, staring at our hands.

I shrugged. "Can't hurt to ask."

Six days later when my alarm went off, I watched a hand reach out from my bed and hit "snooze." *That* was not my hand. I waved it in front of my face. The warts had begun to disappear from my hand and over the next few days I was privy to the progressive work of God as they all disappeared. Bright flesh-colored skin, smooth and pristine, emerged. Not one single wart remained. Every morning that week I woke eager to see what God was doing, and on the day they were all gone, I ran out to the car where Lydia waited to drive my sister and I to school.

"Look!" I shouted.

Lydia waved two hands above the steering wheel. Clear! Hers were gone, too.

Every single knobby eruption, gone. Every single black seed sprouting a new wart, gone. I rubbed my fingers across the smooth skin on my palm, the silky backs of my hands, my fingers, uninterrupted by lumps and crevices.

In that instant, the God I'd committed to became profoundly personal. I don't know how to reconcile prayers for wart-healing with prayers for world peace. I don't know why a God of miracles from raising Lazarus from the dead to cleansing a teenage boy's hands doesn't cure every case of cancer or eliminate poverty. But I do know that God is powerful, present, and personal. I know God is not hampered by my doubt or embarrassed by the smallness, or greatness, of my prayers.

A year later, I was at church again. I sat in the middle, not an overachiever, front-row kid and not a super slacker back-row kid. Services were predictable: sing songs, pass the offering plate, listen to a sermon, go home. But this Sunday, before the sermon started, the pastor left his pulpit and came down the aisle. All eyes watched him. Regular attendees knew what was about to happen. On rare occasions, before starting his sermon, the pastor would walk up to someone and speak about something personal in their life and then pray. It was brief: a five-minute conversation, prayer, and then he began his sermon. Today, he came closer and closer to me.

He stopped in front of me.

"One day," he said, "there's going to be millions of dollars flowing through your hands." My eyes widened, and I held my breath. He turned to my parents. "Make sure he gets a good education so he can steward this. The money won't belong to him. He will be stewarding the Lord's money. Watch for that."

He returned to the pulpit, finished his sermon, and we went home.

I don't know if I believed him or not. Millions of dollars? *Really?* My mother wrote it all down. I figured if that kind of thing built her up, praise God, she's built up. Figured if that got me a better education as my parents ensured I took challenging math and accounting courses, praise God. Nothing wrong with being built up or taking quality math classes.

Over two decades later, my mother showed me what she had written down.

And your son, God has gifted him. He has gifted his hands. He has skills in a way that whatever he touches will prosper, and his hands are full of gold. God will use his hands to save others. Take care of him. Take care of all your children but be careful with him. His heart is tender but strong. He is intelligent, and wisdom will be his portion.

When she showed me this journal entry, it was happening. God provided abundant resources for the ministry God had entrusted to me, and I had a responsibility to make sure they were being stewarded well.

Was it a miracle? A word of knowledge? The hand of God? Charismatic, Pentecostal, Spirit-led, anointing. Does it matter what we call these experiences? They are evidence of God, and they launched me into the adventure of expecting the unexpected.

2

FEAR IN YEMEN

Ancient Romans nicknamed Yemen "Arabia Felix," happy or blessed Arabia, perhaps because of its regions with abundant rainfall. In the late twentieth century, Christians in Yemen struggled to experience this happiness. The Najrān massacre centuries before had nearly eradicated Christianity from Yemen. The handful of surviving Yemeni Christians dreamed of living in Arabia Felix, like what Jesus promised in the Beatitudes.

Happy are the hopeless, because the kingdom of heaven is theirs.
Happy are people who grieve, because they will be made glad.
Happy are the people who are humble, because they will inherit the earth.
Happy are people who are hungry and thirsty for righteousness, because they will be fed until they are full.
Happy are the people who show mercy, because they will receive mercy.
Happy are the people who have pure hearts, because they will see God.
Happy are people who make peace because they will be called God's children.
Happy are people whose lives are harassed because they are righteous, because the kingdom of heaven is theirs.

Happy are you when people insult you and harass you and speak all kinds of false things about you because of me.
Be full of joy and be glad, because you have a great reward in heaven."[1]

But in the 1980s and 90s, instead of happiness, isolation and fear dominated Yemeni Christians' lives.

Shaadi's father, Ibrahim, had been arrested along with several others. They were probably sent to the Political Security Office. Some were tortured. Eventually, Ibrahim was executed. Most of the others arrested with him disappeared with no news of what had been done to their bodies. Shaadi wouldn't find out the details of his father's torture for decades, the electrocutions, the upside-down hanging, the deprivation of water, and being doused in freezing liquid. But what Shaadi knew immediately, the night of the arrest, was the way fear could become a physical presence.

For years, every time a police vehicle turned down their street, if a stranger pounded on the front door, or if he drove by a Toyota Hilux with a machine gun mounted to the back, memories flooded Shaadi of the armed guards, their cheeks bulging with *qat*[2], taking his father away in the middle of the night. His heart would start to race, and he felt his stomach constrict. In the future, Shaadi would cower beneath bus seats and refuse to tell people his real name. He dreamed of a different future, one free from fear.

Was such a life possible in Yemen?

The fear of that night was compounded by the fear Shaadi's mother tried, and failed, to hide four years later when they fled from his home village under cover of darkness on a stormy night. Her hands shook as she wrapped the gold she received when she married Ibrahim, a small bundle of cash, a few items of clothing, and a stack of mysterious books into a cloth and balanced it on top of her head.

---

1. Matthew 5:3-13, CEB
2. *Qat* is a leafy amphetamine commonly chewed by men and women in Yemen and the Horn of Africa.

"Yalla, yalla[3]*."* Her voice trembled as she urged Shaadi and his little sister to hurry, hurry.

Fear emanated from her body, shrouded in the black *balto* and *lithma* that allowed women to move nearly anonymously. The black robe and face veil concealed her as they darted through shadows.

The doors of the old Peugeot they scrambled into, colloquially nick-named *flying coffins,*[4] rattled as they drove over the bumpy cobblestone street to smoother pavement on the road out of the city. Once they reached the highway, they drove on sharp switchbacks, fifty-five of them, Shaadi counted, further and further from the mountains of Ibb he loved, and into the foothills overshadowed by Saber Mountain. Shaadi had never been so far away from home.

It was all enough to brand fear deep into his young body, like the branding marks his grandfather seared into his animals' hides. Joanna Burke writes, "Fear is fundamentally about the body – its fleshiness and its precariousness. Fear is felt."[5]

In a place like Yemen, it would require a miracle to get rid of such felt fear. Either you are a marginalized person or your uncle fought for the Houthis or your brother worked in Ali Abdullah Saleh's govern-ment or you lived in an al-Qaeda neighborhood or ISIS had your name on a list for reasons you didn't know or your mother touched a Bible once, or even worse, carried one when you fled your village under cover of darkness on a stormy night. You didn't know who to trust; didn't know which side people were on. Most people didn't want to be on a side; they simply wanted to survive. But survival could require taking a side, depending on what the dominant forces in one's family or neigh-borhood demanded. Yes, in Yemen, there always seemed to be a good reason to be afraid.

Other than his father's arrest, Shaadi had few memories from before the night his mother shook him and his sister from sleep and rushed them out of the house without saying goodbye to anyone. Not even to

---

3. An informal Arabic expression that means "let's go" or "hurry up."
4. Peter Crooks, *Yemen: Heartbreak & Hope* (Raleigh, NC: Lulu Press, 2013), 38.
5. Joanna Bourke, *Fear: A Cultural History*, 1st Shoemaker & Hoard ed. (Emeryville, CA: Shoemaker & Hoard, distributed by Publishers Group West, 2006).

her own father, Shaadi's grandfather, the village sheikh. Especially not to her own father.

Rumors had spread in the village that Ibrahim had become a *masīḥī*, a Christian. Many Yemenis said it would be better to be Muhamisheen, the despised outcast people. People said it was better to eat with a dog than with a Muhamisheen, and Christians were worse than that. Ibrahim had formerly worked for a British oil company, and villagers envied his training, travel, and income opportunities. A dispute arose over land, the cause of nearly eighty percent of local conflicts before the civil war broke out. To make trouble for Ibrahim in response to this land dispute, someone reported to Shaadi's grandfather that Ibrahim participated in Christian gatherings and had a pile of Bibles in his house.

Shaadi's grandfather was a hard, fundamentalist, Aloweeyen tribal leader. Aloweeyen were educated and preached and taught the Qur'an and poetry honoring the prophet Mohammad. They served as judges and were devoutly religious. Conversion was a deep betrayal of this proud, ancient lineage. Did he betray his family and turn Ibrahim over to the authorities?

Shaadi's memories of his grandfather included running among his herd of Baherie cows in the wadi in the Ibb governorate, surrounded by terraced fields of wheat, sorghum, and barley. And *qat*, always *qat*. What for centuries had been grape vineyards were now transformed into the more lucrative *qat* crop.

Qat is a leafy amphetamine chewed by ninety percent of Yemeni men and between fifty to seventy percent of women.[6] Some said it helped them forget their trouble, others said it gave them clarity of thought. No matter how it made them feel, *qat* was an opiate for the masses, and Yemenis claimed it brought a release from ever-present fear. Chewers strip leaves from the stalk and shove them into balls in their cheeks. They slowly chew and suck out the bitter juices which lead to a mild buzz. Some estimate that chewing *qat* accounts for "a million hours of wasted labor every day"[7] across Yemen.

---

6. https://www.ncbi.nlm.nih.gov/pmc/articles/PMC4412450/
7. Crooks, *Yemen: Heartbreak & Hope*, 27.

Shaadi could picture his grandfather presiding over *qat*-chewing sessions during which he resolved minor village arguments and larger conflicts by relying on his vast historical knowledge. To keep peace and maintain justice, Shaadi's grandfather issued *hukm*, rulings calling on each side of a dispute to compromise. Sometimes Shaadi's grandfather had religious questions too.

"Why don't you pray?" he would ask sharply. "Why don't you read the Quran?"

The villagers slumped their shoulders under his grandfather's hard gaze and turned away with their heads lowered. Many were illiterate or could read Quranic Arabic but didn't understand it. The poorest Middle Eastern nation, with eighty percent of the population living in poverty, Yemenis struggled to feed their families and worked such long hours that, for many, prayer and reading the scriptures weren't a priority. By the time of this writing in 2025, rather than improving, statistics grew worse. As recently as 2024, the United Nations Development Program (UNDP) found that "more than four in every five people in Yemen, nearly 83% of the population, lived in multidimensional poverty."[8]

Shaadi studied the Quran with his grandfather, who took over the role of male authority after Ibrahim's arrest. Boys sat on the floor of the mosque in long rows, each with a wooden stand holding a Quran. His grandfather made them memorize endless portions of it, and Shaadi could never recite the portions perfectly. His grandfather beat him for each failed word with a wooden stick.

"When I was your age, I had memorized the entire Quran!" All 6,236 verses, making him a *Ḥāfiẓ*,,[9] an honor to which Shaadi fostered no ambition.

Shaadi wanted to forget the beatings but didn't want to forget his grandfather's face. He loved him, even as he feared him. The other tangible thing Shaadi feared was what was inside the cloth bundle his

---

8. "Nine Years On: Economic Poverty Plunges Millions into Poverty in Yemen," *Norwegian Refugee Council*, March 26, 2024, https://www.nrc.no/news/2024/march/nine-years-on-economic-downturn-plunges-millions-into-poverty-in-yemen.
9. A title given to someone who has completely memorized the Qur'an.

mother carried on her head when they fled. The terrible books with their dark green covers and swirling golden Arabic script. Shaadi didn't know what the books contained, but he knew they had something to do with their flight, and he hated them. Or feared them. It could be hard to tell the difference in Yemen.

∾

Shaadi, his mother, and his sister settled in a small apartment in Taiz, in the southwestern highlands of Yemen. Every morning, he woke to the high-pitched voices of children shouting,

"Wahid! Itnayn! Thalathe!"[10]

Shaadi poked his head out the room's only window and watched students in school uniforms lined up on the side street below, counting out their calisthenic stretching exercises into a microphone. Shaadi stared at the bustling city, filled with the background rumble of motorcycles. Shopkeepers rolled open their stalls, revealing more objects than he'd ever seen. Mounds of chili peppers and coarsely ground spices, tools laid out on tarps, hand-woven baskets full of dried orange lentils and black-eyed peas, bananas hanging from knotted ropes.

At first, they survived on money his mother earned by selling her gold jewelry. It didn't take long for the gold to run out, and the landlord evicted the family. The three slept on the street, huddled together for warmth, using the cloth bundle as a hard pillow. For the first time in his life, Shaadi was truly hungry. Where was Allah? Wasn't God supposed to look out for them? His dreams filled with images of gooey dates, deep red watermelon, and fire-roasted chicken on a pile of rice. He ached to be back in the wadi, roaming free with his grandfather's cows, even if that life did mean occasional beatings for failing to study the Qur'an enough.

"Are you going to sell the books?" Shaadi asked his mother.

"No!" she said. "Never touch them and don't mention them again."

Shaadi's mother found work cleaning at a hospital, and she rented a small room nearby. In the village, Shaadi never saw his mother tired. She

---

10. One! Two! Three!

worked all day with the animals, then cooked and cleaned the house, fetched water from the well in buckets carried on her shoulder. The few leisure hours she had filled with visiting friends and family. Shaadi remembered her dancing at weddings and ululating with joy at the birth of new babies. In Taiz, she hadn't danced or celebrated in months.

Now, exhaustion marked her body. She came home from the hospital with a bit of stale bread and a slice of cheese, then lay down for the rest of the evening. She started coughing, and sometimes it kept her up all night, her body wracked with deep, shaking coughs.

Cut off from their village and tribal ties, Shaadi and his mother and sister now lived at the mercy of their neighbors. Tribal belonging equaled security in Yemen. "Were one looking for a single attribute that characterized tribalism in the present setting, it might well be this moral reciprocity that turns on protection."[11] Without this covering, they were vulnerable strangers with no one obligated to help them, and no place to turn for refuge.

Shaadi's mother still had the mysterious books. Sometimes she put them under the thin cushion she slept on. Sometimes she locked them in a cabinet. Sometimes she put them on the ledge over the window behind a curtain. They never stayed in one place for long, but Shaadi always knew where they were because she would glance nervously toward the last spot where she had hidden them.

Shaadi's curiosity got the best of him. While she was at work one day, he slid the cabinet away from the wall just far enough to take out the books stowed behind it. He could almost hear his grandfather's voice, cautioning him, "Whoever seeks the jinn will be chased by them." Don't go seeking trouble. But Shaadi couldn't resist.

Three books and one magazine. One book was brand new. It had a green cover and the plastic wrap around it had never been opened. The older book was the largest. The title was printed in an old Arabic script, like the *Qur'ans* his grandfather kept in the mosque, but this book was thicker. Inside the front cover was an inscription in fancy calligraphy:

Kinesat al-Lubnania.

---

11. Philip S. Khoury et al., *Tribes and State Formation in the Middle East* (Berkeley: University of California Press, 1990), 255.

Kinesa, meaning a church and *al-Lubnania* meaning Lebanese. Why would his father have these books and why would his mother keep them?

Shaadi never found another opportunity to ask. His mother's cough worsened and started producing blood on her pillow at night and on tissues during the day. She tried to hide it, but her body grew frail and bent. She stopped eating and one night, five years after they fled the village, she died.

Orphaned and away from their tribal village, Shaadi and his sister moved into the home of their landlord, a shopkeeper. Shaadi worked for him, delivering oranges or tomatoes to customers all over Taiz. In exchange, the shopkeeper housed the siblings, fed them, and paid Shaadi daily wages. He enrolled Shaadi in school and eventually trusted him enough to let him operate the cash register, something he didn't trust his own son to do.

Shaadi felt a flicker of hope that he could be happy living with the shopkeeper, working and studying.

If only Jamila didn't exist.

Jamila, the shopkeeper's petite daughter, hated Shaadi. Maybe because he was an orphan, or from another tribe. Maybe because he was poor and dependent, and she resented her father's investment in him.

Jamila didn't want Shaadi in the house and provoked and antagonized him at every opportunity. Shaadi worked long hours hauling produce for Jamila's father. When he came home for dinner, instead of meeting him with a hot plate of beans, Jamila would perch on the balcony above and dump dirty dishwater or hot tea over the ledge right when Shaadi stepped up to the door.

Shaadi had seen how useless nonresistance had been for his mother, and now, he fought back. The two disagreed on everything, and the home filled with insults.

"*Ya kalb!* You dog!" Jamila shouted.

Despite the obvious tension between them, one day the shopkeeper approached Shaadi with a proposal.

"Shaadi, you are like a son to me," he said. "We should be family, and you need to settle down. Why don't we marry my son to your sister? And you can marry my daughter, Jamila."

The prospect of marrying the woman who dumped dirty dishwater on him repulsed Shaadi. But then he thought about his sister. She had no prospects, and he had nothing to offer a suitor. There was no gold, no money, no blood connections. At least this way, she would have a roof over her head and food, hopefully children. Shaadi reluctantly agreed.

Jamila was as horrified as Shaadi had been and protested vehemently to her father.

"I hate Shaadi," she said. "He's an orphan and has no *'uṣūl*.[12] I even heard his father was a *masīḥī*." She almost spit as she said the word. She didn't know what it meant, but she heard people who were *masīḥī* made cross signs with their hands and prayed in strange, probably sinful, ways. Not like Muslims.

"*Masīḥī* or not, he has never stolen, lied, or cheated in the shop. He has good character."

"I hate him." She cried and shouted, and when Shaadi gave her a simple engagement ring, she gnawed on it and threw it away.

The marriage began as turbulently as Shaadi expected. Jamila threw herself diagonally across the bed and refused to let him sleep beside her. She spent days at her father's house. They fought, often both using their fists, or throwing things. Shaadi began to spend as much time as possible out of the house, and then he agreed to guarantee a loan for another merchant. The loan was worth half the value of the shop, and the other merchant fled without paying anything back. Shaadi failed to guarantee the loan and was thrown into prison.

Prisoners were served a miniscule amount of food. Many survived on food that visitors passed through the bars at the edge of the prison yard. Shaadi had little hope Jamila would show up and hand him bread

---

12. Family background or noble origin

through those bars and hunger gnawed at his insides. He remembered sleeping on the street, using those cursed books as pillows, dreaming of watermelon and pomegranates and roasted meat.

A hand pressed onto Shaadi's shoulder, and he looked up, startled to see an African man offering him an egg sandwich. He grabbed it and devoured it before the man could change his mind. Then he watched as the man passed sandwiches to others who hadn't received enough to eat.

"Be careful," another prisoner said to Shaadi. He gestured at the African man. "He's a *Naṣrānī*.[13] He's dangerous."

Shaadi didn't care what the word meant. He was just glad to have something to eat. He learned the man's name was Eli, and he was Ethiopian. Every day his friends came to the prison with baskets of food for Eli to distribute.

"Why are you sharing your food?" Shaadi finally asked. "You aren't even Yemeni. Why would you care about other prisoners?"

"Because of *al-Masīḥ*,"[14] Eli said.

Shaadi felt more confused. Yemenis continued to warn him against Eli. Eli continued to be merciful. Shaadi needed the food. He also needed the companionship. Eli wasn't dependent on him, wasn't beating or insulting him, wasn't using him for labor. Shaadi had nothing to offer in exchange for the food but even after Eli was released, he continued to bring food for Shaadi, until Shaadi was released.

Out of prison, Shaadi visited Eli in his home. Eli seated him in the *maglis*[15] and left to prepare coffee. As Shaadi waited, he noticed a green book on a shelf. He read the gold print on the cover. A chill rose from deep in his bones, and he dropped the book on the floor.

Shaadi liked visiting Eli, but that book was always there. Sitting on the shelf. Pulling his attention. Reminding him of the night flight, of his mother's fear, his father's absence, his grandfather's rejection. That book brought pain and division. Then why was he so drawn to it? What terrible secret could it contain? What secret could be powerful enough to destroy generations of a family?

---

13. Another word for Christian, often derogatory.
14. Christ
15. A Middle Eastern, Arab-style sitting room

Finally, his curiosity bubbled over. "What is that book, Eli?" he asked. "I have one like it, buried in the dirt." He didn't say he was afraid of it. What kind of man is afraid of a book?

Eli pulled it from the shelf. "This is the *Injil*," the New Testament. "Do you want to read it?"

Shaadi couldn't tell if the burning in him was desire or hate or fear. Maybe all of it wrapped up together. Should he read this book that had ruined his life? He wanted to, maybe he needed to.

"I won't tell anyone," Eli said. "Bring your book next week and we will read together."

The unlikely pair read the Bible together for over a year.

"What do you think about Jesus?" Eli asked one afternoon.

"He is a prophet," Shaadi said. He liked what Jesus taught but didn't know what to think beyond that.

"You need to make a decision," Eli said. "Either follow Jesus and commit your life to him or leave my house."

"What?!" How could Eli demand such a thing? Shaadi wondered if they were only friends if he believed what Eli believed. He mumbled something vague about believing Jesus was the savior of his life, enough to satisfy Eli, but Shaadi didn't understand what his own words meant. Savior of his life? Savior from what? For what? Why and how?

The overwhelming emotion of Shaadi's life had been fear. He couldn't articulate it at the time, but what he longed for was a release from the shadow of that darkness. Shaadi loved reading the Sermon on the Mount and stories about Jesus healing people and raising the dead and casting out demons and feeding thousands of people with only a bit of bread and fish. But what did that have to do with being a savior? He needed to discover and experience the promise of Isaiah 41:10, "Do not fear, for I am with you; do not be dismayed, for I am your God. I will strengthen you and help you; I will uphold you with my righteous right hand."

How could he commit to or believe in something he didn't understand? How could he love something he hadn't yet experienced?

3

THE OBEDIENCE OF GOING

If someone is raised from the dead, do they have bad breath? Does their body bounce back to its predeath state or has rigor mortis set in to some degree?

In the late 90s, while in high school, I met someone who claimed to have raised the dead in Mexico. This man's team moved to Northeastern Peru and continued their miraculous ministry. This, I had to see for myself. I spent every chance I could running through Amazon jungles, following a local church planter and these veteran American missionaries, hoping to learn everything I could from them. They were some of the hardest-working people I ever met, and they loved Peruvians. I didn't mind the adventurous parts either. I hunted caimans, peering through darkness for the bright eyes of the ten-foot-long alligator-like creatures. I watched pink Amazon dolphins frolic in the river and swam with piranhas. I feasted on catfish the size of a Peugeot.

As a close-culture member and fluent Spanish speaker, I preached the gospel and baptized people by the dozens in those rivers filled with caiman, piranhas, dolphins, and catfish. Who knew mission work could be so thrilling, that I could have so much unadulterated *fun*?

During bible school, I had been close to people who prayed for miracles as part of their ministry. I had faith for miracles but also carried a degree of skepticism and intended to explore, research, and interview people involved in the healing ministry. In Peru, I did the same thing. I brought skepticism, research, and an intent to interview those involved in every healing story I heard. I peppered people with questions about what happened before the healing, during it, and in its aftermath.

I never saw someone rise from the dead, and I never saw missing limbs regenerate spontaneously, but I talked to a dozen people making these claims, in the name of Jesus. Were they fooled? Charlatans? Did they have overactive imaginations or egos demanding human praise? Or were the stories true? I learned that wherever the Spirit moves, genuine miracles occur. And, wherever the Spirit moves, the flesh is still at work. But the flesh does not negate the miraculous. It just reminds us that we aren't yet perfected in paradise.

Once, when I preached in Mexico, I visited a rural village where a woman had recently died. This was the first time I had seen a dead body up close. The villagers covered the woman and laid her body on a table, leaving only her face exposed. I walked into the room where the woman's body lay, and prayed,

"Lord, if it be your will, raise this woman from the dead."

I didn't speak loudly, didn't make a scene, didn't call down angels and powers. But I trusted God would work if God chose to.

"May your name be glorified, in Jesus's name, Amen."

Nothing happened.

I walked out of the room and visited the family. I felt good about the experience and trusted God knew best. I wanted to be a man who obeyed God's prompts, and when I wasn't sure if the nudges I felt came from God, like in this case, I prayed in faith anyway.

It was not up to me to judge the veracity of the stories of healings but I could examine the fruit. A healthy tree cannot bear bad fruit and nor can a diseased tree bear good fruit.[1] Were lives changed in the wake of these miraculous claims? Did people repent and confess their sins, move toward forgiveness and restoration? Was the result an increase in justice, mercy, and love of neighbor? Did the people increase in the fruit of the Spirit and did they grow in humility? If the answer was "yes," and

1. Matthew 7:18

a transformed life the result, I decided the specifics didn't matter. My responsibility was to follow Jesus and obey his voice as I learned to discern it. In the end, what was important were hearts in love with Jesus and devoted to the Kingdom of God. I would get no benefit from discrediting stories of healed diseases, financial windfall, or dead children returned to their parents.

Two decades later, in a world as opposite to the Amazon rainforest as I could imagine, a Yemeni told me his son had been raised from the dead.

In April 2015, the Houthi militia began a siege of Yemen's third-largest city, Taiz. They prevented anyone from entering or leaving the city, and blocked all humanitarian aid for more than three thousand days, leading to massive, widespread suffering. Abdul Rahman, his wife, and their daughter suffered under this siege, including enduring a complicated surgical delivery of their son. They named him Murad, which means wanted, desired, and yearned for.

When Murad was one month old and while Abdul Rahman was away for work, the baby came down with meningitis. Staff at the Swedish Hospital in Taiz worked tirelessly to battle the disease in his small body, but it did no good and the baby died. His weary heart stopped during a failed medical procedure.

Abdul Rahman's wife, still recovering from the c-section and now overcome by grief, called him with the devastating news. She had wrapped the infant in the white *kafan* herself, binding him in the traditional burial cloth from head to toe, much like Jesus would have been in Joseph of Arimathea's tomb.

Abdul Rahman raged in grief as he rushed to the hospital. He alternated between praying for strength and vowing vengeance on the doctor responsible for the medical failure.

At the hospital, though, God was at work. The baby's mother couldn't tear her eyes from the body of her son and, suddenly, she noticed the slightest twitch of a tiny toe. *He moved!* The medical team swooped in and performed lifesaving procedures and within seconds, Murad's heart started beating, color flooded back into his limbs, and he gasped for breath. He lived, with no long-term damage to his brain or body.

"You should change his name," one of the doctors said to Abdul Rahman. "Call him Muntasr." Victorious and triumphant.

Was the son raised from the dead? The father and mother believe it. The son was going to be put into the dirt and is now crawling, giggling, and bringing delight to his family. There could have been a random medical fluke. There could have been supernatural intervention. Does it matter? Without the fluke or the supernatural, the boy would have been buried, dead or alive. Abdul Rahman's faith solidified and his character has changed. He is more loving toward his wife. Muntasr's mother started following Jesus, and the family stands as a living reminder of the power of a personal God.

I asked several Yemenis to interview the family multiple times, documented the story, and did my best to understand. In the end, the boy is alive and who am I to argue? On the contrary, I thank God for the miracle and, that through it, the family are now following Jesus.

Traipsing around the jungle following miracle stories and preaching the gospel in Spanish delighted me. I could easily imagine doing this work for the rest of my life.

Lydia was not so easily convinced. We weren't married yet but were heading that direction and her opinion mattered to me. Lydia embodies discernment and wisdom. I am often stubborn, pragmatic, and determined. When I was younger, especially, I would kick and kick and kick at doors until they crumbled, or until I moved on to a new door, which I kicked and kicked. I tried to make things happen, and often my logic was that if God doesn't want it, then even if I kick, the door won't open. Lydia calmly listens for God to make things clear, no kicking and no bruised toes, and then obeys.

After high school, she and I attended the same small bible school. I wanted to focus on my studies, not girls. I knew God was calling me to one of the hardest places on earth, though I didn't know where that was yet. I repeatedly told Lydia she would be better off marrying someone else. I couldn't picture taking her away from a comfortable American life to endure a mountainous village or a desert hut. My life would have no guarantees of security or peace. I had no money. My parents helped me through college by sending $100 every month, which didn't even cover groceries. I worked at The Olive Garden to cover expenses, and there was no time or cash leftover for romantic gestures or dates. Not that Lydia demanded security, peace, or romance, but a life with me would be one of trouble, hardship, and pain, and I didn't want that for her.

Which is simply to say that I didn't understand Lydia well enough, yet.

She visited Peru one summer to see what this was all about. I suspected she would realize that kind of life wasn't for her. Or maybe she would be inspired. Who knew?

She went, observed, prayed, came back, and she knew, "Peru is not the place." She didn't tell me that for years. She also didn't tell me that she knew, "Peru is not the place for Lydia *and* Daniel."

Where was the place?

~

The first year at bible school, a Palestinian man came to campus and shared where Christians face the most severe persecution. He also spoke about the 10/40 Window.

The 10/40 Window was a concept that took off among Christians in the late 1990s. In 1990 Luis Bush coined the term 10/40 Window to refer to a geographic region from ten degrees north to forty degrees north latitude across Africa and Asia which contains the world's largest populations of Muslims, Buddhists, and Hindus. The 10/40 Window highlighted where the fewest number of people loved and worshipped Jesus and where the fewest number of Christians wanted to live and serve.

This visiting speaker gave a moving call. He urged students to commit their lives to serving God in the hardest-to-reach places of the earth: the Middle East and North Africa. Lydia and I sat in the auditorium and watched as other students stood up and walked down the aisle, committing themselves to at least pray about going to these places.

I felt no stirring in my heart or spirit or body. I raised my hands to pray for those who walked forward, blessing them in the name of Jesus. But I wasn't going to the Middle East. I was going to Peru. I wasn't called to work among Muslims.

~

But . . . as much as I loved working in Peru, it didn't feel quite right. It was too easy. Other people could do this, and other people wanted to do this. What people didn't want to do was move to those harder locations, the 10/40 Window, or the countries on the World Watch List.[2] The seed had been planted in my mind, and I couldn't shake questions like: Where did no one else want to go? Where had the gospel not yet taken root? Where were generations not yet following Jesus?

I needed to spend concentrated and undistracted time with God. I wanted to discern where I should go and needed to figure out what to do about Lydia. I hadn't stopped thinking about her, even as I tried to convince her I was a bad idea for her future.

My parents had started a ministry training center in northern Mexico, just south of the Texas border. It was isolated, quiet, and felt sacred. I decided to spend a year there, fasting and praying for direction.

The training center was on Egido land, meaning local people used it for agriculture and productivity, but didn't own the land outright. It was also located in the middle of Narco country, in the wilderness of the American-Mexico border, on the Mexican side. Drug dealers regularly traversed this land but never bothered the center, and I was never consciously aware of their presence. There was no nearby city, no social media to alert us to trouble or to distract me. This was the ideal setting for a restless, seeking wanderer.

In the morning, I led a group devotional and then retreated to my room. I had no work responsibilities and spoke to almost no one. I had the Word of God, peaceful tranquility, and nothing to do for days on

---

2. The World Watch List is an annual ranking published by *Open Doors*, documenting the 50 countries where Christians face the most severe persecution for their faith. It assesses religious freedom, violence, and pressure experienced by Christian communities worldwide.

end other than seek God's will. From time to time, I would stare at the map on the back of my door and contemplate each country, waiting to feel a nudge or to hear that small whisper or to have a fly land on a specific nation.

Here is where I wish I could write about the incredible, mystical revelation I received. I would love to write a story so captivating and compelling that it would lead every reader to devote weeks to prayer and fasting simply to stir up such a profound encounter with the divine. But that's not my story. My story is practical and logical.

I pulled out the map and circled all the countries where Arabic was a primary spoken language. Twenty-two countries, across North Africa and the Middle East. Here was the tiniest of directions, not toward a nation or people but toward a language. Arabic would give me options.

I reached out to a friend and asked if he knew anyone in the Middle East. He gave me the email of a young woman who was there studying Arabic. I wrote and asked about her studies. She told me about an Arabic Institute, and I decided this could be a first place to land. Once there, I was sure that God would show me the next step.

I'd been waiting for a spiritual sign to move me, and when nothing came, I made a decision. Which I suppose is a kind of sign, it just doesn't sound as spiritual as a dream or vision. But I believe God knows me and if God didn't want me in the Middle East, he should have made it more difficult to get there.

I had no special "call" to Muslims, no warm and fuzzy love for a generic billion-sized demographic. I loved God, and the Bible says we are to go and make disciples of all nations. My default mode, all Christians' default mode, should be to *go*. Then the question becomes, should I stay? Many people do have a clear calling, but for me, the call came in allowing myself to surrender to God and follow the hints and direction that came to mind.

Theologian Frederick Buechner famously wrote about how to discover one's vocation, *"By and large a good rule for finding out is this: the kind of work God usually calls you to is the kind of work (a) that you need most to do and (b) that the world most needs to have done. ... The place God calls you to is the place where your deep gladness and the world's deep hunger meet."*[3] I was looking for that place.

∾

While I fasted and prayed and poured over the map, Lydia waited. She also, wisely, remained quiet about what she knew. Because she knew. Throughout high school and college, Lydia had seven dreams about marrying me. She didn't say a word about these dreams until after we were married and settled in the Middle East. If she had, I would have run in the opposite direction.

"God told me I'm going to marry you," makes a person look borderline insane and is an irresponsible use of *God told me*.

Lydia is not someone who stakes her life on dreams, not even seven of them. She had the dreams, thought, *okay, we will see, maybe, maybe not*, and went on with her life. She didn't claim the dreams as entitlement, tools to coerce, or warnings but took them as something to consider while she pursued a career and followed her heart. My father also seemed to understand she and I were designed for each other, and he occasionally offered Lydia encouragement to wait for me to catch up with everyone else.

Once I made the decision to move to Jordan for Arabic language school, other decisions came more easily, the first one being to marry Lydia. I had no dreams. I had no yearbook map of young women to pray through like I had done with the world map. I had the desire of my heart and years of knowing the steady, wise, adventurous spirit of this woman, and I loved her. I proposed without a ring a few weeks before leaving for Jordan. She said yes, our families said, "It is about time," and I left.

History is a strange mix of small events and earth-shattering events. Boy meets girl. Hospital staff murdered. The intersection of these events is impossible to predict, the impact of that intersection rippling out over generations in ways no one can anticipate. What would it mean for this

---

3. Frederick Buechner, *Wishful Thinking: A Seeker's ABC*, rev. and expanded ed. (San Francisco: HarperSanFrancisco, 1993), 118-119.

boy and girl, newly engaged, in southern Texas, that a gunman entered the Jibla Baptist Hospital in Yemen and murdered three American missionaries? What would it mean for people in Yemen that this boy and girl decided to study Arabic?

Chaos theory calls it the butterfly effect, one thing impacting another in infinitesimal ways, changing the trajectory of a life, or a nation. As people of faith, we call it God's plan. The proposal and the murders occurred within days of each other. The people in Texas knew nothing of the people in Yemen. The people in Yemen knew nothing of the couple in Texas.

4

SEEDS OF THE CHURCH

The blood of martyrs is the seed of the church is a commonly cited platitude when people talk about the persecuted church. The people saying this are those who are still alive, naturally. They often say it from behind a Western church pulpit in suburban America or Europe, or share it on an Instagram post or send it in an email.

These words attributed to Tertullian in his *Apologeticus* written in 197 AD, need to come with several caveats. Yes, the church will grow out of the ground watered with the blood of martyrs, but it might take a long time—decades or centuries—and it is impossible to know if it would have grown without their blood. And, maybe. It is also possible that the blood of martyrs causes other believers to hide, separate, flee, or abandon faith. Children of martyrs might reject Jesus. Wives or husbands might sink into depression. And sure, as long as it is *someone else's* blood, over there on the other side of the planet. Or yes, the church will grow out of this, but we must be wary of glorifying death while neglecting to care for those who survive and live in ongoing pain and persecution. To some, it is easier to go out in a blaze of glory than to slog through endless days of sorrow and challenge and still cling to faith. A martyr's death means dying once, and in Yemen, it can be easier to die once than to live daily the way Jesus instructed Christians to live. Only by God's grace and the power of the Holy Spirit can anyone die to self every single day.

This idea of blood birthing movements might not even be true statistically. Researcher Justin Long documented cases of martyrdom and tracked the growth of the church. He found that "across 221 nations and territories, Operation World's tally of church growth does not strongly correlate with Pew Research Center's tally of government and social persecution."[1]

The cliché phrase is simplistic and serves its purpose, intending to inspire. But the reality is more complicated. What nudges outsiders toward Christ when a Christian is killed for their faith is not *that* they died, but how, and how they lived previously. Did they live a moral and upright life, exemplified by loving God and loving neighbor, and still, someone killed them? Did they model the love of Jesus in their families and work and character before they died with Jesus? The church grows out of the seeds of a life lived with Jesus too.

Shaadi was taking a second wife; Jamila knew it. He had stopped fighting so much with her, and mostly responded to her insults with silence, but he left the house every Friday with his hair well-combed and wearing his best shirt. He even used a splash of his precious cologne. Fridays were when husbands and wives visited family and spent time together. Or when men went to the mosque to pray. She knew he wasn't going to pray, and the only other reason he would abandon her and their sons on the weekend was for another woman.

Jamila didn't exactly want Shaadi to stay home with her but how dare he make a show of seeing another woman? How dare he refuse to tell her where he was going?

Jamila became pregnant again and developed a high fever she couldn't shake. One Friday afternoon, after being gone most of the day,

1. Morgan Lee, "Sorry, Tertullian," *Christianity Today*, December 4, 2014, https://www.christianitytoday.com/2014/12/sorry-tertullian/.

Shaadi barged through their front door with a trail of foreigners behind him.

"They are here to pray for you," Shaadi said. He didn't explain how he knew them, what they were saying as they spoke in other languages, or what he meant by "pray for you." But before Jamila fully comprehended the situation, she found herself sitting in the middle of the room, with the foreigners forming a circle around her.

Someone reached out a hand and placed it on her shoulder and started speaking. The others closed their eyes and nodded from time to time. Were they performing a magic ritual? As abruptly as the gathering began, it ended. Someone said, "*Ameen*," a word Jamila understood. They opened their eyes and walked out.

That night, her fever broke, and with her newfound energy, Jamila yelled at Shaadi.

"Which one of those women are you chasing? You don't love me and never loved me and now you hate me enough to take another wife! There is not enough money for one wife!"

To her surprise, rather than angry, Shaadi looked frightened. He inhaled, long and slow.

"I have to tell you something," he said. "I go to meetings on Friday."

"With these foreigners?"

He nodded. "We read the *Injil*."

Shaadi told Jamila, finally, about his father and why his family had fled all those years ago. He told her about the terrifying green book with gold lettering and about Eli. He showed her the Bible he kept hidden beneath a cushion in their room. Eli had introduced him to a group of Christians who gathered on Fridays at the clinic to worship. That was where he went every week. He told her he was afraid she would turn him in, that he would end up like his father, betrayed by the people closest to him.

Jamila tried to process his story. This was not what she expected. Maybe it was worse. Christians. Bible. Betrayal. She saw true fear in Shaadi's eyes and felt, for the first time in their marriage, that he was being honest with her and showing his true self, his vulnerable self.

"Will you come with me to the meeting?" Shaadi asked.

Jamila surprised herself by saying yes. She wanted to learn more about these people who prayed away her fever and who drew in her husband, despite his fear.

Shaadi felt a mixture of relief and anxiety now that Jamila knew. He didn't have to hide anymore, but what would she think about Jesus? About Christians? His fear wasn't unfounded, and some of the foreigners were afraid too.

A teacher leaves an inheritance to their students. While Shaadi received many spiritual treasures from those who discipled him, he also inherited fear, distrust, and separation from some of his spiritual teachers. Shaadi said, years later, "If a father tells his son every day, 'don't go out the door, the dog is going to eat you! The boogeyman is out there!' the son becomes afraid."

In his experience, foreigners came to bring Christianity to a place it hadn't yet taken root, and what they brought was beautiful. But in many cases, it was incomplete; it lacked courage rooted in faith and trust in God. He noted that most expatriates required Yemenis to make appointments with them and spoke in cryptic terms. If another Christian experienced trouble or persecution, the others often hunkered down in their homes rather than rushing to help.

Many of these foreigners and Yemenis would claim they were not fearful but wise. There is a fine line separating the two, however, and wisdom provides a lovely spiritual façade to place over fear when Christians fail to examine their hearts and motives. One way to perform this examination is to look at the fruit. Are new believers afraid, like Shaadi? Do they struggle to trust one another? How are they miming what they see in those that first discipled them?

Jamila started to join Shaadi every Friday. At first, she simply watched as people prayed, read the Bible, sang songs, and shared a loaf of bread and small plastic cups of grape juice. She was surprised to see people from all over the world, including women who didn't cover their hair. They greeted her with warm hugs, which made Jamila cry. Her mother died when Jamila was young, and her father raised her well but had never been physically affectionate. The gentle touch on her body poked at a hardness in her heart.

"There are angels here," she told Shaadi, and she committed to follow Jesus faster and with fewer doubts than Shaadi had. Services were mostly in English, and the few foreigners who spoke Arabic didn't speak it well enough to answer Shaadi's lingering questions.

One week someone read from the *Injil*: "For by grace you have been saved through faith. And this is not your own doing; it is the gift of God, not a result of works, so that no one may boast."[2]

Shaadi remembered the lessons his grandfather taught him and the beatings he received if he didn't memorize the assigned Quran passage or if he missed prayers. No matter how well he performed or how hard he worked, his grandfather reminded him forgiveness was not guaranteed.

Shaadi had carried the fear of damnation along with his other fears for as long as he could remember. He had experienced little security in life and could find none in death. No guarantee that suffering on earth would not be followed by an eternity in hell.

Now, Shaadi wondered if these words from Ephesians could be true. Could he receive God's grace based on mercy, not works? Why would God offer such a gift? How would God deal with his sin?

An internal struggle began. Christianity, as it was being described to him, was inviting. That same contrast between the stories in the Bible and those in the Qur'an, Shaadi saw between the people he met at the clinic and those in the society. There were similarities but he saw love and promise in the Bible and in the Christians.

Shaadi longed to follow Christ. He knew he would face hardships, but the Bible promised God would always be with him. Islam had never given him that guarantee. Christianity seemed too good to be true, and Shaadi feared the awful consequences of leaving Islam if it turned out to be a mistake. Leaving Islam was an unforgivable sin. If he confessed Christ as Lord and later realized he had made a mistake, the God of the Qur'an would never forgive him. He had to be sure.

Shaadi made peace with God slowly.

He loved the words of Jesus in Matthew 11:28: "Come to Me, all you who labor and are heavy laden, and I will give you rest." He wanted that rest. A rest of freedom from fear, doubt, and guilt. A rest that promised God would be with him through all of life, hunger, sorrow, loss, poverty. Life in Yemen could be harsh. Shaadi knew from experi-

---

2. Ephesians 2:8-9

ence that before a person could respond spiritually, their physical hunger needed to be satisfied. He needed to know that if he chose Jesus, Jesus would be with him in prison and with his wife and children if he were taken.

Some Western Christians see Christianity as a get out of hell free card, meaning the hell of eternal conscious punishment. Once they are "saved" they aren't much concerned with God in the mundane details of living. Shaadi wasn't looking for a get out of hell free card. What he needed, what was gospel good news to him and attracted him to Jesus, was this promise of Immanuel, God with us. God who was in the prison cell, in the hunger, in the tribal conflicts and coming wars, in the painful marriages. God who was with them communally. Not just with me, but with *us*.

This was a God Shaadi yearned to follow, and this was what he found in Jesus through the Bible and the guidance of the Holy Spirit.

The Southern Baptists ran a hospital in Jibla, in southwestern Yemen. The hospital was a bastion of high-quality healthcare and answered prayers over sick bodies. Foreign Christians worked alongside Yemeni Muslims, and they also gathered for worship in the chapel located on the hospital grounds.

On December 30, 2002, hospital administrator Bill Koehn attended an early morning chapel service on the compound, walked fifty meters up a slope to his home for breakfast, then returned to his office. Dr. Martha Myers and Kathy Gariety, a woman in charge of running the hospital's medical supply store, met Bill in his office for a mid-morning meeting.

While they spoke, a Yemeni man entered the hospital grounds through the front gate. He carried a bundle in his arms. Michael Francis Babbage, who was set to fly out of Yemen and return to Australia later that afternoon, wrote in his book *On the Way: An Australian Doctor in Yemen & Pakistan* that people assumed the bundle was a swaddled infant.

It was not an infant. The man brought a loaded pistol, wrapped and tucked up under his armpit, into the hospital compound.

He strode directly to the administration office, where he pretended to purchase a phone card. The clerk asked him to wait while she found the card, but the man didn't wait. Instead, he pushed past her and charged through the open door of Bill's office.

Bill sat at his desk. Martha was beside him, using the phone.

The man shot Bill once in the head. He shot Martha in the head. Kathy raised an arm to protect herself and was shot first in the arm, then twice in the chest.

The gunman strode into the courtyard. Don Caswell, a pharmacist, poked his head out of his office. The shooter saw Don, who had ducked down and was crawling away beneath a bench, and shot him twice. All four of the victims were American. The gunman pointed his gun at a Filipino radiographer and a Russian pharmacy assistant but didn't pull the trigger either time.

By now, the Yemeni guards had responded. They surrounded the shooter. He threw the gun down and put his hands behind his head. While they apprehended the shooter, hospital staff burst into action and raced to help Bill, Martha, Kathy, and Don. Two loaded Don onto a stretcher and carried him to an operating theater. They had to pass Bill's office and could see Bill with his head thrown back, Martha on the floor, and Kathy tipping out of her chair in a half-kneeling position. No one was moving.

Someone called Bill's wife, Martie, who sprinted from home to be with her dying husband as he took his final breaths. Someone else wheeled Martha and Kathy into operating theaters. Martha died before arriving, and Kathy didn't survive the early stages of surgery. Within fifteen minutes of the shooting, all three were gone.

Only Don Caswell survived.

According to one report, the terrorist's aim was to eliminate the threat to Islam that he perceived Martha Myers to be. Myers, who had lived in Jibla nearly a quarter century, had provided medical care to the man's wife eighteen months earlier and his wife had been touched by Myers' gracious and effective care. He saw this as a threat that needed to be removed to "cleanse his religion and get closer to Allah."[3] He believed employees were converting Muslims to Christianity and sterilizing women.

Hundreds of Yemenis watched the funerals for Myers and Koehn (who wanted to be buried in Yemen) through the hospital fence, many of them in tears. Muslim parents named their children Martha, Kathy, and Bill in loving memory. The remaining foreign hospital staff, who willingly returned after a brief respite to receive counseling, received an outpouring of support from the Yemeni and international community. This attention surely blessed them, but also drew the attention of those who wanted Christians out of Yemen and resulted in an increasingly tense security crackdown on local and foreign Christians.

After the Jibla Hospital massacre, the foreign missionaries modeled more courage than they had before. They stepped out from behind the tall fence surrounding the hospital, literally walking into the streets to talk about forgiveness with Yemenis. They were required to have more security but didn't let that hinder their spiritual conversations. They brought Yemeni Christians together, and some Yemenis declared new faith in Jesus after watching the response of the Baptists.

Shaadi watched the missionaries and the Muslims and the Christian Yemenis. Sure, the foreign Christians exhibited newfound boldness, but they could leave anytime if the situation worsened. And, while some bravely stayed, many left. They could grab their navy-blue American passports or maroon French passports, pack up their house, and go home, taking resources with them and leaving behind hurting and confused locals. Shaadi understood, as anyone watching would, why foreigners left—psychological reasons, liability, grief, issues of family and children. But understanding didn't assuage the sense of abandonment. He, and the few other remaining Yemeni Christians, lacked a critical mass of people modeling how to stay even in suffering, how to thrive in community and with hope.

Shaadi couldn't fathom shedding his fear and trusting people, including other Christians, even now that Jamila stood with him in faith. It would take years, and more bloodshed, for the Yemeni church

---

3. Gregory Tomlin, "First-Person: The Difference," *Baptist Press*, January 30, 2003.

to grow into a cohesive and courageous body, but a foundation that could pass through fire was being laid.

The seeds out of which the Yemeni church would grow were being planted and watered. Not only seeds of the blood of those who died but seeds of the love shown by those who lived.

❧ 5 ❧

FULLY ALIVE

L ess than a week after the Jibla hospital shooting, in January 2003, I landed in Amman, Jordan. I shared a flat in Jabal-Ashrafieh, the highest urban hilltop in the city and a twenty-minute walk from the Arabic Language School, with a Korean student. After the 1948 war and the displacement of Palestinians from their homes, many settled in Ashrafieh, with tents strewn throughout the serpentine streets and staircases navigating the steep hills. Today, the area has developed into a vibrant Ammani neighborhood with hospitals and schools, and a diverse religious population of both Muslims and Christians.

I had no furniture, no bed, no wardrobe, and no desk. Ready for anything and anticipating a grand adventure, I was not interested in furnishing the apartment. I had no coworkers or organizational obligations. I had no wife or children yet. I only had eyes for Arabic.

My roommate kept the fridge full of kimchi,[1] which he offered me daily to make sure I ate. I never cooked at home, and after school, wandered the streets where I ate *sfiha*, a kind of Arab pizza—dough topped with minced lamb or beef, amply doused with spices and

---

1. Kimchi is a traditional Korean fermented vegetable dish, usually made with napa cabbage and radish

onions, and baked. I devoured shawarma, bread and *za'tar*,[2] and for a special treat, *maqluba*. I loved the upside-down rice and vegetable dish, especially when the cook topped it with fried almonds and onions. It would be flipped over before serving, and I often ordered it with chicken or lamb, making it an affordable and hearty meal. Then, I studied until night fell. After dark, I roamed the streets again, looking for someone to practice Arabic with. Inevitably, they fed me tea, falafel, and hummus.

Perched on narrow wooden stools, surrounded by sacks of spice and assortments of fruits and vegetables, sipping tea and bumbling through Jordanian dialect, I learned raw Arabic. In class, the teacher understood my mistakes and adapted, modified her language to dumb it down or translated my convoluted sentences into something comprehensible. But the Palestinian *shab*[3] shouting out what he was selling, "*bandora, bandora*,"[4] and the curious, scruffy kids running errands in the market couldn't be bothered with linguistic modifications. They engaged with this out-of-place foreigner naturally, colloquially, and quickly.

They also had no mercy on my ego. "Daniel!" the kids would shout, "Why is your Arabic still *mukassar?*"[5] Or they would compare me to a student who arrived just two weeks ago. "Daniel, your Arabic is so much better than his!" Their comments made me laugh. Yes, my Arabic was terrible in the beginning. And yes, it was so much better than someone just two weeks in. I *had* been working hard, *shukran*.[6] Slowly, slowly, my ears grew attuned to the melody of the most beautiful language in the world.

People tend to think the goal of studying a language is fluency, an admirable goal. But language learning is really about relationships. Relationships with native speakers, with oneself, with God, and with the language. If the goal is exclusively grammatical correctness, one could

---

2. Za'atar is a Middle Eastern spice blend made from dried thyme, sumac, sesame seeds, and sometimes other herbs like oregano or marjoram.
3. Young man
4. Tomatoes! Tomatoes!
5. Broken
6. Thank you

study Modern Standard Arabic from books, memorize grammar rules and apply them in the most accurate way.

The fun part of learning a language, though, is the human element. Poetry, folk tales, tribal history, body gestures, and facial movements are all important aspects of a language. Can you say *no* without speaking a word? Do you know all the words for camel? The different types of *qat* and coffee and regions where they are grown? Can you identify the different tribes, their dialects and folklore?

These aren't subjects taught in the classroom. Learning Arabic requires street conversations and football and vats of tea. It requires humility, even humiliation, and a willingness to laugh and be laughed at. Learning a language puts the learner at the mercy of native speakers who choose what to teach, and how, and how far to let the foreigner inside. Learning a language builds perseverance and faith, and it leaves the learner feeling exposed and vulnerable, prideful or envious.

I attacked Arabic with a vigor matched by the endless patience vendors, church members, and neighbors demonstrated toward me. What I lacked in methodological training, I made up for in intensity. Even class felt like a competition, against myself, against the other students, against an invisible timeline toward the day when I would feel less clueless, less overwhelmed.

Language learning is always an exercise of character, an opportunity for spiritual growth. The more Arabic I learned, the more spiritual refinement occurred in my spirit and the more I was convinced this was a part of the world I wanted to commit to.

Was Lydia ready for this?

I returned to Florida at the end of December 2003. Lydia and I got married in early January, and within ten days, we were in Jordan together. We had $1,000 a month, donated from our church in the USA to cover rent, language school for two, food, and travel. Every few months we had a break and took those opportunities to renew our visa and to explore Jordan and the countries nearby: Iraq, Syria, Lebanon, and Egypt.

Where should we settle? We sensed Jordan wasn't the place, not any more than Peru had been the place.

That summer, we returned to the United States and itinerated, missionary-speak for going to a different church every weekend to spin a compelling story of God at work internationally, gather vital prayer support, and to beg for funding. It was draining and far from what we wanted to do. We wanted to be with family and enjoy the beach in solitude, not burn ourselves out trying to please an American Evangelical audience that often struggled to understand our context. Our hearts were not there; they were rooted in the Middle East already. I realized I needed a job that would pay a salary and not be dependent on the spiritual or emotional whims of Christians on the other side of the planet.

In India in the 1700s, William and Dorothy Carey lived under William's conviction that cross-cultural workers should aim to be self-supporting. He wrote to England that underlying this conviction was his hope that "money raised at home be used to start new endeavors."[7] Hudson Taylor had conflict with his supporting churches and wasted countless hours and money on ships traveling between England and China attempting to persuade these churches that he understood the situation in China better than they did. This led him to develop the conviction that ministry needed to be field-led and workers needed to disengage as much as possible from their home churches, to be more fully engaged without distraction in the local work.[8] Lydia and I were in good company, though our decision to live without a traditional missionary organizational affiliation rendered us confusing to more traditionally minded Christians.

We returned to Jordan to finish our Arabic studies, determined to find work upon graduating. One afternoon the director invited us to a prayer group.

"We're praying for Yemen," he said. "You should come and pray with us."

I wasn't about to be the lazy heathen student ignoring the request of

---

7.   Timothy George, *Faithful Witness: The Life and Mission of William Carey* (Birmingham, AL: New Hope, 1991), 106.

8.   Joseph Cumming, *Field Governance*, unpublished draft, 56.

his school director. Of course, I went to the meeting. I had not thought about visiting Yemen. I knew next to nothing about the culture or people. I did know Yemen was what Western Christians called a Wild West, backward type of country. That intrigued me. Hard? Very few people wanted to go there? Almost no Christian presence? Sign me up.

Lydia and I visited Yemen shortly after the prayer meeting. We had a single contact in the country and started our month-long exploratory trip in the north, in Sana'a, one of the highest capital cities in the world, at 7,500 feet. A local legend claimed the mountains surrounding Sana'a's plain had flown there from Sinai in shock after Moses asked to see God's face.[9] Each contact we made connected us with someone else, and we traveled from Hajjah to the Saudi border town Abs, from the west coast of Hudaydah down to Taiz.

Rural Yemen was the stereotypical Arabia of the Western imagination. Men slung AK-47s over their shoulders and sauntered through dusty market streets. Most rural homes had weapons—daggers, rifles, rocket-propelled grenades—almost as décor, and people spent afternoons chewing *qat* and discussing the daily news. Men wore traditional ma'awaz, wrap-around skirts ideal for Yemen's hot climate, and the *mashadah,* a headscarf similar to the keffiyeh worn in other parts of the Arab world. Eventually, I started to distinguish someone's region by how they wore the *mashadah or* the color and fabric of the *ma'awaz.* We definitely noticed what we thought at the time was a local weapon openly on display, the *janbiyya.*

This traditional Yemeni dagger is notable for its distinctive short, curved blade and ornate handle that features decorative patterns. The blade is usually made of steel, and the handle can be crafted from various materials including wood, horn, or even embellished with precious metals and stones for higher status or ceremonial versions. The sheath is decorated as well and made to fit the curve of the blade perfectly.

We learned it was not actually used as a weapon, but men wear the *janbiyya* at the front of their waistband as a cultural symbol of

9.   Tim Mackintosh-Smith, *Yemen: The Unknown Arabia*, illus. Martin Yeoman (New York: Overlook Press, 2014), 10.

manhood, honor, and social status. Years later, I would get a good laugh out of watching a video recording of one of Yemen's prayer warriors. He wore a huge *janbiyya* around his waist, the sheath, a bright grass green and tucked into a massive golden belt with the curved blade tip jutting out at his side. His head was wrapped in a white turban and he wore a white kaftan robe and a black tweed suitcoat. He rested his hands on the knife while he spoke with passion about the power of praying Jesus's name.

Women wore black *baltos*, a floor-length robe also known as an *abaya*, and black face veils. Some wore black gloves and black stockings as well. The rich scent of jasmine and frankincense followed them as they walked, wafting out from the robes or from *fool*, strings of jasmine women wore around their necks on their way to a wedding or other special occasion.

In villages, we observed women who bore the brunt of hard labor to feed their families and maintain clean homes. They walked kilometers to find firewood, carrying it home in bundles balanced on their heads. Then they walked to water wells, filled containers, and hauled them home.

The villages we visited were tucked in the crevices of rugged mountains and dry riverbeds cut through stone valleys. Camel trains traversed the land, the lumbering beasts nearly as tall as the spreading acacia trees they walked past. Mosques were ubiquitous, even in the tiniest villages a minaret pierced the sky. But there was no indigenous thriving church at the time that I knew about.

From the villages, Lydia and I traveled back to Sana'a, a city embodying much of what we would come to love about Yemen. One of the oldest continuously occupied cities in the world, it was declared a UNESCO heritage site in 1986. The architecture of multistory buildings made of mudbrick or rammed earth and burnt brick with ornate latticed windows resembles a Hansel and Gretel-like gingerbread house. Intricately carved wooden doors, stained glass, and minarets poking up in every neighborhood contribute to the city's striking appearance. The streets are narrow and winding, intentionally designed to shade citizens from the harsh sun and to protect against invasion. Now, they give the city a magical medieval aura. Sana'a's great mosque was built during the lifetime of the prophet Mohammad. Walking in the history of Sana'a and gazing at the remains of the Al-Qalis church building made me consider all the people who had lived and walked here before, and I couldn't help but wonder how many of them had experienced full life.

St. Irenaeus of Lyon said, in the first century, "A person fully alive is the glory of God." I felt fully alive in Yemen. Yemen was not a safe country. It wasn't officially at war in 2004, but it wasn't entirely peaceful either. Ali Abdullah Saleh had been President since North and South Yemen united in 1990 and had been president of the North since 1978. Starting in June 2004, Saleh began arresting Houthis aligned with Hussein Badreddin al-Houthi after he had led a revolt against the president. Al-Houthi had been killed that September, shortly before our visit.

No, Yemen was not safe in the eyes of the world. But God did not promise safety and we were not seeking safety. God promised presence, comfort, and the power of the Holy Spirit. God promised to be with us to the very ends of the earth. How many Yemenis had never heard these precious words? How many Yemenis longed to feel fully alive in the presence of a tender, loving God made known in Jesus and embodied in Jesus's followers?

Feeling fully alive was not about guaranteed safety, comfort, or even life and breath, but about jumping into experiences with my whole being, risks and all, with the hope of being a blessing. I was ready to leap.

I was under no illusion that we would be the catalyst of a movement of faith. Throughout our trip we'd heard the story of the Jibla Hospital massacre over and over, as brothers and sisters were still processing their grief, doubts, and fears. Studying Arabic had only further impressed me with my weaknesses as an imperfect human being. But I also knew my life was not my own. I knew I didn't want white picket fences or financial security and the deceit of an imaginary comfortable life free of challenge, devoid of adventure, and empty of purpose.

Lydia and I didn't share our impressions of Yemen until the end of the month-long trip, so as not to influence the other. With three days remaining in the country, I turned to my wife of less than a year. We'd been around the world together already, through Peruvian rain forests and Mexican drug cartel territory and in Damascus markets of Syria. We'd visited the old city in Jerusalem. We spent our honeymoon at Arabic language school in Jordan, and now we were plodding through the stone streets of ancient Sana'a in backwater Yemen.

"I like Yemen, and I sense God calling us to move here," I said.

Lydia laughed. "I knew we were moving here in the first week. I've been waiting for you to say something."

A language institute in Taiz hired me. My contract allowed a six-month transition period in which I worked to turn my Jordanian Arabic into Yemeni dialect, followed by six months of teaching English since the school was short on teachers. Lydia would continue to study Arabic. By April 2005, we were living in Taiz.

THREE IN ONE: DISCOVERING THE GOD WHO IS LOVE

It was the early 1990s, and Jamil had a love-hate relationship with media. He loved listening to the radio and watching television with his family. He loved that his parents asked him to translate programs from Modern Standard Arabic into their Yemeni dialect, and he loved how easily the languages flowed on his tongue. But when a radio program said that Jesus was the Son of God, rage exploded out of him.

Jamil slammed his hand down on the radio to switch it off and kicked it across the *maglis*. *Jesus was just a prophet, like all the other prophets.* Associating Jesus, or anyone, with God was an unforgivable sin. And the suggestion that God had a son! As though God procreated like a human. The mere thought disgusted him. Jamil found two ice cream sticks, formed them into the shape of a cross on the floor, and stomped on it over and over.

"You're quite the *muta'wa'a*," his brother said.

Jamil wasn't a fundamentalist, but he was loyal to Islam, like every Yemeni he knew. He had been raised to despise anyone who wasn't a Muslim, especially a Naṣrānī and Yahoodi, Christians and Jews. He didn't know any, but if he did, he knew he would hate them.

But then, Jamil had an unsettling dream.

There was an earthquake and people were running, frantic and wild, terrified. He understood it was Judgment Day. A thin man wearing a white robe stood in front of Jamil and he somehow knew this was Jesus.

"What can you do?" Jesus asked.

"I can't do anything," Jamil said. "What can you do?"

"Everything."

"Can you make time go backward?"

There was a clock in the dream and Jamil watched as Jesus turned time backward.

Jamil's fury at Christians instantly dissipated and he became fascinated by Jesus. Whoever he was and whatever he had done, Jamil decided, Jesus was the Messiah. Did that make him a Christian? If he was a Christian, how should he pray?

Jamil made another cross, this one out of wood, and knelt before it in the *maglis*. His father saw him, and started to beat him, punctuating his blows with words. "You're a Muslim! Stop this foolishness."

Jamil tried and failed to put aside thoughts about Jesus. Even without a Bible or any specific knowledge, he decided he was a Christian, and that he must be the only one in all Yemen.

Jamil kept these ideas to himself but one day while sipping tea with a friend named Rauf, his friend said, "Look at those Muslims fighting," and pointed at a group of men shouting at each other across the street.

"Aren't *you* a Muslim?" Jamil asked.

Rauf lowered his voice. "I am a Christian. I want to learn more about it. I've been reading the *Injil*."

Jamil couldn't believe it. Maybe he wasn't alone, after all. "Do you have an *Injil*?"

"In my bag right now."

Jamil stared at Rauf's bag. The *Injil*! Right there, inches away from him.

Rauf reached into the bag and pulled out a small green book with gold lettering. "Would you like to borrow it?"

Jamil's heart pounded as he took the book and tucked it into his own bag. Was anyone watching them? Did they know what book they were talking about? What would he discover inside? It took all his patience to stay seated and finish his tea with Rauf, while his body burned to rush home and read this book that had miraculously found him.

When he was finally able to open it, Jamil fell in love with the Sermon on the Mount and the story of the Good Samaritan. This was a book of love. Love from God, love for people, even love for enemies. He had been taught to seek revenge against his enemies. Forgive them? No way. Love them and pray for them? Double no way. For weeks, he read the New Testament and met with Rauf to discuss what he was reading.

"Today is Christmas," Rauf said one afternoon at the beginning of Ramadan. In 1998 the two holidays fell in the same month.

"How do Christians celebrate Christmas?" Jamil asked.

"I don't know."

"We should go to the foreign health clinic. I bet the Christians there are having a Christmas party like in movies."

"What if someone sees us?" Rauf said. "What if someone at the clinic reports us to the government? What if they refuse to let us in or suspect we're spying on them?"

Rauf's concerns were reasonable but Jamil's hunger to know more about Jesus was stronger than his fear, and he convinced his friend to go. They walked to the clinic and knocked on the front metal gate.

When Jamil tells this story, two decades later, I can still feel the tension. Two young Yemeni men, irresistibly drawn to Jesus with no foreign intervention or direction, no Christian vouching for them, knock on a door after dark on a high spiritual holiday.

Walter Brueggemann writes in *The Journey to the Common Good*: "It turns out that the wilderness, contrary to our fear and our conventional expectations, is securely governed by God who dispatches angels of mercy at points of need to the faithful."[1] Holidays would become points of grace in the wilderness for Christians in Yemen. Holidays provided an excuse for calling, visiting and checking in on those in remote regions. Common traditions like serving *bint al-ṣaḥn*, a buttery, honey-drizzled layered bread symbolizing warmth and hospitality, and creating indigenous music would bring a sense of bonding and shared culture.

---

1. Walter Brueggemann, *Journey to the Common Good*, updated ed. (Louisville, KY: Westminster John Knox Press, 2021), xxiv.

How to consider Muslim holidays like Ramadan is personal for each believer. Some of the early believers developed a kind of Ramadan-phobia, feeling like they would be consumed by it or hunkering down and ignoring everything going on around them for the entire month, rather than engaging with their family and friends. Sometimes expatriates contributed to this, unintentionally passing on a negative attitude or the idea that Ramadan is a spiritually oppressive time for Christians —overlooking the potential for meaningful engagement even amid spiritual challenge. Ramadan *is* a spiritual time for many Muslims, and Christians are free in Christ to fast and pray during this month as they are during other times of the year. This becomes an opportunity to talk about how Jesus fasted, or to share how they experience God while fasting. Ramadan is a highly community-oriented season and an opportunity for families to spend copious amounts of time together. Today, many Yemeni Christians practice fasting throughout the entire year, have mostly gotten rid of Ramadan-phobia, and have refocused their efforts on sharing the gospel with family members during this month.

But that first Christmas, Jamil hadn't thought about any of this, he was just curious and eager. He knocked on the door and the director opened it, a startled look on his face.

"We are Christians," Jamil said. "We want to celebrate Christmas but don't know how." He shrugged, feeling nervous and a little silly.

The director invited the young men into his office to hear more of their story, then gave them each a copy of the *Injil*, and welcomed them. He took them up to the roof where there were men and women from all over the world, singing together. They didn't see any other Arabs, though. Until they met Shaadi several weeks later, the two believed themselves to be the only local Christians.

Jamil and Rauf began coming to the clinic on Fridays to participate in a weekly Christian worship service. But questions plagued them, questions neither could answer no matter how long they discussed them. None of the foreign Christians spoke Arabic well enough to explain things.

Jamil wrestled with questions as wide-ranging as how to explain the trinity to Muslims, why Mary was held in such a prominent role, how was he supposed to pray now, what was the deal with so many denominations, and what were behavioral expectations of a Christian? He wondered about contradictions he saw in Islamic apologetics, and had a persistent question about how it seemed to him that some foreigners actually encouraged Yemeni Christians to drink alcohol. He realized that when Yemeni Christians asked if they were free to drink, many of them were really asking if they were free to get drunk. Foreigners usually failed to understand this nuance and emphasized freedom in Christ. Jamil wondered if a wiser response would be a stricter teaching, considering Yemeni's contextual background. The more Jamil read the Bible, the more he gained clarity, but he also recognized his need for fellowship and other believers to help him understand even more deeply.

Jamil and Rauf finally met Shaadi at a Friday service and tried to ask him their questions. But Shaadi seemed cagey, fearful, and secretive. Although he introduced them to his wife immediately, he introduced himself as Naser. Jamil viewed everything in an idealistic manner. It never crossed his mind that Naser wasn't Shaadi's real name. For Jamil, with his eager and optimistic outlook, the concept of protecting himself or using caution wasn't at the front of his mind. For Shaadi, who had young children and a wife to consider, and who had his own baggage of losing his father because of this faith, the stakes were evident. They would learn the fine balance between trust and security over the next several years together, even as in the beginning they were both ecstatic in their private ways about meeting other Yemeni Christians.

Finally, one Friday, an Iraqi couple came to the service. Rauf and Jamil pounced on the husband with their questions and tried to memorize his answers. He explained the trinity like this,

"God the Father is like the sun high in the sky at *dhuhr*,"[2] the man explained. "It is so bright and powerful, if you stare at it, you'll go blind. It is also far away from us, and if it were any closer it would destroy us because it burns with such a great fire. We cannot come near the sun in the midday sky, and we cannot come near God the Father physically, or even look at him with our eyes, because his glory is so great it would destroy us."

God as remote and destructively powerful was easy to understand

---

2. Noon

for Yemenis from Muslim backgrounds. Jamil and Rauf nodded. They had been taught about God's absolute transcendence from infancy.

"Jesus is the light of the world," the Iraqi man went on. "The Quran says that God gave Jesus the Gospel in which was guidance and light.[3] Jesus is like the light of the sun, the Holy Spirit is like its warmth. If the heat of the sun did not reach earth, the earth would be covered with ice. As we feel the warmth of the sun, the Holy Spirit allows us to feel the presence of God. The sun, the light it shines, and the warmth it gives, cannot be separated, so God the Father, Jesus the Son, and the Holy Spirit cannot be separated."

His words resonated with Jamil's and Rauf's experiences of being drawn in by the warmth of the Holy Spirit and of learning about God by reading of Jesus's life: healings, miracles, and the way he loved everyone from women to the oppressed and the ill.

Their questions are common to people from Muslim backgrounds. The trinity, especially, is a confusing and contentious barrier for those interested in Christianity, and Christians have historically struggled to explain it. Even this illustration from Jamil's Iraqi mentor falls short, as do all human efforts to explain God.

Dr. Joseph Cumming addresses Christian and Islamic perspectives on this doctrine in his seminal dissertation, *God, Word, and Spirit: the Doctrine of the Trinity in the Qur'an and Islamic Interpretation*. He concludes that the heart of Christianity is found in the statement that God is Love and that this is necessarily a triune statement. "The very heart of Love is to give oneself for the other. When we speak of Love as existing eternally in God, free and prior to creation, we must understand that Love not as self-love, but as Love that gives self for the other, as God and God's Wisdom rejoice together in eternity. Thus, to say that God is Love is to say that God is Triune."[4]

---

3. And We sent, following in their footsteps Jesus, the son of Mary, confirming that which came before him in the Torah; and We gave him the Gospel, in which was guidance and light and confirming that which preceded it of the Torah as guidance and instruction for the righteous.
    — Saheeh International, (Al-Ma'idah) 5:46

4. Joseph Cumming, *God, Word, and Spirit: The Doctrine of the Trinity in the Qur'an and Islamic Interpretation* (PhD diss., Yale University, 2020), 425.

Whether a person approaches the doctrine of the trinity from a metaphorical, academic, theological, or allegorical perspective is not of eternal importance, and doesn't fully remove all the mystery of who God is. What matters for Yemenis is what Jamil and Rauf experienced: love, as seen in the power of God, the life of Jesus, and the tangible presence of the Spirit.

After months of growing spiritually together, including sharing their baptismal day which the friends dubbed their new birthday, Rauf moved across the country for a job. The new city, Mukalla, was ten hours away by bus, a lifetime to Jamil.

Jamil had no way of knowing the blood that would flow when he became friends with Rauf. Community is vital for Christian growth, but community also brings the possibility of pain and sorrow. I had no way of knowing the blood that would flow when I invited a European friend and his team to come to Yemen. None of us understood the way shared losses would bond us and motivate us for kingdom work.

❧ 7 ❧

LEARNING DEPENDENCE

In 2005, Lydia and I lived in Ṣalāḥ, fifteen kilometers outside downtown Taiz. I worked at a school owned by a Muslim sheikh. Foreigners—aid workers, travelers, businesspeople—came to study Arabic. Local people attended to study English. I received a small salary and our residence visa through the school, with the sheikh as my local sponsor. He didn't know that within months of hiring me, my life would be in his hands.

Lydia and I lived upstairs and our landlord lived downstairs. I upgraded my living conditions from the sleeping bag and floor mattress of my days in Ashrafieh, Jordan, but only slightly. We bought a refrigerator and used the cardboard box it came in as a table. The living room area had two cement walls that jutted out and we set the box in the middle. No couches, no *maglis*, nothing to sit on other than the cheapest quality carpet that I could find.

"A friend is coming over tomorrow," I told Lydia one afternoon. "Time to buy a cushion."

That evening we spent one thousand Yemeni riyals on four cheap, thin foam mattresses, $5.00 each. I put two on the floor to sit on and propped two against the wall, for leaning back against. One for me, one for the guest, and just like that, we had our *maglis*, our sitting area, albeit a woefully inferior one.

Historically, Arab Bedouins set up goat hair tents in which they hosted tribal leaders and distinguished elders. Guests removed their shoes and perched on low cushions, designed for comfort and outstretched legs, as these gatherings could extend for hours at a time. The *maglis* was a room intended to promote social interaction, free speech, constructive dialogue, and to mediate disputes with an aim toward reconciliation. Even today, televisions are rarely turned on in a *maglis*, as they would distract from the communal purpose of the room.

Symbols of Yemeni hospitality among the middle class or wealthy, a modern *maglis* is furnished with the best a family can afford: carpets, opulent curtains, and low mats with back cushions in an array of red, gold, and brown fabrics. Men and women often have separate sitting rooms, each with an entrance and a bathroom that is separate from the rest of the house.

Scents of coffee and incense waft throughout a *maglis* and seep into the fabrics. *Qahwa* (coffee) is brewed in the kitchen, while incense burns in a *mabkhara* set nearby in the *majlis*—the gathering space where guests are received. The steaming coffee is then offered fresh to each guest in palm-sized, handleless cups. When burning incense, Yemenis place the incense on top of the coals and the scented smoke swirls through the house, similar to how it was burned in the days of the Queen of Sheba and the frankincense trade.

We didn't own a television. We didn't own luxurious carpets or curtains. But we had our cushions, we knew how to brew coffee and tea, and we were ready to practice Arab hospitality, a gift we have yet to master to the Yemeni standard.

Other than those cushions, a stove, the fridge, and a mattress we set on the ground to sleep on, every bit of extra cash went toward our vehicle, a 1981 Land Cruiser with only four gears. We still own it, twenty years later.

We hadn't taken a vow of poverty or voluntary suffering. Voluntary suffering without purpose, vision, or meaning is foolish. But choices compound. Our choice to love people and love God brought us to Yemen. Our choice to not do traditional fundraising in the United

States brought us freedom and autonomy as well as limited resources. We sat on cement walls that formed makeshift chairs and ate off a cardboard box. Our choice to spend time on language study and learning the country meant we prioritized a vehicle over the distraction of a television.

It was a beautiful life of simplicity, clarity, and stewardship. I felt free to focus on my strengths of relationship-building and learning without being concerned about household management or building bigger barns to hold an ever-increasing hoard of worldly goods. Yemenis belong to the rich Bedouin heritage of wanderers. Owning only necessities, they are able to quickly pack up and move through the harsh landscape of the Arabian Peninsula. Even for city-dwelling, settled Yemenis, the urge to possess is less important than the delight found in relationships and community. Many Yemenis sleep together in empty rooms with a dozen small mattresses spread across the floor, and spend their day chewing *qat* while debating and arguing over the day's news. The Bedouin example challenged me to find contentment in Christ and to be a wise steward of God's good gifts.

This early lesson of simplicity brought on by necessity through our financial limitations and modeled by the local people, showed me the learning process was going to cut deep. Not only would I be learning about this new place, but I would need to reevaluate my own ideas, ideals, and habits of life in ways that might become uncomfortable.

Yemen was safe, or not safe, depending on the context and the person asking the question. What does safe mean and how can it be guaranteed in a world of tornadoes and earthquakes, Covid and malaria, drunk drivers and school shooters? My early years in Yemen were the nation's golden years of peace. Internal political tensions raged, most of which I remained ignorant of, but the majority of Yemenis lived in peace. Their children attended school, the sick in major cities had access to basic medical care, employees received salaries, albeit meager. None of this seemed precious. None of it seemed precarious.

I didn't pretend to understand local politics, nor did I discuss politics or get involved in politics. Politics never led someone to Jesus and, more often, relationships are broken over political views that hold no eternal purpose. My role was to stay out of the way in that regard, to not become part of those problems, and to not become a problem myself. I could be empathetic toward friends who suffered, but my vision was to make every attempt to live at peace with all, as far as it depended on me.

People who have lived in places like Yemen, or Syria, or Afghanistan, or Iraq talk about safety and peace differently from people who have never left their Western security bubbles. We don't expect it or demand it, and we learn how to weigh risk. We know that we are new on the scene and have none of the necessary historical knowledge or national buy-in to engage in local politics.

Lydia and I hopped in our Land Cruiser on weekends or school breaks and drove all over Yemen. The country is stunningly beautiful, nearly untouched by foreign tourism, rugged and earthy. We walked through the old city in Sana'a, over cobblestone roads. We stood on a cliff, looking down at the wadi below on our way to Daar Al Hajar. We took countless trips to Aden as a family and played on the beach and in the crystal-clear waters. We went up Saber Mountain in Taiz and enjoyed the views on clear days and days when the fog would cover the city below us. We went as far east as we could to Mahra and luxuriated in the lush mountains of Al Hawf, so green I could imagine we were in Scottish Highlands, not southern Arabia. We stood as close as possible to the waterfalls in Ibb and Taiz and let the spray cool our faces. We picnicked along the Red Sea coast and vacationed on Socotra and roamed through city alleyways, delighted by the vibrancy of a vivacious culture.

Bread bakers slapped dough against wooden tables to knead it, vegetable sellers promised low prices, children chanted school lessons, donkeys pulled clattering wooden carts over uneven roads, and behind the cacophony was the steady hum of the call to prayer.

We didn't fool ourselves into thinking our travels were entirely safe, kidnapping of foreigners didn't begin with the war in March of 2015, or with the outbreak of the revolution in January 2011, or with the formation of Al-Qaeda in the Arabian Peninsula (AQAP) in 2009. But we didn't let fear stop us either. I don't remember feeling fear, only curiosity and a hunger to know more about this country that had so quickly captured my heart. Still, even in those golden years, there was always the risk of being in the wrong place at the wrong time. People weren't targeted specifically, that would come later. No matter what, where, or when, we were in God's hands. "The Lord brings death and makes alive; he brings down to the grave and raises up."[1]

Men carried AK-47s over their shoulders like prayer beads, and strapped daggers around their bellies. They were more for show than violence, and we would not have been the intended target anyway, which provided a sense of security, even if it was a bit naïve. Occasionally a foreigner would be kidnapped, but upon bargaining with the government, they were released. In those years, the risk was low of ending up on the next Al-Qaeda video with your head chopped off.

On October 12, 2000, Yemen caught the world's attention when a small boat pulled up alongside the USS Cole, a massive naval destroyer docked for refueling in the port of Aden. Two Yemeni men in the boat waved warmly at the American servicemen and then blew themselves up. Four hundred and fifty kilograms of C4 explosives ripped a forty-foot hole in the side of the USS Cole, right above the waterline. Seventeen American sailors were killed and nearly forty injured. Al-Qaeda eventually claimed responsibility for the attack. A number of men have been accused of being the masterminds behind the attack, including two who are still, in 2025, being held at Guantanamo Bay, Cuba by the USA. Another of the alleged planners of the attack is also accused of being behind the 9/11 attacks in New York and Washington.

While these events ushered in the "Global War on Terror," which we continued to live under in 2005, with the addition of the Afghanistan war and the Iraq war, civilian life was largely unaffected. The majority of Yemenis differentiated between governments and individuals. Large-scale operations among militaries and politicians trickled down in terms of conversation over tea and *qat* but they did not hinder our welcome by Yemeni people.

Until the Arab Spring reached Yemen in early 2011 and more widespread terrorism, until regional violence became uncontainable and foreigners became specific and desirable targets, we thrived in Yemen and learned how to recognize and respond to risk. Anna S. Hampton, an American Christian who worked in Afghanistan for years wrote,

---

1. 1 Samuel 2:6

"The risk-adverse culture of North America does not lend itself to a generation of cross-cultural staff able to be resilient and withstand extreme danger."[2] We were shedding our risk-adverse Americanness and part of that was coming to understand the geography of risk. We understood that if there is a battle between the Houthi and President Salah's forces in Saa'da, and we live in Taiz, the equivalent safety concern is that there is a shooting in New York and you live in Florida. You're fine. You're safe. Later we came to understand that even with missiles and bullets falling in our neighborhood, God was with us, and God's presence is a safe zone, even in death.

Often people ask me, why Yemen? Aren't you afraid? Especially when Lydia was pregnant with our first child, questions about our decision to stay in the region increased. Lydia delivered Esther in a neighboring country of Yemen, but both Lydia and I recognized that, of course, Yemeni women give birth in Yemen every day, even during times of upheaval, chaos, and war. For the birth of our second child, we remained in the country. Lydia delivered a baby boy in a hospital near our home in the heart of Taiz. She delivered at 10:30 a.m., and we were home by lunchtime. Yes, in answer to all of the concerns, the hospital lacked Western amenities and, yes, we felt safe. Even more importantly, we sensed God's presence, tangible through the care and kindness of our Yemeni community.

Still, questions persisted. People want to know: How have we stayed so long, and through so many trials? Risk forces us to confront our fears, hopes, expectations, and even our demands and misconceptions of God. Yemen taught me to turn toward God with a thankful heart, becoming aware of God's presence in every situation.

In those years, the largest risk to me personally was myself. Danger is different when it is broad in scope versus when it becomes targeted. The response is also different and requires dependency on local relationships. I learned this when I was thrown in jail for accidentally killing a man.

≈

2. Anna E. Hampton, *Facing Danger: A Guide through Risk* (New Prague, MN: Zendagi Press, 2016).

My boss at the time introduced me to a Yemeni businessman, the first Yemeni disciple of Jesus from a Muslim background I ever met. There was not yet a gathered indigenous church and he began to dream and envision one with me. I imagined all the ways I could contribute, serve, and bless. That's what I was in Yemen for, or at least that's what I thought I was there for.

A few months later, I drove our Land Cruiser through the Taiz streets, limping along in second gear, through the narrow streets. I had just turned a corner. Suddenly, an elderly man with a neck brace leaned forward and lurched right into the intersection in front of my truck. I couldn't swerve away and struck him directly.

There was no 911, no emergency ambulance to call, and no one wanted to help because they might be held liable for whatever happened. Blood was everywhere, on the man, on the truck, on the road. I picked him up, placed him in the vehicle, and drove to the nearest hospital, five minutes away.

Medical staff brought him into the ER and I followed behind the gurney. There were no protocols keeping me from staying by his side. I stood next to the doctor and watched this man die.

My mind was reeling. I had just killed a man. I was living in a tribal society. How much time did I have before his family found out and came to get vengeance?

I was in serious trouble, and the police knew it. They threw me into a holding room—a mostly empty space with a single chair and a small window. There weren't any other prisoners with me, partly to give them time to determine if I had acted maliciously, and partly for my own protection.

In prison, I was a show. Everyone wanted to know what this foreign man sitting in a Yemeni jail cell had done. Police officers and cleaning women and administrative staff, even other prisoners who could walk about freely, came to stare at me in my holding cell. People from the man's tribe did come to the prison to get a good look at me. They would remember my face, and if the police found any mal intent in the accident, they would take matters into their own hands.

Alhamdulillah, there were witnesses at the scene. They swore I had been going slowly, that the man sort of tipped over in front of the car, that I couldn't have done anything to avoid it, that it had not been intentional, that I'd braked but he'd come out of nowhere.

"It was his time," someone said.

"He was very old," another said.

Death is always death, but this was not the same as if I had struck a sixteen-year-old or a young mother.

"*Qadr* Allah," someone else said. God predestined it.

Qadr is an Islamic doctrine asserting all events and outcomes are predetermined by God and are unalterable. God ordained this to happen. I could not have stopped it, so they tried to convince me that God caused it. The man could not have stopped it. We were puppets in the hands of the conductor of the universe and had simply been playing our roles as fallible human beings. This was my first interaction with this strict form of fatalism. Later, Yemeni Christians would develop a biblical perspective on *qadr* as we dealt with grief and lament, but for now, my basic understanding of it was that Yemenis saw all of life through this lens and complaining or striving against it was meaningless, even faithless.

The Christian businessman I had been building a relationship with, the man I thought I'd come to serve and bless in his trial of being a Yemeni Christian, became my Good Samaritan. Western Christians imagine themselves as the Good Samaritan in this story Jesus told. We will help. We will stop and look at the wounded man and care for his needs. We will love our neighbor well. On a more honest day, we might examine our conscience to see if we are perhaps the priest or the Levite who hurried past the wounded man, on the opposite side of the road. We rarely consider that we might be the wounded man, lying helpless and broken in our own blood, at risk of being attacked again or blown up in the police station by the family seeking revenge. We do not want to be the one in need. It is painful and awkward, and like language learning, another exercise in humility. Yet there I was, in need, and a man considered a pariah by his community on account of his faith, was the one who neighbored me.

He placed his business on the line, offering it as a guarantee for me, essentially as bail, and got me out of prison. Home to Lydia, away from staring eyes, and out of legal trouble.

The Muslim sheikh who had agreed to sponsor us as foreigners in the country for our visa application was my second Good Samaritan. Even more important than the legal issue, was the family and tribe issue. I needed to restore honor to the family members of the man who died. There had to be peace or there would be revenge. I wouldn't fully appreciate the risk the sheikh took on my behalf for years, but when he told me I needed to go with him to visit the family, I went.

Although the insurance had already paid the blood money on my behalf ($6,000) the sheik knew we had to make peace in person. We visited the home, and after greeting the family and being seated in their *maglis*, he said,

"We desire peace, tell us about this man's life."

The elder pointed around the room at the man's relatives: a cousin, an uncle, a brother, a granddaughter. They told us about his father and mother, where he was born, his employment history, his marriage, his love for tea, and his sense of humor.

I could never restore the man to his family, but I could offer my presence. I understood, though, that my presence was not what carried the weight of reconciliation. It was the sheikh, and his entire tribe, putting his reputation on the line to vouch for me. As a lone American, I was like dust in their eyes, easily blown away. But as part of an ancient and respected tribe, my life mattered. Peace between tribes mattered.

Nadwa Al-Dawsari, a conflict analyst specializing in the Middle East, describes tribal law as, "designed to protect the interests of the collective over those of the individual and offers protection for tribesmen so long as they respect tribal rules. Therefore, tribal conflict resolution is largely based on compromise. In addition, empathy, the culture of apology, and the admission of wrongdoing are deeply rooted in tribal mediation, which promotes reconciliation beyond the resolution of conflict itself."[3] Clearly, I was not in Yemen to be a kind of Joan of Arc out to save the world, leading great victories or creating massive

---

3. Nadwa Al-Dawsari, "Peacebuilding in the Time of War: Tribal Cease-Fire & De-Escalation Mechanisms in Yemen," *Middle East Institute*, April 1, 2021, https://www.friend sofsouthyemen.org/analysis/tribes_in_resolving_conflict.pdf

breakthroughs but to learn and to experience these powerful local social dynamics.

Interdependence became foundational. Building peace among people of all religious convictions mattered. Muslims and Christians should not consider ourselves in competition but in partnership, striving to create a beautiful, peaceful world together. Today, we know stories of Nigerian Muslims defending Christians from being massacred by extremists. We have stories of Muslims standing outside churches to protect them from being burned. Christians surrounding Muslims during times of violence so they can pray safely. We should not be divided by denominational barriers. When four Catholic nuns were decapitated in Aden, Protestants needed to share that pain. When Baptists were murdered in a hospital, Muslims named their children after them in honor and solidarity.

❦ 8 ❦

SEEK AND YOU WILL FIND

Yemenis didn't have easy access to the Bible, and having a physical one in their possession was dangerous. People had been killed for less. And yet, the Bible had a way of finding true seekers. Seek and you will find, Jesus promised. In Yemen, those who sought the Bible found it in miraculous ways.

Tariq was a seeker. In middle school he intensively studied the Quran and pestered his teachers with questions. In one instance, he asked the teacher about a verse in Surah Al-Ma'idah 5:73, "They have certainly disbelieved who say, 'Allah is the third of three.' And there is no god except one God." The teacher explained that there was God, the Messiah, and Mary. Tariq couldn't make sense of that answer.

"What about the idols that Arabs worshiped in the early days?" he asked.

"There were stones and other idols," the teacher said, frustrated with Tariq's constant questioning of Islam. "Stand up," he said and motioned for Tariq to get out of his desk. "Are you a Muslim?"

"Yes," Tariq said.

"Is your father a Muslim?"

"Yes."

"Is your mother?"

"Yes."

"Do they pray? Do you pray?"

"Yes, and yes! I just want to understand."

"Your words have Satan in them," the teacher said. "Get out of this classroom and don't come back without your father."

This exchange and others like it, or others in which the teachers simply refused to answer, was the beginning of Tariq's search, and then he decided he wanted to study Christianity but from a Christian source, not an Islamic one. This was impossible. In rural Yemen, with no internet access, he couldn't find a Bible or a Christian person or a book that didn't have a strong Islamic bent. Tariq was convinced his search for Christian materials was futile.

Even among scholars and theologians who attempt to present a different religion, faithfully representing the other is a challenge. Everyone studies and thinks about the world and religion through particular lenses. This is important for foreigners to keep in mind. When studying Islam or Yemen, what are the sources? Are they Westerners who visited Yemen for a few weeks? Are they theologians who studied Islam at a Christian seminary? Or are they Yemenis? Foreigners who have lived in Yemen for decades and acknowledge their lingering outsider status and perspective? Muslim scholars and theologians?

Tariq had friends traveling outside of Yemen and tried to get them to bring him a Bible, but they refused, telling him he would get into trouble. Others didn't want to get caught with a Bible at the airport. He turned to the radio but his heart burned for access to a Bible.

When he was thirteen years old, on a dusty night after one o'clock in the morning, he heard a military truck pull up outside the house. He and his father woke up, startled by the intrusion at this hour. Tariq wondered if someone was coming to arrest his father? For what?

He watched from the window as one of the soldiers climbed out of the truck and approached the front door. Suddenly, he kissed Tariq's father on the head in greeting.

"*Ahlan wa sahlan ya walaid!*" His father said, welcome young man.

Tariq realized it was his relative who worked for the central security in Ibb. He wore his uniform and openly carried his weapon. He told the family he had the day off because the previous day he had successfully raided a group of Yemenis in Jibla.

When the relative entered the house and saw Tariq, he said, "Do you read? I heard you liked to read."

"I love to read," Tariq said.

The man still wore his tactical vest. He reached inside and pulled something out from beneath the ammunition magazines. He held a book in his hand and pushed it toward Tariq.

"Don't let your dad see this!" he said. "I was going to burn it, but then I remembered you liked to read so I saved it and brought it to you. If you see that it will cause you issues, just burn it."

Tariq glanced down and saw that it was the Bible. "Where did you get this?"

"There was a group of people that had been meeting and we were going to arrest them. Maybe they were part of a rebel group trying to overthrow the government. When we arrived at their location, we didn't find anyone but did find a crate of material. We confiscated piles of books and materials. My officer told me to take them and send them to headquarters so they can understand who this group is. I was curious about what kind of publications these were and before turning the materials over, I snatched one book from the top of the pile of confiscated items." He slipped it into his ammunition vest and pulled it out that evening to read.

"I expected to find political writings or which country was giving them money," he said. "It wasn't political at all. It was religious. These people were Christians. I thought about returning the book to headquarters, but how would I explain why I kept it? I thought about burning it inside the headquarters, but people would see the smoke. I thought about flushing it down the toilet, but was afraid the toilet would clog up and then when they sent someone to fix it, it would be clear it was from the raid, and I would get in trouble . . . then I remembered you."

He looked at Tariq. "Will you read it?"

Tariq tried to shrug nonchalantly.

"If it causes you trouble, promise me you will burn it."

Tariq nodded and took the book, hiding his excitement. He began to read the Bible late at night in secret. Parts he understood and other parts he didn't, but this was the beginning of Tariq's search for truth in the scriptures. Many believers are under the illusion that their family will have no issue with the Bible. Relatives don't care what they watch on YouTube or what images fill their minds as they scroll Instagram. They imagine their family is more secular and lenient than they truly are, and the Bible can trigger a strong, even violent reaction, especially if someone brings it inside their home. Tariq did not suffer that illusion. He knew he needed to be cautious.

When a believer receives their first Bible, other Christians can help them think through the implications so that they can practice wisdom. Do they have a safe place to hide it? Have they talked with their spouse or mother and father about reading the Bible? Do they plan to carry it with them outside the home? In recent years, is a Bible app best for their situation?

Tariq had no Christians to guide him, but he knew his family would never accept him reading the Bible. He needed to be careful, but there was no possibility of him burning the book.

The relative visited a few months later and asked Tariq if he had destroyed it. He asked over and over and Tariq promised him the book was gone.

Gone from the room, yes. Gone from being a concern for this relative, yes. But burned? No. Tariq had hidden the Bible in his bedroom and began to read it late at night. He couldn't get enough. The deeper he went into the Word of God, the deeper the Word of God cut into him. He felt overwhelmed each time he opened the book. What a miracle! Tariq had been asking questions about faith since childhood and actively sought news of Christianity for six years. God used a government security officer to deliver a Bible to him here, in rural Yemen. God used the persecution of Christians hours away from Tariq to deliver this precious book into the hands of a seeker.

I spent hours zipping along narrow roads, switchbacking through Yemen's northern mountain passes with an experienced expatriate veteran of Yemen named Kevin. Acacia trees blurred as we passed, and the occasional blue and red billboard advertising Abu Walad's biscuits, vanilla crème sandwich cookies, pierced the cloudy sky. Yellow barriers, dented from previous accidents, marked steep drop-offs, and row after endless row of gray mountains stretched out before us.

I drove with no idea where Kevin and I were going. I turned when he said turn. I stopped when he said stop. I backtracked when he changed his mind, which wasn't often, though he hadn't been this way in months and was over eighty years old. Kevin had spent his life here, loving Yemenis and loving Jesus, he had even buried one child in Yemen's soil. I made it a point to get time with him, to glean wisdom from his experience. He wasn't one to put up with being pestered by questions, though, and if he sensed I was pressing for stories, he clammed up. So when Kevin called and asked me to drive him into the mountains, the only reasonable response was, "Of course."

The best way to learn all the things I didn't know about living in Yemen, which was *all* things, was to sit at the feet of Yemenis and established expatriates. I was at their mercy; they could help me learn or could try to force me to conform to their boxes of predetermined expectations or could ignore me. And because I wasn't one of them, with a mission organization to report to and no prefield orientation to taint my thinking with Western constructs of religion and culture, I could pick up what I found helpful and pass over the rest.

Kevin didn't believe in intentional discipleship or follow-up when people came to faith. He prayed and he relied on the Holy Spirit. I believe in doing both.

"If God doesn't send a Philip to an Ethiopian," Kevin said, "God will reveal himself without a human agent. Otherwise, it would be unjust to condemn someone to hell. They have not rejected Jesus; they never met him." He described discipleship as a relay race in which the foreign Christian needed to relinquish the baton and let God do God's work. God was in Yemen, with or without foreign Christians.

"Let the Spirit disciple them," he said. "Come with me to meet Ali." The invitation was not to conduct a Bible study or to teach someone how to pray, it was to visit a friend. He believed people who hungered and thirsted for God would hunger and thirst for God without a foreigner's perfectly designed discipleship program, and that God would prove faithful to meet these believers without outside intervention.

I took Kevin's reliance on the Holy Spirit and the patience he embodied and added my own conviction about the importance of community and intentionality. I believed in following up with all Yemeni believers and seekers, and intentionally teaching them, but at times I discerned that once I had done my part the believer needed a week or a month on their own, so the Spirit could address them. He or she didn't need my interference at this time and giving them space and time allowed God to deal with them on God's terms, not mine. Eventually, though, I would follow up, and over time, the church developed a discipleship program so believers wouldn't be left wandering in the desert after they had discovered water.

Still, Kevin's underlying principle played out over and over, exemplified in Tariq's testimony. The strongest believers were those who had, in their original seeking journey, been relentless in their pursuit of God. They chased after a relationship with Jesus with a zeal that continued into their life as Christians. They were the ones who didn't rely on the Westerner to show up on Friday, to preach a nice sermon, or to explain the way of the kingdom. They took charge of their faith and trusted the Spirit who had initially prompted them.

Tariq, who encountered the Word of God when the persecution of other Christians brought it to him, taught me to trust that God is doing something intentional, even when trials come. In Acts, the stoning of Stephen and suffering of believers led to a scattering of Christians, carrying the gospel with them. In Yemen today, migration caused by war, poverty, natural disasters, and political unrest, means Christians are moving about the country, bringing the gospel with them to new governorates. In *Migration and the Making of World Christianity*, scholar Jehu Hanciles argues that "migration has been an indispensable element in the advancement of the Christian faith from the earliest beginnings and a prime factor in the plural frontiers of cross-cultural engagement that mark the world Christian movement."[1]

Gospel spreading happens as Yemeni Christians stay in Yemen but bring their traditions, rituals, ideas, and beliefs across community borders and enter a new society. Internally displaced believers carry Jesus to new regions and enact incarnation as "Christ becomes 'flesh' in different cultures and territories."[2] Of course, this happens in international global migration as well, but if migration takes a Yemeni Christian out of Yemen, it takes the gospel incarnated in that person out too.

But when a Christian stays inside Yemen and moves from Dhamar to Sana'a or Bibles are confiscated in Jibla, a young man in a remote village meets Jesus.

Tariq loved what he was reading and hoped to find someone who could help him understand it better. He knew the Yemeni saying, "The one who doesn't have an elder, his elder is the devil." Eventually, Tariq discovered a Christian radio broadcast. One day, he went to the post office to mail a package and noticed the man next to him acting strange, clearly nervous. Tariq edged closer to him and saw that the address on the envelope he was mailing was the address of the Christian radio show. Tariq tried to speak to the man but he avoided making eye contact with Tariq, quickly slipped his letter into the mailbox, and dashed out of the post office.

Tariq realized there were other seekers in Yemen, maybe even other Christians. But if they all lived in fear and isolation, what would happen to them? They needed community and leadership and training. They needed each other. What if there were no more radio programs? What if foreign Christians were all kicked out? Would Christianity die in Yemen?

---

1. Jehu Hanciles, *Migration and the Making of Global Christianity* (Grand Rapids, MI: William B. Eerdmans Publishing Company, 2021), 1.
2. Ibid, 68.

9

GROWING PAINS

Tariq called the radio program, hoping they could help him meet other believers. They sent him more material and asked if he would like to meet someone face to face. He began meeting foreign Christians and thought, like most new believers, that inside the Christian community he would discover only peace, beautiful relationships, moral character, and sincere pursuit of God. Instead, he found a community of human beings, sinful and saved by grace, and people who loved one another and had opinions, personalities, and foibles. People who were all still learning to embody the fruit of the Spirit.

Around the time Tariq came to faith in 1994 and into the early 2000s, the fledgling Christian community was in a stage I compare to the Corinthian church in I Corinthians 3, caught up in a dispute about leadership, arguing over fruit, and not ready for solid food, but behaving as infants in Christ. This description applies to both local believers and foreign Christians, as the primary focal point of the disagreement was the role each should play during the church's formative years.

Discussing the building of an indigenous faith community between expatriate Christian workers and local believers is a fraught endeavor. The complicated and nuanced issue is far too often oversimplified. It can be easy for either side to accuse the other of pride or control, spiritual immaturity, or greed. Foreigners can tend toward unhealthy paternalism and an insistence on maintaining their leadership roles beyond usefulness. Some locals can tend toward insincere motives for demanding indigenous leadership or may prefer an outside expat, a visitor who comes and gives them money, but then leaves and isn't involved in their daily lives.

Tension around the topic of indigeneity swirled during my early years in Yemen, though I remained an observer and a learner. Maybe these tensions are growing pains, necessary for any developing movement. Because of this commonality and historicity, it is valuable to explore what was going on in the early years of Yemeni church growth and where the church leaders are now regarding partnership between foreigners and locals.

I believe any foreign Christian if asked, "Do you support an indigenous church?" would say, "yes." As would any local believer. Yes, of course, they all long for the day when the seven selves of indigenous churches are fully practiced: Self-governing, Self-supporting, Self-propagating, Self-identifying, Self-teaching, Self-expressing, Self-theologizing.[1]

But they may disagree with it when that point is reached, or how it is reached, or how to be part of the international body of Christ, or the role of the local and the role of the foreigner over time. Each group brings concerns and issues to the table that must be addressed with humility, transparency, and courage. Issues of paternalism or a colonialist mindset must be faced head-on and repented of. Foreigners need to be humble and willing to submit to local leadership. Locals need to discern when a call for indigeneity is sincere and timely, and when it stems from someone eager to end a relationship with one specific foreigner or is premature.

A clear sign that a church is moving toward healthy indigenous leadership is when local believers joyfully partner with foreigners, and vice versa. There can be no hint of negating the global body of Christ. As the

---

1. Jervis David Payne, *Discovering Church Planting: An Introduction to the Whats, Whys, and Hows of Global Church Planting* (Milton Keynes, U.K.: Paternoster Publishing, 2009), 18-24.

local church grows and develops leadership teams and generationally established leaders who are multiplying their faith, there must still be room for international partners in God's work. That is the model of the church in scripture, a beautiful tapestry of diversity, each one benefiting from the unique giftings of others to bless the whole.

Yemenis told me about the discussions they had during these years and I had heard a bit from foreigners. There was hurt on both sides, even as they all ultimately wanted the same thing. Two key lessons and two hard truths emerged from this time that Yemeni believers continue to carry forward.

First, there was an emphasis on shared faith commitments and the eternal reality of the body of Christ, no matter where a person resided geographically. This applied globally as well as within Yemen, across tribal and regional boundaries. Believers came to recognize that they needed one another. There were roles the foreigners needed to relinquish and there were roles the Yemenis needed to be encouraged and empowered to take on. Spiritual gifts in both communities transcended ethnic heritage. Believers needed to submit to one another and partner for the sake of the kingdom, not for the sake of anyone's agenda or ego.

Second, the church, even the early church in scripture, is made up of human beings with personalities, preferences, annoying habits, struggles, and sin. Of course, the more the church gathers in community, the more conflicts could arise. But along with those conflicts come opportunities for growth and for practicing the fruit of the Spirit. These are vital, though painful, refining experiences that will inevitably be part of any church growth process. Rather than this being something to hide or feel ashamed of, it is an opportunity for sanctification.

The two hard truths were that some new believers would struggle upon realizing that inside the church community, life wasn't idyllic. When faced with the reality of arguments over money and positions, differences in priorities, and other humans they might not naturally get along with, they could easily become disillusioned. This realization helped Yemenis recognize the importance of a broader community, trust, and transparency, and they created discipleship lessons on topics of forgiveness, reconciliation, and mercy.

The second hard truth involved the existence of a "Judas," the reality of betrayal. During the years of discussing indigenous church leadership, specifically in 2009, a man who had been a leader betrayed the community. Anything can lead to this—disillusionment, bitterness, money, family pressure, envy. The repercussions were dire as the group struggled with hurt and anger, confusion and broken trust. The situation could have added fuel to the fire of the leadership discussions. Instead of increasing the heat, however, people wisely responded by beginning to teach about the reality of facing a Judas-like betrayal.

The expectation became that every community would have a Judas eventually. Jesus didn't avoid it, how could we expect to? But neither did Jesus walk in fear or refuse to trust people. He loved Judas and gave him charge over finances until the very end. Like the father in Luke 15, faithful Yemenis stand at the door, ready to run in welcome when the prodigal son makes his way home, hoping he will choose the path home and not the self-destructive path of Judas.

The more I learned about the discussions, the clearer it became that this work would be a partnership. This was not My Show or the Expat Ministry or the Yemeni Alone Church. This was for, in, by, and through locals in partnership with the global body of Christ, of which I was a part.

These were people I wanted to partner with through fire and blood, through celebration and trial.

❧ II ❧
LEADING
ARISE, SHINE!

¹Arise, shine, for your light has come,
  and the glory of the Lord has risen upon you.
² For behold, darkness shall cover the earth,
  and thick darkness the peoples;
but the Lord will arise upon you,
  and his glory will be seen upon you.
³ And nations shall come to your light,
  and kings to the brightness of your rising.
⁴ Lift up your eyes all around, and see;
  they all gather together, they come to you;
your sons shall come from afar,
  and your daughters shall be carried on the hip.
⁵ Then you shall see and be radiant;
  your heart shall thrill and exult,
because the abundance of the sea shall be turned to you,
  the wealth of the nations shall come to you.
⁶ A multitude of camels shall cover you,
  the young camels of Midian and Ephah;
  all those from Sheba shall come.
They shall bring gold and frankincense,

and shall bring good news, the praises of the Lord.
[7] All the flocks of Kedar shall be gathered to you;
   the rams of Nebaioth shall minister to you;
they shall come up with acceptance on my altar,
   and I will beautify my beautiful house.

Isaiah 60:1-7

10

WELCOMED BY MUSLIMS, NOT MANUALS

In October of 2005, after six months of teaching and continuing my own studies, I often found myself encouraging incoming students. "Language learning will expose your character," I told them during orientation.

"I'm going to be preaching in Arabic in six months," one of the students said.

I thought to myself, *"You will not be preaching in six months."*

Another, a surgeon with a PhD, was brought to his knees in humiliation by language study. He acted out in class and lost his temper, like a toddler in need of a bowl of Cheerios.

I urged them to focus on the relationships they were building, not only the linguistic content.

Often Western—usually highly educated and professionally competent—foreigners were ill-equipped for the character-refining process of cultural adaptation, of which unlearning is the hardest part. People come abroad with five-year strategies: two years to learn the language, one year to plant a church, one year to train leaders, one year to pass it on. Never mind that language learning alone will take more than five years. Never mind that there may already be a church with well-trained leaders, the foreigner just can't recognize it. Never mind that "passing it on" is never going to happen the way one imagines.

There is the enmeshed team structure: one leader, three couples, maybe a single woman or two. They intend to learn language together and model church together. Then they have conflicts over money or parenting or eschatology. Someone gets sick. Someone falls behind in language. A child rebels. One family pulls out. The team leader is blamed. Another family leaves. Pretty soon, they are all back in the USA working at Starbucks, either filled with resentment or nursing an inflated story of glorified persecution.

Of course, not everyone leaves disillusioned or resentful. Some wrestle deeply with God over their time abroad. Some experience unexpected and surprising personal transformation as a result of their pain. They believe God was preparing them for something beautiful through those hard seasons. It matters that people and organizations are alert to the reality of possible ways people respond to this kind of life.

Then there is all the extra luggage of finely tuned methodologies and frameworks that often accompany cross-cultural ministry. Some, like the Camel Method and chronological storytelling, are prescriptive tools designed to guide practitioners. Others, such as the C-scale, Insider Movements, and Disciple Making Movements, were originally intended as descriptive observations of what God appears to be doing in various contexts according to their authors, and which were later adopted as methodologies to be followed. While these approaches have sparked both enthusiasm and debate, it's important to acknowledge that God has used a variety of means to bear fruit in different places. Convictions on theology or specific strategies sometimes lead practitioners to focus narrowly on replicating what they've learned, translating seminary ideas into local languages without fully engaging the context.

People come burdened by ideas of Westernized Islam or, worse, Christian Westernized Islam, and think of Muslims as homogenous. Yemen alone, divided by mountains and tribes, is not homogenous even between neighboring villages. One village celebrates Mawled, the prophet Mohammad's birthday. The next village teaches it is a sin to celebrate Mawled. One village requires mothers to stay inside for forty days postpartum. The next village over requires new mothers to be back in the fields working within seven days or less. Which is "Yemeni culture"? This diversity applies even to learning Arabic, with widely variant dialects across Yemen. What Yemenis say in Taiz might be indecipherable to someone from Hajjah.

The best thing a foreigner can do upon arrival in Yemen is to take on the posture of a learner. Grab local leaders. Grab experienced expatriates. Listen, observe, and absorb. You are welcome to not mimic any method of the foreigners or locals. You are welcome to try something new. Stand on your head as you talk about Jesus, if you want. But find out what has been going on before you came, what people have struggled and bled to learn, and let that launch you into the next season, your season.

Although I didn't have an official team or organization, I sought out experienced expats and benefited from the body of Christ but didn't have to sit through meetings detailing the next conference or an interpersonal conflict. No one was determining what was acceptable or unacceptable for me to do according to a globalized, and thus irrelevant in my specific context, team plan, and no supporters were waiting for an inspirational report in the mail.

To some, this may look irresponsible, like I thought I had Yemen figured out, or didn't need accountability. To me, it was the opposite. I wasn't trying to be a solo maverick. I knew I was clueless and dependent on input but was determined to keep the source of that input as local as possible. Even when I struggled against the counsel Yemenis gave.

One incident in 2014 brought home how essential and beautiful this was. Motorcycles have always been ubiquitous in Yemen, but during the war years, their presence took on a new sense of ominous foreboding. Al Qaeda operatives had a particular preference for motorcycles, frequently using two riders—one driving and the other on the back with an AK-47 at the ready. There were dozens of incidents in the city where they would drive by, turn a corner, and assassinate their targets.

My neighborhood and I decided to ban motorcycles and put up signs at the ends of the streets.

One afternoon a fundamentalist decided to test the signs and the determination of the guards around my house. He drove a motorcycle straight through, aiming directly for my house. My guard, Sabat, heard the moto coming and watched its approach on the security cameras. He grabbed his AK-47 and climbed to the rooftop.

"Stop!" he shouted. "Stop!"

The driver didn't listen. Sabat lifted his assault rifle, aimed at the motorcycle, and shot. He sprayed the motorcycle until it split into two pieces. The driver rolled to the ground, shaken but uninjured.

I heard the commotion and was not about to leave my house if this was an attempted attack. I called my security team to see what had happened. The motorcycle had been shot up, the man was lying on the ground, and Sabat stood nearby with his gun slung over his shoulder. Walid, my head of security, concluded that the man wasn't al-Qaeda. He had the same kind of religious DNA but, after speaking to him, Walid concluded he wasn't exactly al-Qaeda.

"Look," Walid said to the driver, "you are clearly in the wrong. The sign says no motorcycles. But the man who lives here," he pointed at my house, "a foreign Christian, is going to help you."

"How can he help me?" the man shouted. "I almost died! And my motorcycle is ruined. It's my only source of income. I drive deliveries around town and now my family will starve."

Later, Walid called to tell me what the best solution would be.

"You should pay for the motorcycle," he said.

He was in the wrong, not me, I wanted to protest. "That's ridiculous," I said.

"It *is* ridiculous," Walid said. "But we have to show him that he has false ideas about Christians."

"He came into *my* street, maybe to kill *my* wife or *my* kids, or me. Yemeni tribal code says no way do I pay for his stupidity."

"This is your opportunity to choose the path of peace," Walid said. "You represent Jesus in this country, and this is your chance to send a message about what that means to you."

How could I argue with that? Eventually, this Muslim friend convinced me to pay $3,000 to buy a new motorcycle for the man whose actions had nearly provoked a deadly response—in the name of Jesus.

A Yemeni proverb says, *Ahl Makkah adra bi-shi'ābiha,* the people of Mecca know its mountain paths best. At times, my Yemen Muslim friends—men of peace— have helped me understand how to represent Christ faithfully in this context. They have not only been trusted voices, but also an integral part of my team, inspiring me to love the way Jesus would.

❧ II ❧
BEYOND HEADS OF
HOUSEHOLDS

A thir's father thought the busy village road was dangerous and forbade his ten children from playing near it. Instead, the siblings spent hours playing on the third-story rooftop of their home. Athir was almost the baby, the ninth child, and one of her favorite games was a version of blind man's bluff, where a blindfolded child chased after and tried to capture the others.

Athir, blindfolded, raced around the unwalled rooftop, arms outstretched, searching for a brother or sister, and she fell straight off the roof to the ground below. By the time her siblings and neighbors raced to her in the dirt, she was sitting up and laughing, without a scratch on her. Her parents insisted she go to the hospital anyway, where doctors could find nothing wrong.

Her mother urged her father to put a wall around the roof but he didn't. He had seventeen other children, with other wives, and didn't seem to take the safety of these ten seriously. Athir rarely thought about him. Instead, she considered her older sister's husband as a father figure. He had always been kind, had helped raise her, and encouraged all the women in his life to speak their minds and to work and study hard. She felt respect and care from him.

One day, Athir climbed to the rooftop to retrieve a metal bucket.

She put it over her head and it covered her eyes and nose. She headed for the stairs but misjudged and fell off the roof again. When she hit the ground, the bucket dislodged from her head and ricocheted all the way down the slope behind the house. Once again, Athir was unharmed.

The third time Athir fell off the roof, no one can remember the exact circumstances other than the reality that, yet again, Athir didn't sustain a single scratch. If multiple people hadn't observed every fall, no one would believe her stories. In high school, Athir tripped over a low step, fell, hit her head, and passed out. An ambulance took her to the hospital, where her brother told the doctor, "She'll be fine. She's used to falling off the roof."

An elderly woman in the village still whispers, "Praise God!" every time she sees Athir. Apparently, God did not want Athir to die yet.

Athir's mother prayed the salat regularly but when Athir tried to maintain the five prayers a day, she grew exhausted. She would barely finish one prayer when it was time for the next and, essentially, gave up. She identified as a Muslim but didn't take practicing her faith seriously. At university, other girls seemed to use Islam to judge and criticize each other, comparing how many times they had prayed or demanding to know why someone wore fingernail polish. Athir felt disgusted and dissatisfied with religion as she had experienced it.

Athir's nephew often visited her at university, or she visited his home in the village. She noticed that he had a strange book which he tried, and failed, to hide from her. His effort at secrecy only piqued her interest, and Athir grabbed it one day and started to read. That afternoon, her nephew showed her a compellingly beautiful movie about Jesus. Over the next few months, her nephew sent voice messages or MP3 recordings to Athir in which he talked about Jesus and what he had read in the Bible. By the time Athir sat down with another neighbor to read Surah 3 in the Quran, which talks about the birth of Jesus to Mary, she had decided she loved this Jesus.

The first person she told was her nephew, and it wasn't for several more months that she learned other members of his family were also believers. Then, she learned about the broader Yemeni church community. She wasn't alone! Athir eagerly joined Bible study groups and prayer meetings. She got baptized and learned about the Lord's Supper. She started to brainstorm with other educated women about ideas for helping illiterate women learn and memorize Bible stories.

Athir's parents did not know she had become a Christian, and they started to encourage her to get married. This was around 2009, Lydia and I had started to get to know Athir, and she talked to me about her marriage prospects.

"I want to marry a foreigner," Athir told me.

"You'll have a lot of trouble with cultural differences," I said.

"I want to study and get a job. I want to serve in the church. What Yemeni man will allow that?"

I tucked her words into the back of my mind and kept on the lookout for a local man for Athir. Interfering in marriages or arranging a meeting is serious business. These are people's lives, and if things go badly, the matchmaker can walk away while those in the marriage are wounded or damaged. Setting people up should be done in community, bathed in prayer and approached with fear and trembling. The man, especially, needs to be vetted regarding his faith, employment, history, and character.

Believing Yemeni men in the Gulf and the West want to marry Christian Yemeni women and have made countless proposals. The first thing the local church and I say in response is, "Are they willing to move back and serve God in Yemen? Or, if they are serious, will they return to Yemen so we can pray and discuss together in person? We never hear back from these men. They have chosen a different path, not one these Yemeni women in the country desire. They have seen the beauty of God's work and experienced God's miracles in Yemen. They see entire families put their faith in Christ and recognize this is far more meaningful than a "safer" life in Europe or Australia—where, despite access to churches, many find themselves isolated from a rich community, and attending service on Sunday while distracted by worries of the world throughout the week.

Athir's father was also on the lookout for a local man, a Muslim. Family pressure to get married increased. There was a man in another city who expressed his desire to marry Athir. She refused the proposal. She'd changed her mind and decided she never wanted to get married. Not to a Yemeni, not to a foreigner, not to a Muslim, not to a Christian.

Athir's faith, leadership, desire and then waning desire to marry, called to my mind the common perception of the Middle East: that it is impossible to share the gospel as a family because the region is segregated by gender. Historically, Christians have adapted to this with a gender-segregated model of reaching male heads of households. Fran Love called this "gender blind missiology" as it leaves women out of strategic church-planting and ignores their unique needs and gifts. It is also condescending, as it places women and children downstream in priority. What about when a woman doesn't have a so-called head of household? What about when she is a gifted leader herself?

I learned about working in Yemen by observing both locals and other expatriates. One self-nicknamed "black sheep" of a large mission organization had lived in Yemen for years but still spoke broken Arabic in a thick, Southern American accent. His work entailed delivering food to poverty-stricken villages, where he also met with believers.

"How many believers are there in your area?" he would ask a group of Yemeni Christians.

"Thirty," they would answer, because they thought he had asked them how many people in their area had received food aid. He could then write, "thirty Christians" on his organizational report. Was miscommunication one reason some organizations reported such large numbers during the early 2000s? I wouldn't take my language-learning standard from him, but he had other lessons for me.

When he visited a village, he brought his entire family.

It was certainly easier, as a man, to visit and share Jesus with only men, especially once my family grew to four children. But ease has never been a value for me, and I learned that the effectiveness of reaching male heads of households first was a false assumption. It was easier *initially* to engage in spiritual conversations with only men. But in the long run, it was far easier to grow a movement with whole families.

This Southern American brother showed me how to include my family. At first, Lydia and I would visit families together, but eventually, we started bringing my oldest daughter Esther, too, and then all our children as they were born. Ministering together was about more than simply including family, though. I learned to develop intentionality around family. If we visited a home, men and women would be separated into gendered *maglises*. But if we went to the beach, husbands and wives and children played in the water and sprawled on the same blankets laid out over the sand, all together. If we went to a restaurant as families, we would be seated in the mixed-gender section behind curtains or particleboard walls.

Healthy families form the core of healthy churches. Whole families entering the kingdom would require whole-family interactions. New believers would see seasoned Yemeni believers discuss issues together, make up, serve one another, laugh together, and work and worship alongside one another. They would see the parenting, children's behavior and misbehavior, and respect for elders.

One afternoon in July 2009, several families, including Shaadi and Jamila, traveled to a forest in the foothills of a mountain. Lydia, eight and half months pregnant with our third child, and I drove in my Land Cruiser full of Yemeni Christians. Several Yemeni families rode in the trucks behind us as well. It had rained the night before and part of the road was washed out, but I couldn't tell through the thin upper layer of sand.

I was driving, and then all of a sudden, I wasn't driving and the car was tipping over onto its side as the passenger side slipped into a sinkhole. It happened as though in slow motion until the car stopped once it had flipped entirely onto one side. Lydia was the only passenger wearing her seatbelt, as there were more people than seatbelts, and everyone tumbled on top of one another.

The people in the cars behind watched, horrified and helpless. They scrambled out of their vehicle and rushed to see if anyone was injured. They reached our car and were astonished to find that not only was no one hurt, the only sound was uproarious laughter as arms and legs and feet and hair and scarves twisted all together.

We quickly got everyone out of the truck, I waited for a winch to take the car to the mechanic, and everyone else continued to the forest for a Bible lesson and fellowship.

Later, the family who had been driving behind said they decided in the moment that they approached our tipped car and heard only laughter, to follow Jesus. Not because we had been spared injury but because of the joy that spontaneously erupted in what looked terrifying. They wanted to experience the peace that passes understanding in the middle of danger.

Yemenis had plenty of experience with danger, and little experience with peace, whether in politics, regional and tribal tensions, economic security, their families and marriages, or their own spirits. Religious teachers could do little to assuage anxiety with their offer of eternal rest *insha'Allah*, if God willed it. Politicians couldn't guarantee peace and struggled to maintain the slightest semblance of control and good governance against a rising tide of extremism as the years inched toward the Arab Spring. Fathers, brothers, and husbands wielded inordinate control over their daughters, sisters, and wives, sometimes relying on violence to enforce that control. And tribal tensions were all too often "resolved" with vengeance, resulting in a never-ending cycle of retaliation. Peace was a rare commodity.

Living in proximal and authentic relationships with Yemenis allowed them to witness peace in action, like the joy of a family inside a tipped-over car, finding delight in chaos.

A vision toward kinship in Christ makes more sense than a vision of reaching heads of households to Yemenis, especially when interpreted through their existing tribal allegiance lens. The biblical models both of families coming to faith as families and individual Christians being grafted into the family of God will strengthen the church by providing natural networks in which the gospel flows. It promotes unity because they are often also family or from the same social network and will be required to see each other at holidays and social gatherings, they are more likely to seek full reconciliation when there is conflict. As families come to faith, they have preexisting places in which to gather for fellowship—their own home. No one will question why cousins or nieces and nephews visit one another regularly or why large families host meals and parties together.

A household paradigm is not the definitive solution that applies universally to every Yemeni church planting initiative. Nor is it my intention to offer a simplistic strategy while ignoring the nuances of each context. There are instances in which the Gospel spreads through non-household social networks. Even when the focus is placed on households, there are occasions where trust is scarce within families and tribes. However, to my knowledge in Yemen the gospel spreading outside the household "oikos," social network is more exceptional than commonplace.

Tribal culture is rich with principles and stories passed on orally that can aid in communicating the gospel in this country where nearly fifty percent of women are illiterate, and thirty percent of men. Kinship theology guards against the isolation new Christians feel in many Muslim-majority countries. It urges them to share the good news with their blood family and welcomes them fully into a new family of believers.

My Muslim Yemeni chief of security once said to me, "When a Muslim is approached by a Christian, they are skeptical as to why the Christian is not evangelizing their family first. If the Christian found such a valuable life-changing treasure, why wouldn't he share the treasure with his family first?" Kinship evangelism in countries with such an emphasis on family, gives credibility to the gospel message.

When I watched the Yemeni families respond to our tipped-over car and when I thought about the delightful sound of my wife's laughter at the absurdity of the situation, I remembered Athir and her wrestling with the idea of marriage. What might it look like for two Yemeni believers to get married? Two people already in the kingdom? Two people entering marriage without fear or anxiety of being caught, but able to fully and freely live out their faith in partnership? *Lord, let it be so*, I prayed.

BUT DO YOU LOVE ME

R adio programs had a long reach into Yemen. I often drove across the country to respond to people who had contacted the radio stations. Sometimes I went alone, and other times I took another expatriate with me. If I felt uneasy about an encounter, I brought a discerning and trusted Yemeni along. People contacted the radio program for various reasons. Some requested Bibles or visits, while others didn't clarify why they reached out. We responded to every request. That meant we often drove three or four hours to meet someone who wanted a visa to the USA, who was curious to meet a foreigner, didn't show up, or had been tasked by the government to find out what foreigners were doing. Responding to those Yemenis seeking God required taking risks. Once in a while, we met a sincere spiritual seeker.

Saif's story is one of many that demonstrate the challenges and rewards of stepping into uncertain situations to spread the gospel. Saif was born in the northeast of Taiz Governorate. His mother was a devout but uneducated Muslim, while his father, unconvinced by Islam his entire life, eventually began observing Islamic rituals under the weight of family and societal pressure. Still, the prayers and rituals never satisfied the deep longing in Saif's father's soul.

A year after his father's death, Saif encountered Jesus Christ. His newfound faith filled him with joy, but it also brought a deep sadness. Saif grieved that his father never heard this life-changing news, never experienced this joy. Sorrow didn't paralyze Saif; instead, it spurred him on. He became deeply attached to the Word of God and spent countless hours studying. One day, Saif read Acts 1:8: "But you will receive power when the Holy Spirit has come upon you, and you will be my witnesses in Jerusalem and in all Judea and Samaria, and to the end of the earth."

Emboldened by what he understood to be a command to share the news of Jesus, Saif began introducing his family to the Word of God. Their initial reaction was harsh and violent. Some refused to eat with him. Easily, the most painful moment was when Saif's wife demanded a divorce and took their child away. Saif was heartbroken but his love for Jesus and his resolve to share his faith remained unbroken. He shared the gospel with his friends, even as one grew increasingly hostile. On one visit, anger overwhelmed this friend. He pointed a gun at Saif's head.

"If you ever speak to me or anyone else about Jesus again, I will blow your head off," he shouted. "Snap out of it; you've lost your mind!"

The shock of this moment drove him to retreat into prayer and solitude. Saif prayed fervently for the salvation of his family, friends, and community and continued to speak about Jesus. Gradually, God answered. Eighty percent of his family came to faith, some of his friends believed, and many others in the region embraced salvation. Today, this area boasts a large, influential church that continues to see people coming to faith.

Saif rejoiced in the newfound spiritual fellowship he shared with his blood family members and began to ask God for a believing wife. During one visit to his family, he met Amira. She was the daughter of a strict village cleric. One of her relatives was even a member of al-Qaeda and had once tried to recruit her, going so far as to teach her how to put on a suicide belt. When Saif first met her, Amira had been suffering for years from a bleeding disorder. At first, motivated by compassion, Saif pursued treatment and care for Amira, and over time, the two began to fall in love. Amira wasn't a Christian, but when Saif told her what happened to his first marriage, her response was compassionate.

"That doesn't seem like a good reason to ruin a marriage," she said.

Saif took that as a hopeful sign. He proposed marriage but Amira's father hesitated. He knew Saif was a man of good character, but because he was a Christian, the family had concerns. Her father investigated Saif and, eventually, to everyone's shock, approved the match.

"Amira has the right to choose her own path," he told her mother and brother, both of whom opposed the marriage. To Amira, he said, "Will you bear the consequences and responsibilities of this marriage?"

"Yes," she said with confidence.

"Then we will respect your decision," he said.

Saif hoped to be married in the church community and began to pray Amira would meet Jesus before they got married.

Walid, my chief of security, was never enthusiastic about my ventures to meet strangers, though he did understand why I insisted on taking the risks—and why other Yemenis like Saif did as well. A faithful Muslim, Walid has worked alongside me for over twenty years and can now articulate my reasons and motivations almost as clearly as I can. His grandfather was the first man of peace in our network who built relationships with foreigners. He vouched for them during times of trouble and gave them refuge, welcomed them into his family home with true Yemeni hospitality, and showed remarkable patience as expatriates like me stumbled through learning language and culture.

Walid wasn't hired in the traditional sense; he was, in some ways, inherited. When I became the last foreigner standing in our circle, it fell to me to take up the foreigner's role in this partnership, just as Walid was next in line in his family to take on the role of man of peace, protector, and mediator. Neither of us chose the other—our paths were decided. When the great exodus of foreigners began in 2012, circumstances thrust us into closer collaboration. Our shared history became a story of resilience, trust, and a partnership that neither of us could have foreseen but both have come to value deeply.

"Christians love and respect us," Walid told another foreigner who asked why he would put his own life on the line to protect Christians.

"Christ compels them to love and I can see it in their actions. I feel loved by them."

As a young boy, Walid sat in his father's majlis where he witnessed hundreds of *hukum*, rulings, over disputes related to water, land, and tribal conflicts. His father, grandfather, and the long line of ancestral sheikhs[1] from which they came modeled a unique ability to discern whether someone was sincere or had ulterior motives.

Walid has been evangelized by foreigners through word many times, but what impacts him most deeply is living in intimate relationships with foreign and Yemeni Christians. He can easily differentiate sincere love from friendship, contingent on whether he follows Jesus or not. He knows my commitment: I will serve the Yemeni people alongside him until the very end. Our families are bonded by common ground, and neither of us doubts that we would give our lives for each other. Walid has proven this numerous times, not only for me but even for Christians who have wronged or used him.

Muslims sense a Christian's motivation. They know if we love them or if we love our strategy. They know if we love them or if we love an end goal that looks more like a Westernized church building than the kingdom of God sprinkled with local flavor. Are we visiting Muslims to check a box? Or are we motivated by the love of Jesus? Are we engaging in a reciprocal relationship or solely an attempt to pitch our evangelistic model? What happens when our friend rejects Christ? How our posture shifts in that moment reveals everything about why we relate with them.

Of course, I want my Muslim friends to meet Jesus as I did. But Jesus calls me to follow him in loving them and in sharing the gospel in action and word, never as a project or assignment but an overflow of authentic affection. The night he was betrayed, Jesus said, "My command is this: Love each other as I have loved you." This is a work of the Spirit.

The highest compliment paid about a Christian was when a Yemeni said, "No one taught us as he did. Others taught us to refute Islam; he

---

1. "Sheik," here, refers to a tribal leader rather than a religious leader, signifying authority within the tribe and including responsibilities such as mediating disputes and guiding communal decisions.

taught us how to love Muslims." To that, the Anglican Bishop of Egypt, Dr. Mouneer Anis, added, "they will forgive you your cultural insensitivity, and they will overlook your awful Arabic if they believe that you really love them. But they will very quickly sense if you do not."

While Walid and I don't share all the same faith convictions, we do share the belief that faith should not be forced upon anyone. That people should have access to resources for answering their questions, and that every human being has inherent dignity and is worthy of being shown love and care. This is what compels him to protect Christians, and it is part of what compelled me to pursue the radio contacts.

Some expats accused me of hoarding contacts from these radio follow-ups. They thought this was easy work— plucking up people primed for the harvest. There was jealousy and accusations of seeking glory based on long lists of Muslims we were following up. Few people understood how discouraging the visits were. Four hours on bumpy roads only to be met with a gun in the chest is not how I define glorious.

We were not chasing our own glory. Not only because there are far more effective ways to hear the praise of humans than to disappear in backwater Yemen. But also, and primarily, because none of this was about us. It wasn't about our strategies or courage or flow charts and end of the year reports. It was about the love of God, God's love for the people of Yemen and his desire for them to know him.

I was not looking for personal glory and was not under any illusion that I had the silver bullet church-planting strategy. God was leading me on this adventure in Yemen, though, and I loved zipping through mountain passes with great expectation of who God would have me meet next. I was enjoying myself, beginning to understand the Yemeni people, and always looking forward to the next adventure.

Christian stories of cross-cultural life tend to emphasize darkness, trial, and suffering. Some practitioners choose to portray Yemen as a stronghold of Islam, a place dominated by evil, with terrorists lurking and no safe haven for outsiders. While I don't doubt the evil caused by wicked humans during the worst of Yemen's wars or that parts of it felt close to hell on earth, I refuse to define an entire nation or place as "hellish." There are beloved children of God there, God's self is there, through the ever-present Holy Spirit. That light is always more powerful than any kind of metaphorical darkness.

Darkness and evil cannot be the default description thrown at difficult locations by outsiders. One danger with focusing on the darkness and not the light of God, is that it becomes an excuse for why families are not coming to faith. We excuse the lack of multiplication by saying to ourselves *I am in an Islamic nation, oppressed by the devil, where there is a stronghold*. I do not mean to ignore the reality of the work of Satan. But Jesus's resurrection power is greater, as Yemeni disciples testify to what God is doing in the midst of darkness. The focus on evil and wickedness is not the way local people describe their lives or experiences with God and it is worth learning from their example. When mission organizations focus solely on narratives of torture, graphic photos, and highlight pain, all outsiders see is suffering, horror, demons, and darkness. But that is never the full story, nor is it the focus of the church in these harsh places.

Later, when bombs fell and friends died, the story we told and the story that kept us holding to faith and committing to one another is the story of the light that overcomes. A spiritual narrative focusing on the dark is a significant reason why Christians from Muslim backgrounds in places like Iraq, Syria, Somalia, or Yemen flee. They are in contact with foreign Christian organizations who look at the pain and conclude the empathetic response is to get them out, and that is the story they tell, rather than the story of the light that moves and spreads.

I don't want to minimize suffering. But who said following Jesus requires a dour expression, severity, and discussions of hell around every corner, metaphorical or spiritual? Life in Yemen was a grand adventure rife with unpredictability, uncertainty, and challenge. Rich with beautiful friendships and creative, resilient people. Kathleen Norris wrote in *Dakota, a Spiritual Geography*, "The basic principle of desert survival: not only to know where you are but to learn to love what you find there."

I loved what I found in Yemen.

❧ 13 ❧
JESUS LOVES ME, THIS
I KNOW

Hussein met Jesus in an internet café in June 2007, two years after I moved to Yemen. He had spent his entire life searching for love, something he never experienced as a child. His father died when he was two years old. His mother abandoned Hussein to her abusive brothers who beat him bloody. Hussein comes from a Hashemite family of the Sayyids, affiliated with the Zaydi Hadawi sect which traces its lineage to Imam Zayd ibn Ali ibn Husayn ibn Ali ibn Abi Talib. The sect was established in Yemen, in Saa'dah, by Imam al-Hadi ila'l-Haqq Yahya ibn al-Husayn in 897 CE. Sayyid families follow their ancestral line back to the prophet Mohammad through his daughter Fatima, also the wife of Ali ibn Abi Talib.

Sayyids enjoy great authority and respect in Yemen and are considered the primary religious and legal authorities in matters of Sharia and religion. Only they are supposed to hold leadership positions in the nation, including political, religious, and judicial roles, unless there is no Sayyid available to assume these positions.

The respect paid by the community for his genetic heritage wasn't the same as love. He wasn't allowed to play with kids who didn't share his status, leaving him without the love of friendship. His first marriage was to one of his uncle's fourteen daughters and it was a miserable relationship. With no experience of love from his family, Hussein hoped to find it in religion and aggressively searched for a loving God.

The search led him to memorize most of the Quran and study complex Islamic theological texts, such as *Risālat al-Ghufrān* by al-Maʿarrī (973–1057 CE). He eventually embraced Sunni Islam and subscribed to the strict Wahhabi sect that originated in Saudi Arabia. Typically, the Zaidis would not have accepted such a conversion, but due to internal disputes among the Zaidi leadership, they dealt with him with more leniency.

Hussein hoped that if he could be perfect in obedience, he might sense God's affection. He went on Islamic mission trips within Yemen, primarily in the northern governorates and the coastal towns of the Tihama, where he taught in neighborhood mosques. He preached Friday sermons and gave the call to prayer. Eventually, he was recruited into extremism by Jamaʿat Dammaj, a group centered around the Dar Al-Hadith Institute in Dammaj, a small village in the Saaʿdah governorate in northern Yemen. This Salafi institute is closely associated with Sheik Muqbil bin Hadi al-Wadiʿi, a prominent Sunni Salafi scholar. Yet, despite all these efforts, nothing could satisfy the deep ache in his heart to experience the beautiful and loving side of God.

Extremism led to disillusionment and Hussein's faith became a façade. He prayed for people during Ramadan as they fasted but didn't fast himself. He didn't perform ablutions. People were so moved that they wept at his preaching, but he went home after sermons and cried out in despair, "God, where are you?"

Dissatisfaction led him to study other religions: Buddhism, Zoroastrianism, Confucianism. He avoided the vile religions of Judaism and Christianity. He had read books as a child that convinced him Christians gave their children to Jews to eat. The Jews murdered the children and ground up their bodies into their Passover meals. Christians believed in three gods, a grave sin and an intellectually ridiculous concept in his opinion.

Hussein spent twelve years on this quest for a God who loved him, a God who knew Hussein's problems and still cared, a God who was present in a tangible way. The quest was futile, and Hussein gave up all hope.

One day, he went to an internet café to chat with an American woman in her sixties that he had met on Skype to continue his search for God. They had talked previously about faith. She identified as Catholic but had little knowledge of the Bible. Still, when Hussein admitted to abandoning his faith years earlier, she urged him not to give up hope and would search the internet for Bible verses to share, or would Google ways to respond to his questions. This particular day, she asked again about religion. Before Hussein could respond, she left the chat, and suddenly all the despair he had been feeling for years washed over Hussein like a tsunami. He stopped chatting with her and spoke directly to God, "It's over. I failed. I can't find you. I can't understand you. I'm tired. If you are there, tell me."

Suddenly Hussein heard a voice from his right side and from inside his body, speaking in classical Arabic.

"I've been waiting for you for twelve years, and I'm not waiting any longer."

The questions in his chest flew away and he nearly burst into tears.

This was the voice of Jesus the Messiah, he knew it. The search was over. An unnatural pure light flooded the internet café. Hussein got out of his chair and knelt on the floor, right in the middle of the café, and pressed his forehead down. He wanted to look up but was afraid he would be consumed by the overwhelming light of God. At that moment, Hussein knew he had become a Christian. He didn't know what that meant, only that he believed Jesus loved him.

Six months later doubts began to creep into Hussein's mind. How did he know that was the Messiah in the internet café? Since that day in the cafe, he had been reading the Bible online and interacted with some Christians, also online, but it was all in English and didn't pierce Hussein's heart. What if he had been wrong and it was Satan's voice that had spoken to him? What if he had not, in fact, found the fount of true life in Jesus? The thought was even more devastating than his twelve-year quest had been.

One night in his home village, Hussein felt his brain would explode from the tension and the longing, the hope of having found the truth and feeling secure in being loved, and the dread of yet again being wrong about God. He got out of bed and prostrated himself on the ground in the *maglis*. Shoes were heaped into a pile in the back of the room, and Hussein started to talk to God as though he were the shoes, lowly and dirty.

"God," he prayed, "I am less worthy than these shoes for you to speak with me. But I need to know that the voice was your voice."

Just like in the internet café, a voice came from inside and all around him. In the most powerful experience of his life, Hussein heard the same voice as before and it said just two words, "I am."

Hussein knew in the very core of his being that this was the voice of God. He never doubted again.

Hussein's natural thirst for knowledge about God now led him to Christian Google searches, chat rooms, and radio programs. He longed for a Bible in Arabic but doubted he could find one in Yemen and was convinced he was the only Christian in Yemen. Through a Christian chat room online, he asked if there was anyone who could bring him a Bible.

And that was how Hussein entered my life.

～

My father-in-law was visiting from Texas in August of 2007, and I took him along to meet Hussein at a local hotel.

"Do you know this man?" my father-in-law asked.

"No," I said.

"You've never met him before?"

"Never."

"And you're bringing him a Bible?"

"Yes."

I heard the unspoken questions in the silence that followed: *Is he a good guy or a bad guy? How can we trust him? Are we about to get blown up? Arrested? Kicked out?*

I didn't feel nervous but understood why someone new to Yemen might. We were meeting in a public location. I wasn't going to lead with the Bible in my right hand, first thing. We would talk first, drink tea, and hear Hussein's story. I would try to discern if it was a police trap, if he was interested in a visa to the USA, or if he was sincere.

Later Hussein told me he had been thinking similar thoughts: *How do I know I can trust this man? What if it is a trap or a trick? Will he even show up?*

We agreed to meet at a hotel. We recognized each other from the description we had given, and there was no way to miss my tall Texan father-in-law who looked like he had just walked in from the ranch. Any hesitation I felt disappeared as Hussein began to share his story. He could not stifle the eagerness in his eyes when he talked about the Bible and couldn't deaden the joy in his voice when he talked about meeting Jesus in the café. This was a man who had sought after the kingdom of God with all the zest of the farmer who found a treasure in his field and went and sold all he had to buy that field.

Before long, I pulled an Arabic Bible out of my bag. I have never seen someone react to the physical book with such exuberance. Hussein took it from me with both hands, his eyes wide and glued to the green cover with golden lettering. He lifted the book to his nose and inhaled. He kissed the Bible. Tears filled his eyes as he cracked open the cover and ran his fingers along the text. He embodied Jeremiah 15:16, "When your words came, I ate them for they were my joy and my heart's delight."

Hussein was, and remains, a seeker. His hunger to know and experience more of God is never-ending. I have no hard data to back this up, but I believe that if one hundred of the most mature believers were interviewed, I would find that most of them had been desperate seekers, literally hungry to know God. They are relentless in their quest, demanding even, that God meet them. They are discerning when they encounter other ideas and dissatisfied with anything other than truth. When believers from a Muslim background (BMB's) are filled with the Holy Spirit, they realize that no matter how religious they were before, they were empty in their spirits.

This seeking mentality continues in their relationship with Jesus. They take nothing for granted and appreciate grace in life-changing ways. They are like the woman in Luke 7 of whom Jesus said she loved much because she had been forgiven much. They know the emptiness of a life outside Christ and refuse to return to that, even at great personal cost.

~

Hussein's marriage to his cousin ended before he met Jesus. They had no children together, and Hussein began to wonder if he should leave Yemen. No family obligations tied him down. He was highly educated and could get a decent job somewhere else. He was vocal about his faith and became polemical about Jesus. This led to more pain from his family members. His mother rejected him, again. She even shot at him with an AK-47 through the windows of her home. She got off five rounds, trying to hit him while he scrambled away through the dirt. His uncle locked Hussein up in the basement of his home.

When the imprisonment didn't erase Hussein's faith after six full months, his uncle tried to persuade him to sign a paper that he would be silent about Jesus.

"You can worship the devil if you want," he said. "Just don't talk about it."

"I can't stop talking about it," Hussein said. "I won't lie and sign a paper for you. When I leave this house, I will keep distributing materials and talking about Jesus."

"Fine," his uncle said. "Get out of here. God be with you. But if I see you in the future, I will kill you."

This time the rejection of his family felt different from when he had felt unloved as a child. Now, Hussein knew Jesus was with him. He was filled with the Spirit. Peace flooded him to the point that he could laugh and smile when his family insulted him.

"I was even enjoying it," Hussein told me. Not the persecution exactly, but the way the persecution highlighted the level of contentment and belovedness Hussein felt in Christ.

The persecution opened another opportunity to leave Yemen and Hussein began to pursue that possibility in earnest. Several Christian groups promised to help him leave. Their offers were tempting. Hussein had lived abroad earlier in his life and knew how much easier things would be outside Yemen, but he couldn't come to peace about leaving.

One night, Hussein came to see me in Taiz. He fell asleep in my house and had another vision.

Hussein was riding in his uncle's car on a high mountain pass in

Hussein's province. His uncle was driving and all the village elders and sheikhs from his hometown were also in the vehicle. The car swerved and jerked around on the curving road as though Hussein's uncle was drunk and trying to crash the car.

Hussein pointed to a spot up ahead where his uncle could get out of the driver's seat and Hussein could take over. When they stopped, Hussein glanced down and saw a dark chasm. At the bottom was a pool of water and a mosque. The car started to roll backward and tip into the chasm. Hussein grabbed a rock and shoved it behind the tires to stop the car's momentum. Then he got into the driver's seat and began to drive. To his left and his right was only darkness but the way straight ahead was lit up bright white in the shape of a cross. The light pointed across the country toward my house.

Hussein woke up and knew he would stay in Yemen.

"The message was that my ministry was in my own country," he said.

There is an assumption among Western and even Arab Christians that the reason Yemeni believers stay in Yemen is because they don't have the opportunity to leave. Maybe they lack the money or the connections. While this is true for the majority of Yemenis, it does not apply to all Yemeni Christians. In fact, many could leave, and some have. They build new lives in the USA or Europe or other Middle Eastern nations. This was particularly true for the first Yemeni Christians, who were unaware of the existence of a community of believers in Yemen. Yet the majority choose to stay. Some even return, fully aware of the potential consequences and risks they face. They have relatives in Australia or Canada who could sponsor them, and some hold advanced degrees. Still, they stay.

They stay because they have a clear calling from God to serve in their own country. It is not easy, but it is profoundly *good*.

Once Hussein decided to stay in Yemen, he began to build a new life there, one with the gospel of the love of Jesus at the center. Hussein's extensive study of Islam before he met Jesus gave him unique insight into the disagreements and counterpoints he would come across in discussions with Muslims. He found that his first hurdle in a spiritual conversation was convincing the other person that he was sincerely a

Christian, and a Christian on the strength of his own convictions with no money or power or promised visa to be gained. Most often, he relied on his changed character and personal story of growth, including being a former drug addict, to testify along with his words.

Once people believed he truly loved Jesus, the next most common disputes were the ideas that Christians worship three gods and that the Bible was corrupted. At times, when speaking to those that had read and studied the Quran, he referred to reliable hadith and Quran verses to support his points, and then he encouraged people to read the Sermon on the Mount. Matthew 5-7 had left an impression on him when he first heard the words, "Love your enemies" on the radio long before he started following Jesus.

He had considered this, loving enemies, an impossible task. Yet, filled with the Holy Spirit, the first person Hussein was moved to forgive was his mother. Their relationship remained tense, partly because Hussein insisted on storing Bibles at her house in the village. She despised the books' presence, and one year, toward the end of Ramadan, Hussein called her to announce he would return to the village for the *Eid* holiday.

"You can come," his mother said, "but only stay one week. If you stay longer, there will be trouble. And you cannot bring any more Christian books."

"But there are already forty Bibles in your house," Hussein said.

"I burned them all," she said.

Hussein felt like his soul itself had been doused in gasoline and lit on fire. "Do you have any idea how hard it is to get a Bible into this country? I'm not coming without bringing more."

"You are not my son," she said. "I don't know you. But I want you at my house for Eid." In her contradictory words, Hussein heard the mother-pain of loving someone she also despised and possibly feared because of his different beliefs.

"I will bring a Bible," he said.

"Just come. Bring Satan and hell with you, but don't bring a Bible."

Hussein was thrilled to rejoin his family for the holiday. He ran straight to another Christian's home and gathered thirty Bibles to bring along. He didn't have time to hide them in his luggage and prayed through each checkpoint that no one would look inside his bags. Once in the village, Hussein brought a Bible to every single house. Sometimes he waited until the people inside were asleep and then tucked it into a window. He left one at the door of the mosque.

Villagers knew exactly who was delivering these books, and one night he was beaten until his "soul came out," but he remained pleased with his efforts.

When Hussein traveled, he left Bibles in hotel rooms and at restaurant tables. He added them to the bookshelves in mosques. He believed in the power of the word of God, that it would not return without accomplishing the purpose for which God sent it out. He also knew people in Yemen rarely destroyed books. If they were confiscated by the police, they would simply be placed in a giveaway pile or stored in the trash where a seeker might stumble upon them, like how Tariq received his Bible.

Incredibly, in the last three days of her life, Hussein's mother allowed him to visit her in the intensive care unit. He came near her bedside and Hussein held his mother's hand while she took her final breaths. He knew that such a moment of peace would have been impossible apart from Christ. Hussein's capacity for forgiveness and the intimacy he cultivated with Jesus would prove vital throughout his life. The childhood beatings from his uncles were only the precursors to future suffering.

14

THE RELUCTANT LEADER

Back in January 2005, two years after I moved to Jordan and one year after Lydia and I got married, we did our only year of missionary itinerating. We hated it. It is difficult to overstate my gratitude for not being tied to an organization that required regular visits to supporting churches. Without that structure, we had more space—no weekly team meetings or forced and unnatural gatherings to distract from culture learning. No irrelevant training requirements or yearly conferences to take me away. No letters to write, no money to raise, no donors to please, no churches to visit.

When I look back, though, I see God had a plan even in our agonizing treks across the Southeastern USA. I spoke at my former Bible school and started to urge a group of friends to join me and move to Yemen.

"You've had enough Bible school, just come and you'll learn the rest in Yemen," I said. They had already studied a couple of years and most of what they needed to learn they would learn in the field.

I didn't want to be their team leader, didn't want to join their team, and didn't want to participate in all their community-life activities. I didn't have a job to offer them. I told them if they wanted support from churches or training, they should join an organization. I knew I couldn't be that kind of support.

"Your pitch is terrible," Walter, one of my would-be recruits, said.

"Just come," I said. "You'll work it all out when you get there."

Work it out on the ground. Work out your questions about Islam in the context of Yemeni Islam. Work out your convictions about church leadership in the context of indigenous church leaders. Work out your evangelism techniques once you have had years of experimentation and analyzing to see what is effective in a specific context. "Prepare what you are most passionate about but unlearning and relearning is harder than learning."

Walter described his heart in those years of bible school as burning for Jesus and a question he had for me was what was I doing for Jesus?

"You seem like a tourist," he said. "What about the kingdom of God and discipleship?"

He saw me as a tourist because, when we had first met, I had been acting like one, traveling all over the Middle East as Lydia and I prayed about where we should settle and then traveling all over Yemen once we landed there. I hadn't yet committed to Yemen when I met Walter, but I could still talk about, and did talk about, unreached populations in the hostile and challenging locations we had visited. Despite the need, there seemed to be little effective witness. I found myself asking: why wasn't there more? Somewhere, wherever God brought us, would be an opportunity to participate in the building of the kingdom of God from the earliest days.

One point we connected on was that Walter decided I was, in his words, crazy for how I went from Jordan to the United States, married Lydia, took her from the wedding to a three-day layover honeymoon in Paris, to the Middle East, and spent our first year of marriage traipsing around Arabia. He was drawn to that pioneering, entrepreneur, adventuring, all-in spirit.

Walter had grown up as a minority Christian in a Muslim country where both religious groups were persecuted by communists, and the Middle East was the last place he wanted to live. His grandfather had wept when Walter told him he was going into cross-cultural ministry because their family experience had been that when missionaries came to a location, they were more likely to destroy the indigenous fellowship than to bless it.

Walter and two other team members came to Yemen on an exploratory trip. They decided Yemen was the place for them, and within a year they were all living in Taiz. Their wives came without even having explored the country but trusting their husbands' judgement and God's plan for them as couples.

Walter asked me to be their team leader. The couples had made a nearly covenantal commitment to one another and spent hours and days in community together: prayer meetings, Bible studies, strategy discussions, family gatherings, birthday parties, and holidays. But none of them wanted to take on the role of leading the team. I didn't want that responsibility either, or the relational ties of obligation to foreigners. I was happy to invite them and guide them, to consult and advise. I introduced them to veteran foreigners with whom they engaged in lengthy discussions about vision and culture, and others who prayed with them through discerning what their best contribution might be professionally. I was available as a reference and support from time to time, but I refused the request to be the traditional mission team leader. I still refuse this type of leadership role.

I explain to foreigners coming that if they need the support and safety net, okay, join a ministry organization for a year or two. They would teach how to learn a language, offer cross-cultural training, and it would build character. They might provide educational support for children or mental health counsel.

Organizations are not the only resources for these supports, but I understand the appeal of being part of a like-minded community with a global vision. I also think these organizations allow us to forget the value of a "God's team" mentality, Christian lingo for people from different organizations and different Christian backgrounds working together toward the same mission. Even without a formal organization, this group can provide accountability and access to a variety of giftings and skill sets.

An organization is more likely to teach you to toe the party line, to model their preferred method, to buy into a strategy built inside a boardroom on the other side of the planet by people who have never lived in your context long term. They don't know about Islahi neigh-borhoods or Yemeni folk tales. Have they broken *rashūsh*[1] in their hands and dipped it in spicy *sahawaq* sauce, thick with cheese, tomatoes, chili peppers, garlic, and herbs and spices, as they share fresh caught fish on the Mukalla seaside coast? Have they inhaled the *bukhur*, frankincense burned in their honor? Have they kissed the cheeks of broken men, released from prison having spent months in solitary confinement communing with Christ?

I suggested to Walter that if he did join an organization, he should ask himself after a year or two if his time with them has run out. For the sake of both his calling and the health of the organization, it might be wise to release one another, especially if the existing strategies continued to yield limited results.

Walter exhibited more pastoral gifts than I could dream of possessing and he reluctantly stepped into the position of team leader. He later told me that he felt these pastoral gifts were developed over years of growth. Mission team leaders, much like pastors, take on a dangerous role that can lead to narcissism if they believe they are standing in the position of speaking for God to people. In his book *When Narcissism Comes to Church*, Chuck DeGroat writes, "Ministry leaders and churches today are obsessively preoccupied with their repu-tation, influence, success, rightness, progressiveness, relevance, platform, affirmation, and power."[2] Instead of a charismatic person consumed by these things, the reluctant team leader, one who is capable but humble, teachable, and responsive to people's cares and concerns, is a wise choice. That was Walter.

Over the next seven years, Walter, his team, and I developed a mean-ingful connection without having extensive interactions. We all focused on our specific calling and grew to believe in each other. We realized that we could still be a part of the same community identity and could share similar culture and values, while not being on the same "team." We each

---

1. Rashūsh is a traditional bread, often similar to a thick, rustic flatbread, sometimes made with whole wheat flour.

2. Chuck DeGroat, *When Narcissism Comes to Church: Healing Your Community from Emotional and Spiritual Abuse* (Downers Grove, IL: IVP, an imprint of InterVarsity Press, 2020).

worked at different organizations but were all in Yemen to see the gospel of Jesus spread throughout the country. I helped them navigate culture and relate with Yemeni Christians, and our families grew close.

Walter became a kind of buffer and was an indispensable unofficial partner in ways I continue to discover and appreciate. He saw me as a natural concealer, not prone to share news of my family or ministry, not eager to tell people what is going on in my personal, work, or spiritual life. This is probably one reason missionary itinerating didn't work for me. Living in Yemen strengthened this tendency because of security issues. Call it being circumspect, or being wise, some felt I was secretive and exclusionary and complained to Walter about me. He saw this trait as contributing to my ability to thrive in Yemen while also contributing to the conflict foreigners had with me.

Walter became uniquely equipped to translate me to other foreigners and to Yemenis in the diaspora to the point that he developed what he called *The Five Areas You Are Misunderstanding Daniel*. I laughed the first time I heard about the list and laughed even harder when he described the five points because they were so accurate. Thanks to people like Walter, I have been able to develop in these areas.

One: don't expect to be invited. If you sit around waiting for him to call and invite you to join, you will wait forever. Be proactive if you want to engage with him on something.

Two: don't make assumptions. Seek clarification about things he says or doesn't say.

Three: don't expect to be babysat pastorally.

Four: don't expect affirmation. Don't read into him smiling or not smiling.

Five: don't expect transparency. He is a concealer, and just because he is not telling you everything, that is not a sign of him hiding something for a negative reason. Reframe the concealment as him not being aware that he hasn't told you or that he has a good reason to not tell you or that you aren't ready for it.

"You should hire me to translate you to people," Walter said.

Even in small Christian expat communities like in Yemen, there can be a kind of popularity contest, and missionary bubbles form. Walter's team avoided that due to their internal commitments. I avoided it because I wasn't in Yemen to relate with foreigners and had no organizational reason to. And, as Walter put it, I was so removed from people-pleasing that he suspected I didn't even know the term.

John, one of Walter's teammates, was also a concealer, and a peacemaker and an academic. Walter's open-hearted sharing and easy-going-while-focused personality and innate humility contributed to our growing mutual respect. John was harder to get to know, but I saw his devotion to language study and to his professional work as a teacher and believed their team would make a lasting impact on the church. They were willing to learn and work hard, open to hearing from local leaders, and took faith-filled but not foolish risks.

I didn't want to be Walter's team leader, and I also didn't want to be appointed a leader among Yemeni Christians. But I couldn't help but see and do something about issues I saw. One thing that consistently poked at me was the way local Christians remained dependent on foreign investment and foreigners' skill sets, and foreigners' presence in the production of indigenous materials. From music to sermons, recorded teachings and discipleship materials, anything produced was influenced from abroad. Why was no one training Yemenis to do these projects on their own, from designing to creating to producing to disseminating?

Since 2009 a power vacuum had been growing in Yemen, when the central government responded to unrest in the South with hundreds of arrests and lethal force against peaceful protesters. In March 2009, al-Qaeda in the Arabian Peninsula launched several attacks inside Yemen killing four South Korean tourists, two German nurses, a South Korean teacher, and kidnapping six other foreigners. Across the country, people who spoke out or held leadership roles in various political organizations started "disappearing." In May 2009, the government banned distribution of the leading newspapers and imposed informal censorship rules.

In Aden alone, on July 7, so many people were arbitrarily arrested at peaceful protests that they were held in industrial hangars and sports stadiums. In the North, Houthi rebels increased attacks and their use of child soldiers.

Despite the growing insecurity across the country, with the skill of a compassionate Yemeni doctor, our third child, another daughter, was born safely in Yemen. The nurses asked Lydia if we had dyed our baby's hair because of her natural blond highlights. Yemeni traditions around childbirth vary depending on tribe, region, and family, and maybe they assumed that was our "tribe's" tradition. Some families tied their babies to restrict movement, while others adorned them with gold jewelry inscribed with Quranic verses to ward off the evil eye. Others used herbs to protect against spirits. We rejoiced that she was healthy and were thankful that we felt free from these worries about evil spirits. Her birth reminded us of life and hope in the midst of external hardships.

At the end of 2010, in Tunisia, 2,730 miles from Yemen, fruit vendor Mohamed Bouazizi set himself on fire in protest against police refusing to let him operate his cart. His public death launched the Arab Spring, a movement that raced across North Africa and the Middle East, igniting nations from Sudan to Syria, Bahrain. Yemen, already inflamed by the internal issues of 2009, grew even hotter. By 2011, the Middle East and North Africa were raging with protests and tensions.

In January, demonstrations in Yemen called for President Saleh to step down. He had ruled for thirty-three years. He offered some concessions, including not running for president again, but refused to step down and the protests spread. Estimates vary on how many people died in the crackdown on the protests, but between 200 and 2,000 people were killed by government forces.

Jamil, Rauf, Hussein, Tariq, Shaadi, Jamila, and many Yemenis were becoming established in faith and were writing their own music and creating discipleship plans. Ever since he heard that Jesus was the Son of God on the radio and kicked it across the room, Jamil understood the power of radio. He had worked with a Wycliffe translator to put the

Jesus Film into Yemeni dialect and had fallen in love with media as a means of sharing his faith. In November 2013, I brought in a European sound engineer to teach Jamil and others how to record.

One afternoon while they recorded, from outside the studio came the sound of a massive thump. Then boom boom boom. Bang!

"What's that?" the European man asked.

"Nothing to worry about," Jamil said.

"Nothing," I said.

"These are normal sounds for us," Jamil said.

The man looked skeptical, but our unchanged demeanor convinced him to continue the recording. Once we finished, I glanced at Jamil and, with a sparkle in his eye, he opened the blinds on the window. Exactly as we both suspected, less than one hundred meters away, a building had been bombed. Cement blocks had fallen onto the street, smoke and debris and dust filled the air.

"This is normal for us," Jamil repeated. He and I burst into laughter while our guest stared at the destroyed building through the window. We weren't laughing at the senseless destruction, and it was clear from the lack of human response in the streets that, miraculously, no one had been injured. We laughed at the shocked look on our guest's face and at the absurdity of such a thing being "normal." Laughter is a vital coping mechanism in places like Yemen, though often misinterpreted by people on the outside.

This was Jamil's country. Yemen belonged to her people, with their vision and voice. And the church—God's church—needed to be rooted in Yemeni soil, led by Yemeni believers, and shaped by their faith journey. I wanted to partner and train, to equip, challenge, and catalyze. I wasn't refusing relational leadership, but I didn't want the traditional or positional leadership role. I have always been eager for partnership and adding value to one another by being in community. The early days of the Arab Spring increased a sense of urgency for Yemeni leadership. I wasn't sure how long foreigners would survive in Yemen.

That sentiment included me. I was foreign, a fact that will never go away, and which would become more controversial and dangerous as the church grew and violence intensified. Walter and John had dreams about one another when they were in college, before they moved to

Yemen. Walter describes it as a "divine connection," where he says otherwise, they would not likely have been friends.

One night, when Walter was in my house, he had a dream about he and I growing old together. In the dream we connected with a powerful bond. Walter remembers jotting it down in his journal. When I invited Walter and his team to Yemen, I couldn't have predicted that there would be blood on the ground, or that I would be the one to reach the body first.

15

THE SECURITY OF
TRANSPARENCY

"Jeremy needs to leave right now. Like today."

The governor of Taiz stared intently at me as he spoke. I hadn't even begun our English lesson—had barely greeted him—yet something in his tone told me this was serious.

This was March 2012, and Yemen had been growing increasingly unstable. The Arab Spring had rocked Yemen and worsened the power vacuum that had begun in 2009 and spread across the nation. I felt it viscerally in Taiz. I knew I had been a target of extremists since 2010, and over the next two years, security became increasingly necessary and complicated. AQAP had a long presence in Yemen, and Taiz was known as a training center. Many men who fought in Afghanistan had been ideologically trained in Taiz.

"Tell him to leave Yemen," the governor said.

Jeremy was a friend, and I knew he would take this warning seriously, especially considering the source of intelligence. The governor was also a friend, a private English language student of mine, and he didn't want trouble or violence on his watch. It was never entirely clear what Jeremy had done or said, but the details aren't as important as the gravity of the threat against him. Most likely, he was sharing the gospel or a Bible story and was overheard by the wrong person in a *qat* chewing session. These sessions could include eight to ten men, and you never knew all of them intimately, who they were connected to, or what their ideology was. You could never know how something you said might be misinterpreted or used against you. Jeremy said or did something, someone told an extremist who decided to act either as a lone wolf or as part of a more organized team, security forces discovered the plot, and the call came for him to flee.

Following the resignation of President Ali Abdullah Saleh and Vice President Abd Rabbuh Mansur Hadi's assumption of power in February 2012, Yemen faced significant political and security challenges. Optimistic Yemenis saw the nation transitioning toward a more inclusive and democratic administration, but AQAP posed acute security threats and exploited the political unrest and lack of strong leadership. The Southern Movement, which sought secession from the North, added to the complexities. At the same time, Yemen faced a deteriorating humanitarian crisis marked by poverty, food scarcity, and limited access to essential resources.

There was political unrest, armed conflict, and population displacement as people fled violence or searched for food and work. Government officials held decreasing power and were more susceptible to elements working against the nation-state. Even my friend, the governor, eventually left his post after realizing he was being intentionally undermined by other members of the government and security forces in the city. This led to several acts of violence, causing him to conclude he had lost his ability to govern effectively.

I taught the governor English one hour a day and around the time of Jeremy's evacuation, the phone rang during our lesson. The governor answered, glanced at me, and turned away only slightly. By the way he responded, I guessed he was speaking about me. I pretended to be preoccupied with the lesson for the day, flipping through papers, while staying attentive to his reaction to the conversation. I was curious who would call the governor to speak about me but also didn't want to hear it, because it wasn't any of my business.

"You know this man, Daniel?"

"Yes."

"What is he doing in Yemen?"

The governor outlined my work as a teacher and vouched for my character and professionalism. "I know him, and I know his father. They are good for Yemen."

After the call ended, he told me I was under investigation by the National Security Bureau but that there was nothing to worry about. No specific threat, no timing of a proposed threat, no presumed attack planned. That wasn't exactly reassuring but, of course, I didn't think about leaving. My heart had knit itself to Yemen long ago, and it would take more than one investigation to make me leave. Normal life slipped away, replaced by twenty-four-hour armed guards and counter-surveillance measures. Then grief barged in, but Lydia and I never talked about leaving. We chose Yemen. We still choose Yemen.

Of course, there were far more things happening than one investigation. There were threats and attempts, and Yemen grew more dangerous by the week. Living in a country experiencing unrest or even civil war doesn't necessarily require a security detail. But when the threats become personal, when a person starts to be hunted, survival means hiring security. My name started popping up on radical websites, then photos of me, along with posts claiming I was a threat to society. At first, I searched out these posts so I could know what was being said, but that wasn't healthy psychologically, and I didn't want to increase traffic to the websites. I built up a robust safety team. They watched my family and me physically and monitored the internet to track online discussions about me.

This team was composed of men I knew, or men my original sponsor knew and vouched for. They were all Muslims I had known for more than fifteen years and were men I trusted from my early days of the car accident to these treacherous times. Many of them knew me and my work well, including my teachings about Jesus. In some cases, they were so well-informed that on occasion they offered wise counsel to Christians. I once discovered one of my Muslim security detail explaining Jesus's teaching on love and forgiveness to a Yemeni Christian who was struggling in these areas.

Early on, before foreigners develop trusting relationships and meaningful cultural expertise, we tend to revert to security in a secretive way. We don't want Muslims to know our business. We use code words and disguise allegiances and aren't transparent about our motives or intentions, as though any of this would protect us from those truly seeking harm. Kevin Crooks gave sage counsel when he wrote, "Trust more in God's protection than in the doubtful protection of coded messages beloved by some Christian organizations and secure e-mails considered essential by some, which I believe are little deference against those really determined to cause us harm, and which provoke bewilderment and sometimes suspicion amongst those who do not."[1] Better to follow the Apostle Paul's example, "Rather, we have renounced secret and shameful ways; we do not use deception, nor do we distort the word of God. On the contrary, by setting forth the truth plainly we commend ourselves to everyone's conscience in the sight of God."[2]

At the same time, it's important to recognize that full transparency isn't always possible in certain contexts. In environments where lives are at stake, measures like pseudonyms, altered names, and discretion about sensitive information are often necessary to ensure safety. While secrecy should never be used to deceive or distort, there is a balance to be struck between protecting others and living openly in integrity.

When I use the word "security" now in my own context, I do not mean hiding or being fearful. I mean revealing. It is vital for the team protecting me, my family, and Yemeni Christians at baptisms or church gatherings to know what is going on, and why. They need to understand what they are protecting and would feel deceived if they found out another way. Security is about partnership and trust, not secrecy and "cover." These men don't have to work to keep Christians safe, they choose to. If I wasn't being honest, trust would break down immediately.

Those who have historically sponsored us to get visas and legal work permits in Yemen have experienced their own persecution and assassination attempts from extremists because they pursue peace, have moderate views, and support the right of Christians to worship. These Muslim men believe in the right of every Yemeni to worship as they feel led, even when that meant Muslims putting their faith in Christ and identifying

---

1. Crooks, *Yemen: Heartbreak & Hope*, 64.
2. 2 Corinthians 4:1

as followers of Christ or Yemeni Christians. They also believe in the value of Christians and Muslims knowing one another in authentic, reciprocal relationships.

Reciprocal relationships are key to developing trust between Muslims and Christians, as professor of Islamic Studies, Dr. Martin Accad states, "Meaningful, life-transforming conversation can hardly take place outside such respect and trust. But it is important to emphasize that this engagement does not go merely in one direction. The relationship of trust and respect that is developed through the kerygmatic approach should precisely be mutual. Kerygmatic engagement creates an opportunity to listen to what Muslims have to say about religious issues as well, the opportunity to learn and stand corrected."[3]

When I asked my chief security officer why he takes the risks he does to protect Christians, he said, "The things I read about Jesus I see in their flesh. I see *Al-Masīḥ mutajassid fīhim.*" The Messiah incarnated in Christians.

I never wanted to replace this level of transparency, partnership, and affection with a hired privatized company. Those were known for dropping their weapons and running away when things got hot. I needed people I trusted, people who trusted me, and people who came with tribal affiliations, so that anyone who made trouble with me was ultimately making trouble with an entire tribe. Their allegiance needed to be more to the tribe than to me, or the money I paid.

I hired three guards with automatic weapons for our house on the same day a friend was assassinated. We were guarded twenty-four-hours a day. We installed security cameras. We altered our movements, never taking the same routes or leaving at the same times. My eldest had started school in 2010, and while she continued to go, I had security looking out for her too.

The posts online increased in frequency and created a mythology around me. I wasn't just any foreigner in Yemen now. I was a foreigner accused of acting against the government and of evangelizing people.

---

3. Evelyn A. Reisacher, Joseph L. Cumming, and Dean S. Gilliland, eds., *Toward Respectful Understanding and Witness among Muslims: Essays in Honor of J. Dudley Woodberry* (Pasadena, CA: William Carey Publishing, 2012).

Others alleged I had escaped from Hezbollah or even had the power to reopen the Sana'a airport. There was a doctored video in which I met with the former President of Yemen (true story) with the addition that I worked for Mossad and sponsored special meetings between the President and Israel (untrue story).

I told my security team I would happily meet with anyone making these accusations. Bringing people together humanizes them. They would realize in a thirty-minute conversation that I was nothing like who they had built into a threatening caricature online or in their imaginations. I was a *shab*, a young guy who wasn't who they thought I was, didn't believe what they thought I did, and didn't do what they said I did.

No one ever took me up on this offer.

But, at the same time, those seeking to harm me weren't totally opposed to interacting with me when it served their benefit. When war came, electricity was an issue. I had set up solar panels and batteries that generated my own electricity, and when I left the area, neighborhood al-Qaeda members used them to charge their phones. I couldn't do anything to stop them and recognized the irony in the possibility that they would then use those cell phones to plan an attack against me.

During the beginning of the war in 2015, flying bullets and dropping bombs that could strike anyone indiscriminately were the biggest dangers for the general population. But for my family, the primary dangers were always extremist elements with a *taqfiri*[4] ideology or any party that viewed me as a threat to their political agenda. The government, as evidenced by my English student, welcomed foreigners, even Christian foreigners, if we made legitimate contributions to Yemen through business, education, healthcare, development, and other sectors. But the government couldn't effectively monitor, control, or snuff out all these radical networks.

The shooter at the Jibla Hospital on December 30, 2002, had read about the hospital and decided to target the foreigners as a lone actor. It only takes one upset extremist to kill many people. He could be someone watching reports on Israel and Palestine, and he sees a white

---

4.   When a Muslim declares another Muslim an apostate.

foreigner on the street and decides it is time to do his part. It could be that someone drops their guard or has a sentence misinterpreted. The atmosphere was changing, and there were no more exploring road trips through mountain passes or family visits to the beach.

Yemen is like the ocean—calm on top but there are powerful undercurrents. Pay attention and be aware constantly or you might end up dead prematurely. Those undercurrents reared their heads more and more often. This continues to be the case in Yemen. Measuring risk and making wise, faith-filled decisions is one of the most complicated situations expatriate Christians face.

One expat who lived in Yemen for over twenty-five years told me, "You can choose to live in fear, become frozen, do nothing, and get kicked out of the country eventually or you can do something for God and eventually get kicked out of the country, but at least it was for something."

I never wanted to stay just to stay. I desire to actively follow Christ and be obedient to him. And yet, my posture was also to be respectful to the government God had allowed to be in power, to be respectful to my Muslim hosts, and to seek peace with everyone. With that in mind, I had to consider security and things like analyzing the impact on locals if the foreigner stays or goes. Where are the limits, and who decides? The situation is always more complex than it appears on the surface and often looks worse from the other side of the ocean to those who are watching and making decisions but not living it.

One assumption might be that if the foreigner leaves, there will be less risk or violence for the locals because the outsider is the obvious, high-profile target. However, they are also often more protected or are citizens of powerful countries. And, as one of my security staff explained, the foreigner acts as a buffer between extremists and believers. In his experience, the terrorists do view foreigners as a priority target, meaning they would prefer to kill the expatriate, and a secondary priority would be a Yemeni Christian. Thus, the foreigner does shield the locals to some extent.

The contextual complexities around questions of risk and security are one reason why so many organizations develop blanket, company-wide policies. When certain major trigger points are struck or when a critical mass of lesser trigger points are struck, they pull staff out. These large organizations are liable, and most people don't push to stay longer when they probably could and should remain. Most of the time we do not allow for enough risk. We love the people we serve alongside, and are committed to a place, but then we leave. Organizations must weigh liability carefully, but the danger is that it can overshadow the deeper question of what God is asking people to do.

I also recognize that especially large organizations can't trust all their people. They don't know them deeply enough. Home office staff don't know how reliant field staff are on prayer and the Holy Spirit, they don't know what their local security relationships are like, they don't know their real emotional or mental health in response to crises. Some field staff aren't equipped to make wise judgments, and some should be removed from the field. Some refuse wise counsel and make foolish decisions that place themselves and others in danger. Some have extenuating circumstances, or a medical need, or prior hardships that give them less emotional margin.

Life and death are held differently, too, in Yemen and by Yemenis. As immersed as I was in Yemeni community, and without an outside organization dictating my choices, I embraced the local perspective. Life is idolized by many Westerners, to the point that safety, comfort, and security become ultimate. And yet, many in the West crave danger. They skydive and ocean cave dive and climb Mount Everest and drive too fast. Life in Yemen is always on the edge, death lurks from war, poverty, disease, terrorism, accident. It isn't that people don't grieve or dread death as profoundly as a Westerner, but they are less surprised by it, less offended that death should stalk them too.

One of my guards told me it was rare to see someone in his home village die of old age; there were so many assassinations and vengeance killings. Rather than scaring him away from security detail, the deaths motivated him to work for peace even when it meant putting himself in harm's way. Death was a lesser specter than perpetuating the cycle of violence.

The Apostle Paul's words "For to me to live is Christ, and to die is gain"[5] left a deep impact on me. At the point of death, Christ welcomes us into eternal life with him. Yes, life was vibrant and meaningful on this earth, but I was not living for life on this earth. I learned from Yemenis of all walks of life how to be resilient during dangerous situations and, again like Paul in Philippians, how to be content in every situation.

Unbeknownst to me at the time, my life was hanging by a thread in late 2011 and early 2012. I found out about three assassination attempts from a Yemeni friend who had been put into prison for his faith and had been thrown into a cell with al-Qaeda operatives.

"Three times we tried to kill that guy!" the al-Qaeda prisoner said. "We've been trying to kill him for a long time."

My friend didn't manage to get details of one of the attempts, but when he told me about the other two, I remembered the exact days.

Once, I went into a bookshop in downtown Taiz. Two al-Qaeda operatives waited outside and intended to shoot me as I walked out.

A prominent government official visited the bookshop at the same time. When he stepped out, I exited behind him, and his entire retinue of security guards blanketed the area. The terrorists had to pull out, thwarted.

The second attempt on my life occurred on a regular day, during a regular trip to the company I was working at. I alternated my route, as I always did during the years I was targeted. However, there was one stretch of road that couldn't be changed. Several al-Qaeda operatives waited for me at the top of a hill. As they waited, a massive group of protestors marched near the intersection I was crossing and the government sent security vehicles to the area to keep the protests from getting out of hand. I hate being late for work and impatiently watched the minutes tick by until I could continue. The protestors moved toward the would-be assassins' position, and again, they had to abandon their plan because of the increasing military presence.

But then, on March 18, 2012, death came.

---

5. Philippians 1:21

16

IN THE LINE OF FIRE, IN THE HANDS OF GOD

Obviously, I have not gone to be with the Lord yet. But I was one of the presumed targets the day death came. My name was on the hit lists. I'd been a direct assassination target at least three times by then, more in the future. A US military person said to me that once you survive an attempt on your life, *khalas*, finished. Go home. You won't likely survive another, and the wisest thing to do would be to go home and sit in your rocking chair and enjoy whatever life you have left. You are a dead man walking.

Walter was supposed to go to work that morning with John, but the team had been dealing with interpersonal struggles.

"Go to the office without me," he told John. "I need to spend time praying through these issues first. I'll meet you there soon."

There had also been serious and credible security threats recently and the team had changed their travel routes, their departure times, the cars they drove in, and who they rode with. Walter didn't know he had made a decision that would save his life.

Walter had become close with a man, Sa'ad, who held an important government position and who had confided in Walter that he was a fifth generation Yemeni Jew. Being a Jew in Yemen was complicated, danger-ous, and ancient, another marginalized community that could trace its roots as far back as the fifth century BC, the time of King Solomon. The Ethiopian Christian incursion into Yemen and then the Islamic conquest transformed the once-vibrant Jewish community into a population of *dhimmis*, a protected but subordinate class. They paid a special tax and lived under restrictions unique to non-Muslims. In 1679 the "Mawza Exile" saw Jews expelled from their homes. After the establishment of Israel in 1948, approximately 50,000 Jews were airlifted out of Yemen into Israel by the Israeli government in an operation commonly known as "Operation Magic Carpet."[1] By 2020, estimates are that only a handful of Jews remain and the historical memory of Yemenis being Jewish, just as the historical memory of Yemenis being Christian has been nearly eradicated.

And yet, Sa'ad, an open-minded man of peace, remains. When he befriended Walter, he couldn't have known the lifelong impact their relationship would have on him.

While Walter knelt in his prayer closet that morning, Sa'ad was driving with his own personal guard on the same route leading to Walter's and John's clinic. Suddenly, rapid gunfire shattered the morning stillness. Sa'ad looked in the direction of the shooting, just in front of him on the same road. He recognized the car; it belonged to Walter's organization. He couldn't see who was inside the car, but he and his guard started to shoot their own guns into the air, trying to scare off whatever attack was happening up ahead. The driver sped up and screeched to a halt beside the shot-up vehicle. The attackers seemed to have fled.

Sa'ad jumped out of his car and rushed toward the bloody scene. Other onlookers tried to get close but Sa'ad shouted at them to stay back. He couldn't see who was inside the car but could tell no one was moving. He pulled out his phone and frantically tried to reach someone from the organization. Walter's phone rang and rang and rang. John

---

1. "Operation 'Magic Carpet' came to an end on the 24th of September 1950, which involved 450 flights carrying around 50,000 Yemeni Jews to Israel between 1949 and 1950." Ahroni, Reuben, (2013), Jewish Emigration from the Yemen 1951-98, Routledge, New York. p: 1.

didn't answer. He tried Walter again, and to Sa'ad's immense relief, Walter answered.

"I'm at your car," Sa'ad said, trying to keep his voice calm. Later, he would need to address the traumatic impact this event had on him. Now was the time for getting help. "Someone has been shot."

Walter called another coworker. He answered the phone. He was alive. Walter called John. The phone rang and rang and rang. Walter forced himself to breathe. Maybe John was praying, like Walter had been, and ignoring his phone. Maybe he was just injured.

I was in my office that morning and picked up my phone on the first ring. It was Walter.

"There's been an attack," he said. "I think it's John. I've been calling him. There's no answer." His voice shook. "I think John is dead."

I told Walter to stay where he was and I grabbed Mansour, a Muslim employee, and rushed outside to the car.

Jamil watched us leave the office. He knew I wouldn't leave so abruptly without a word unless something terrible had happened. I don't remember why I didn't say anything, I don't even remember Jamil being in the office. There are flashes of memory and then black spaces of nothing. I probably didn't want to frighten anyone. If it was true and John was dead, there might be lingering danger as the shooters waited for spectators and coworkers, friends, or family to arrive. If it was false, there was no reason to raise an alarm. In either case, if I said something, people would have jumped into the car with me, and I didn't want to cause more of a scene than we already would.

Mansour and I sped to the other side of town, and as we drove down the mountain closer to the intersection, I knew. There was John's car, destroyed. All the windows were shot in. Glass littered the street. People stood nearby, staring but not moving.

There was John. His body was riddled with bullets. I didn't look long.

I didn't stay long. Whoever did this was surely watching.

Mansour and I drove to my house. I was frozen. I couldn't stop to feel. I had to be vigilant. This was now a warzone, a hot zone. I needed to pay extra attention to the cars behind me, and the people on the side of the road. I needed to think, plan, and inform people. I didn't need to remember my friend's body.

Mansour wept the entire way to my house. Of the few memories I hold of this day, this one is searingly vivid. My tender, strong Yemeni Muslim friend wept for the death of his American Christian friend.

I called Walter and confirmed his worst suspicion. I called Lydia.

"John is dead, don't leave the house."

She said our eldest daughter was still at school and that it would be wise if she didn't leave the school at the normal, predictable time.

"We need to get her home now," I said, concerned someone would grab her to get to me. "Zayn will pick her up and bring her home, I don't want you to leave the house."

Lydia didn't ask any questions.

When I got home, I told Lydia the details of what happened. Then she and I pulled our housekeeper, an Ethiopian woman who knew John, into the bathroom to tell her. We didn't want the kids to see her reaction, which was powerfully emotional. Lydia wasn't emotionally expressive externally. I was usually the expressive one between us, but during times of danger, I entered a hyper-aware mode that shuts down these external reactions. I would express my emotions later, once the danger had passed.

I remember saying to her, "So, are you okay?"

She stared at me, her eyes wide, and I realized how inappropriate the question was, as though someone had dropped a sack of potatoes. "Are you okay?"

"No," she said. "No. I am not okay."

Her blunt answer shook me out of my stupor. Of course. Of course she was not okay; nothing about this was okay. Not being okay made sense right now and was a normal response to the murder of a friend. None of us were okay.

Walter told Jane, John's wife, and she remained in denial until the two of them went to the morgue to identify the body.

Walter told me they planned to pray for John to rise from the dead while at the morgue, as if asking for my opinion.

"Yes, sure, why not?" I said. "Pray whatever you want, this is her husband and your close friend." They weren't going to put on a dramatic show or draw attention. They would breathe out a sentence or two, unheard by anyone, and then go home to grieve.

Other loved ones of murdered Christians have described this urge to pray for them back from the dead. Probably most people feel the desire when a loved one dies, but there is an interesting commonality among the families of missionaries killed abroad when they tell their stories. Even families who knew this was a possibility, can't avoid the wrestle, the shock, that God would allow this. Someone who gave up their country and comforts to identify with another culture *actually* dying there. *Actually* shedding blood and breathing their last breath. It can feel terrifyingly unjust of God. And yet, isn't that what we are modeled in Jesus? Aren't we called to lose our life for Christ's sake? It is a painful test of faith with no easy balm.

I hoped God would answer her prayer, but John remained dead, and now our company had to figure out how to evacuate over one hundred foreigners from Taiz. John's wife had to figure out how to repatriate the body. Walter's team was there to support Jane and her two young boys. I was managing my own emotions and explaining to my family what had happened while trying to communicate with our Yemeni staff and trying to stay alive.

I remember being close to God during those days, as if I knew I would be next. I had made my peace with God and death and every moment with my children. I thought, *this is the last time I will hug them or kiss them.* I knew I was in God's hands, but even so, when you have small kids and there are extremists intentionally hunting you down, each moment feels precious and raw.

Within minutes of breaking the news of John's death to my family, and making sure my daughter was home safe, I had to go back outside to check on others. This is not a glorification of a martyrdom story, and I certainly wasn't heroic; I wasn't seeking death. But I knew the implications of living in Yemen and had counted the cost. This was me trying to be faithful.

In the days following John's murder, residents of Taiz came out *en masse* to protest the failure of the government to foster a safe environment. They protested the needless bloodshed. They stood in solidarity with the shocked and grieving foreign community, even as that community fled Taiz. Christian and Muslim Yemenis joined to raise their voices in a collective lament, not knowing that unimaginable bloodshed would soon flow throughout their beloved nation.

I still felt frozen, and it would be years before I fully grasped how this traumatic event, among others, affected me, but the impact of these protests was not lost. Extremists were surely watching, taking note of who dared publicly display their displeasure. And yet, Yemenis fearlessly sent a message that they longed for peace. What happens in communities in the United States when a mosque is vandalized, or a Muslim is assaulted? In a nation where there is no risk of being placed on a hit list, are Christians silent about injustice? That, too, sends a message.

After the Jibla Hospital shooting that took place in December 2002, the majority of Yemeni Christians scattered in the region. The church spent the next few years slowly reestablishing trust and community. It had been painful, and stories of betrayal and rejection abound. When coupled with the fear of more violence, the burden of sustaining the community grew overwhelming. Overcoming resentment and bitterness and building trust and loyalty had been church leaders' focus for nearly a decade. When John was killed, the effectiveness of their efforts was revealed.

The church did not scatter like the terrorists intended. The opposite happened. The church stood together in visible solidarity, a clear indicator of their corporate maturity, character full of the fruit of the Spirit, and hard-earned wisdom. Jamil, Shaadi, Jamila, Athir, Tariq, Hussein, and others strengthened their bonds of fellowship even as there was a general premonition that John's death opened a door no one wanted open, and that more violence was coming.

"We were upset," Athir said. "We loved John. But being upset also made us brave."

As Yemen slipped further into chaos, Yemeni Christians responded with a sober understanding of the situation and decided if they were going to die, they would rather be part of a meaningful community before death. They would rather promote healthy practices and unity than die in isolation and fear. They would rather endure together than struggle alone. Before John's murder, small groups had restarted meeting together and his death merely reinforced their resolve to tangibly be the Body of Christ for one another.

Sa'ad provided three vehicles when it was time for Walter and his family to leave the city where the attack had taken place. Sa'ad embodied what I, and Walter, experienced over and over again in Yemen—mercy from unexpected sources. We were vulnerable and wounded, especially Walter and his team, including John's family, and a Yemeni Jew became the Good Samaritan, neighboring us well. Often the help and mercy came from Muslims, like my security team and dear friends. Sa'ad loved Walter and John and put his life at risk to serve them, even calling on his entire Jewish-Yemeni tribe to protect these Christians as they drove away from the city they loved, the city that had broken their hearts.

One Yemeni Christian leader said, "Persecution is not our identity." This is true for Christians in Yemen, it is true for Jews in Yemen, it is true for Muslims who care about and protect Christians and Jews in Yemen. Organizations who highlight the "persecuted church" often seem more committed to a slogan to catch Western Evangelical attention than they are in truly seeing the victorious church. Some of these organizations cherry-pick who they support, attempting to give only to Christians without realizing that in Yemen no one stands alone and in contrast to what Jesus modeled of mercy on all. The Yemeni church partners across religious lines and donations do not remain in a single pocket but spread to a wide network, including Muslim relatives. Yes, there is pain and persecution, but the church is networked, committed to the broad mercy of God, resilient, and beautiful. It is so much more than a persecuted victim.

In faithful defiance and hopeful resiliency, Yemeni Christian leaders made the decision to mark the day of John's death, March 18th, as a National Day of Prayer in Yemen. In a few short years, they would add a second National Day of Prayer.

～

Now I knew. The terrorists were willing to kill. I also knew we were one family of two or three remaining foreign families. Before, terrorists had their pick of over one hundred and fifty people. Now, ten to twelve. We took even more security measures, including rarely leaving the house and pulling our daughter permanently out of school. When I did leave, I used different cars and worked unpredictable hours. Maybe they would go after an easier target. I hate the thought that by being more secure and a harder target, someone else might be hit. But that is the reality. I counseled others on security, advised and gave suggestions, and explained why I relied solely on locals for information and security. Some people took my advice, others didn't. Some were safe as they continued to live in Yemen, others decided to leave and got out safely, others didn't. There is a fine line even Christians walk between *qadr* and human agency, between God has ordained our every breath and God has given us brains to use wisely.

In practice, I believe in doing what I can to keep myself and my family safe, but I also believe that when my time is up, time's up. When God decides it's my time to be with him, death will come. I could be in the West or violence could reach me in Yemen. Don't be foolish, I tell people. Trust God, but don't go stand in front of a lorry in the street. The truck will run you down. God will still welcome you into paradise, but that was foolish.

Lydia and I watched the foreign exodus from behind our guarded home, listened to the increasingly frequent gun battles across the city, tried to create an atmosphere of family and community with our Yemeni brothers and sisters, and wondered how long it would last.

17

PRESENCE AS WITNESS

Most of the foreigners left after John's murder, but by 2012 local Christians hadn't been dependent on foreign leadership for several years. The Arab Spring had come and gone with lingering effects. The revolution and war were arriving. Yemenis didn't need to look only to outsiders for examples of faith-filled courage, they could look to their own communities.

Yes, now they had a fresh visceral understanding of the risk of following Jesus in Yemen, but that surprised no one in this community where most people had spent time in prison or faced pressure from families for their faith.

Preprison training and postprison debriefs became an integral part of discipleship. Believers counted the cost and learned how to stand together through fiery trials. And, while they grieved John's death, the reality is that it felt a bit removed for Yemeni Christians. John was American, a high-profile outsider assassinated by al-Qaeda. Would the reaction be different if a Yemeni was killed? No one wanted to find out the answer to that question, but they were not oblivious to the growing violence.

People outside Yemen asked if my family was safe. As another Westerner in a dangerous location wrote, "Of course we were safe. Of course we were not safe. How could we know? Nothing happens until it happens. Safety is a Western illusion crafted into an idol and we refused to bow."[1] Al-Qaeda had my name on a hit list and operatives lived in our neighborhood. The Houthis waged war against the feeble government. Saudi Arabia sent fighter jets across the border. The United States played an active role in Yemen's conflict, with drone strikes targeting AQAP, offering their allies intelligence, or refueling allies' jets.

But safety has never been the predominant guiding factor in my life choices, or in Lydia's life choices. We were where we were supposed to be. God had promised to be with us always and that was enough.

The question from foreigners is almost always, Why stay? *Why stay?* The default assumption is to flee when danger arrives. I think the question should be, Why leave? *Why leave?* And the follow-up: Is God asking us to leave now? The surprise and the probing questions should come when a person who committed their life to a place or a people with the Kingdom of God in mind leaves.

That doesn't mean the choice to stay is easy, and it certainly doesn't mean it is heroic, or that everyone would make the same choice. Or that it is the correct choice in every season. Clearly, most people didn't stay. Most foreign Christians left the country.

I also can't pretend my motivation for staying was completely righteous, either. Leaving was what the extremists wanted. It was why they terrorized people. I would not give them what they wanted.

They wanted me to leave. I would stay.

They hoped to frighten me away. I would remain.

When I am vulnerable enough to share the whole truth, a driving emotion behind my refusal to leave was my refusal to give in to any extremist desires. Al-Qaeda killed my friend with the intention of scattering, even destroying, the church and Christian witness. The weakest thing I could do would be to bend to their wishes; to bow out. To say, *okay, you win, have it your way, Christ has no place in Yemen.* I couldn't do that.

I would stay and be a disruption. I would be more effective than

---

1. Rachel Pieh Jones, *The Proper Weight of Fear* (Grand Rapids, MI: Plough Publishing House, 2021).

ever. I ached for the power of the Kingdom of God to uproot every wicked scheme, to undo every violent act, to restore every broken heart, and I wanted to be part of it. I carried my competitive streak, for better or worse, into my passion for Jesus to be known and loved in every governorate across Yemen.

Our concern wasn't only al-Qaeda, but also the escalating resistance in Taiz led by Islahi's Sheikh Hamoud Makhlafi who led opposition forces against forces loyal to then President Ali Abdullah Saleh. Makhlafi's opposition gained steam throughout 2012 and, along with later Saudi-led intervention, led to the world's worst humanitarian crisis. War brought more anonymous, less targeted dangers. More than once my family had to run for cover from bombs raining from the sky, stray bullets from nearby street fights, and at night we could hear drones flying nearby. I gathered bullet casings, rocket casings, and shrapnel from the backyard and the rooftop, took photos, and showed them to the security team.

Were we foolish to stay during the war years? Consider the underlying assumption: that we were free to leave because we were not Yemeni. Some would argue it was foolish to die in another country where we did not have to live. No one forced us to stay, no one closed their border to us, or demanded thousands of dollars to help us escape in the dark of night in a rickety boat that might never reach land safely or to coyote us through desolate wilderness stretches littered with bodies.

When the New Testament talks about Christians being brothers and sisters in Christ, does that mean brothers and sisters only during peacetime? When there is enough to eat? Brothers and sisters as long as it is comfortable for you? Brothers and sisters as long as you make no demands on my time, resources, or comfort?

The question of whether I was foolish for staying during a season of war fails to sufficiently address this, and fails to take kinship in Christ theology seriously. However, there does come a point when the human earthly reality becomes a factor. When the color of my family's skin and the color of our passports became more of a liability than the local church should bear. When some nations forcibly extract their people from conflict or danger. I am not saying foreigners must always stay no matter what. But, again, let us challenge the notion that *leave* should be the first response. Maybe stay should be the default.

And so, we stayed.

Lydia homeschooled the kids, mostly kindergarten and preschool. Our fourth child, a son, was born during these years. Lydia and I had to plan multiple possible routes to get to the hospital in preparation for the delivery, in case one or another was blocked or too dangerous. We call him our "child of the revolution." Roughly every three months, we left the country. Partly for a break from the stress of war and isolation but also to throw off anyone who might be planning an attack. They wouldn't know when we left and wouldn't know when we were returning.

We were never certain if or how we would be able to get home again. We flew to Dubai or Cairo or to another city nearby, and two or three weeks later would attempt to go home to Taiz. Lydia, steady as ever, said she knew we were supposed to go back if we got back. She relinquished to God all expectations of how that return would look and trusted that if we were supposed to remain in Yemen, God would bring us home. Sometimes our flights scheduled to land in Taiz would instead land in Aden because of weather or another unknown reason. Then we would take a bus or a taxi. Sometimes the flight would be delayed a few hours or a few days.

If we made it to our house, if we made it inside the front door, we were meant to be there. We were home.

✺ 18 ✺

GOD WITH US

J amil, a partner in endurance over the years even through the anger and grief waiting a few years down the road for him, continued helping lead our company. I rarely went to the office, and it was becoming harder to financially sustain the business as Yemen sank into increasing chaos. I rarely left the house at all. Lydia couldn't go to the supermarket herself and we hired someone to do our grocery shopping. We lived within the confines of our walled, guarded house, with surveillance cameras on twenty-four hours a day. When I reflect on those years from 2012-2015, I still feel gratitude for the fig tree and mango tree in the yard, and for the dirt the kids could play in. I was thankful for the light rain that fell most afternoons, water for weary souls.

We did see our Yemeni friends who were able to visit our home. Rauf, Jamil's friend with the shared baptism birthday, and his wife, Maha, visited. Their children's ages roughly lined up with ours and the kids loved to play together, providing much-needed levity for my family behind our security walls.

Rauf remained bold in sharing his faith, even after John's murder, and his passion was occasionally interpreted as negativity toward Islam. He, like Hussein and Shaadi, came from a generation of believers who carried wounds and trauma from how Islam had been imposed upon them. They were beaten by teachers, shamed for failing to memorize enough or for asking too many questions, and some, like Rauf, were trained in extremism, which he now rejected. The early generation of believers lacked local elders who could help them navigate the pain and anger they carried into following Christ. Later, some believers would carry similar wounds, but Yemeni Christian leaders who stayed in Yemen rather than fleeing were equipped to help them process the pain in healthy ways, rather than using it as fuel for attacking Islam.

Before he rejected his previous convictions, and before meeting Jesus, Rauf had nearly joined a terrorist training center. He started his life of faith as an Islamist, committed to incorporating premodern Islamic law into the modern-day functioning nation-state political and legal system. But when the teachers training him refused to answer his questions and claimed it was forbidden to ask questions at all, he left them to join a group of Salafis. Salafism revered the early years of Islam as the truest and most faithful version. They attempt to replicate the practices of seventh-century Muslims as much as possible.

Rauf became the most religious person in his neighborhood, never missing prayers or a sermon at the mosque. He harassed people who missed prayers or cheated on the Ramadan fast and considered himself a committed fundamentalist, superior to everyone around him. He became so convinced of Salafi doctrine that he believed them to be the only true Muslims. He decided to move to a radical training center in the North.

The center was known for producing Salafi-jihadists, people who espoused divine sanction for violence, even against fellow Muslims they considered apostates. Suicide bombers and several men locked up in Guantanamo Bay, Cuba, had been trained there. When Rauf's father found out about his intention, he refused to allow his son to leave.

Rauf had a choice. Honor his father and abandon his extremist quest or abandon his family and pursue a life of violence in the name of a particular Islamic interpretation. He was torn. No one could top him in religion or debate, shouldn't he use his religious knowledge and zeal for something as important as convincing others to follow the same beliefs? Yet family was everything.

In Yemen, the tribe and family come even before God in allegiance and obedience. Many tribal societies respect tribal tradition and authority more than any other government voice, religious leader, or other social affiliation. Would Salafi brothers be as committed to Rauf as flesh and blood?

Rauf chose to stay in his hometown and not go to the training center but continued to harass neighbors who didn't live up to his standards. A neighbor whom Rauf labeled a socialist began to poke at Rauf with questions about the Quran and the prophet that he couldn't answer sufficiently. Now, Rauf began to not only doubt his fundamentalist convictions but the existence of God at all. Socialism seemed hopeless, fundamentalist Islam had failed to satisfy, and radicalism hadn't been compelling enough to persuade him to abandon his family. Rauf believed Christians worshipped three gods, drank alcohol, and permitted adultery. Did no religion offer peace or hope or help for this life or the next? Rauf felt increasingly empty.

His family home was in a traditional section of Taiz, a place frequented by tourists attracted to the unique architecture of homes, mosques, old markets, and intricately latticed windows called *gamarias*. Rauf's mother often hosted tourists in their home, treating them to Yemeni sweet tea and biscuits. One afternoon an Italian couple sat with Rauf in the family maglis, and they began talking about religion.

"Christians worship three gods," Rauf said dismissively.

"No they don't," the Italian man said. "They worship one God."

They argued for a while, but the man lost interest and the conversation shifted to Yemeni history. Rauf decided to read the Bible but had to first get access to one. His French teacher, an Iraqi man, found out Rauf was interested in Christianity. That teacher gave him the Bible Rauf later showed to Jamil. Rauf read straight through Genesis and then flipped to the Gospels. He was struck by Jesus's words, "Love your enemies and pray for those who persecute you." He had never heard of such radical love. Rauf loved the beauty of the text, and it wasn't long until he began to identify as a Christian.

Rauf's bumpy path to Jesus instilled in him confidence that God cared about him. God had not left him to the Salafi training center where he may have strapped on a suicide vest. God had not let him wander in the desert of never-ending questions but provided an Italian tourist to offer a glimmer of hope. This gave Rauf strength and resolve, which he channeled into building up other Yemeni Christians. Initially, however, some of his faith discussions flowed out of a place of pain and frustration—that his questions hadn't been welcomed, that he had felt duped by radicalism, that he had been told to shut off his mind and blindly obey.

As Rauf grew in faith, his perspective toward Islam shifted. What he had once rejected as passionately as he had embraced, he now understood as something many people were satisfied to follow without questions. His job was not to attack Islam, the Quran, or their prophet. His job was not to force anyone to believe something they did not find believable or compelling. That was not the way of Jesus. The way of Jesus and the message of the life of a Christian was not to disparage or denigrate other beliefs but to present Jesus and elevate the goodness of a message whose very name was *gospel*, good news.

Tearing down someone else's religious beliefs or attacking a revered prophet would not be welcomed as good news. Good news is that God loves you so much he sent Christ to die a dishonorable death on a cross in a society where honor and shame were essential values. Good news is that God sees you and God is with you. Good news is that with Jesus marriages can be restored and children can be blessed. Good news is not that God will keep someone out of prison, but that God will be with the prisoner. Good news is not that God will pour out abundant financial wealth or cure every disease, but that in Christ there is a community of brothers and sisters who will stand together through the deepest trials.

When Rauf visited my family in Taiz during the war years, we often talked about the good news of the gospel, preaching hope to each other through days full of suffering and hardships. He had extensive knowledge of the Quran and the hadith and could be tempted to use only those sources in conversations about religion. I urged him that no matter what source he used to begin spiritual conversations with Muslims, it was imperative to introduce Muslims to Jesus. There is no room in the church to dishonor another's religious belief system. Even if someone is "successful" in sharing the gospel this way, all that is accomplished is the removal of a rug from someone who is now stranded in a wadi.[1] Better to begin with building than to begin with tearing down.

The good news which Christians in Yemen embody doesn't neglect topics of sin, heaven, or hell. Yemeni evangelists discern possible icebreakers, knowing that eventually these complicated topics need to be spoken about. Immersed in Islam, Yemenis are aware of the concepts of heaven, hell, and sin. They believe in versions of the afterlife and the two options: paradise or suffering. They intellectually understand sin as a failure to fulfill all of God's laws. But the felt needs of Yemenis often do not begin with a desire to be freed from sin, longing for escape to an ephemeral happy afterlife, or fear of eternal punishment.

Christian Yemenis live the good news that God is with them every day and that God loves them. There is war and hunger, terrorism and fundamentalism, poverty and natural disaster. There are diseases and cruel neighbors and abusive spouses and wayward children. There are relational conflicts and mental illnesses. There may be years in prison or persecution. There might be murdered friends and raided church services. Through it all, Immanuel. God is with us. God loves us.

Yemeni Christians love to talk about and demonstrate that God is with them in their troubles. And that because of Jesus's death, burial, and resurrection, humans can be ushered into a new family, through Jesus.

This is a message that does not need to denigrate other beliefs or religious systems. It can stand on the power of the Holy Spirit, the beauty of Jesus's life siding with the downtrodden and broken, and the glory of God the good Father.

Here, in the absence of a need to put down or argue polemically about another religion, Christians like Rauf and Muslims like Sheikh Walid and my security team, found common ground. Although they did not all agree about the work of Jesus on the cross, they had all been damaged by Islamic fundamentalism and now wanted to promote peace. Whether Christian or Muslim, they believed in the basic right of individuals to believe as they felt led to believe, to follow God in a personally compelling way. They put their lives on the line to protect

---

1. Wadi - Valley

this right for others, even when they disagreed. These are men of peace, men who hold faith in God with such confidence that they are not threatened when someone disagrees with them.

Not everyone appreciated that message or pursuit of peace across religious divides, and Rauf began to receive threatening messages, most likely from al-Qaeda. He took some precautions, but not many. Not enough.

19

THREADING THE PEARL
NECKLACE

A thir once described the Yemeni church to me as a pearl necklace. "We are individual beads, but all connected in a long strand." A strand of fragile beauty, an ornament of great price. "When the war came, the strand was broken," she added.

When does a war begin? The question is complicated in a volatile country like Yemen, where ancient grudges and a generational thirst for revenge simmer. How much of the current war in Yemen is built on past conflict remains a matter of debate for historians and politicians. For the sake of brevity, let us imagine these old tensions reemerged when the British left Yemen in 1967, the decade during which they left many colonized nations. Marxist forms of socialism were then planted across South Yemen and the leaders banned all political parties other than their own. Socialism and Islam lived in uncomfortable proximity for decades. According to Gregory Johnsen's book *The Last Refuge*, mosques, beer gardens, and bikini beaches were visible symbols of the underlying incongruous values.[1]

During the 1980s, Soviet influence and financial backing of South

---

1. Gregory Johnson, *The Last Refuge: Yemen, Al-Qaeda, and America's War in Arabia* (Carlton North, VIC: Scribe Publications, 2012), 19.

Yemen faded, and cracks appeared in international support for the nation, as the leftists in power supported various leftist revolutionary movements, some of which were labeled as terrorist organizations by Western and regional governments. In North Yemen, President Ali Abdullah Salih treated the country like his own private tribal kingdom, and the government barely functioned. The discovery of oil and the possibility of joint wealth drew Salih and South Yemen's President Ali Salem al Beidh into secret dialogue about unification. Of course, Yemen could never have two presidents, and, in 1990, Beidh took the role of Vice President serving Salih's administration. He didn't last long, and, in 1993, Beidh withdrew to Aden claiming southern interests were being overlooked by Salih.

In 1994, civil war broke out as the South attempted to return to its former independent status. The war was brief and brutal and the South lost, leaving the country united politically but divided ideologically. While the South and North unified, fought, and reunified, a Zaidi-Shia group known as the Houthis rose to prominence in the North. President Salih initially viewed them as useful pawns in protecting Yemen from Saudi Arabian influence. However, in 2000, Salih made a peace treaty with the Saudis and subsequently attempted to disarm his former allies, the Houthis.[2] By 2004, the Houthis angrily responded in open rebellion and despite several attempts at ceasefires, battles continued until the uneasy ceasefire in February 2010, which looked like it just might hold.

I moved my family to Yemen in the middle of these years. In 2004, when the Houthis rebelled, Lydia and I visited Yemen for the first time, and by April 2005 we had rented our first home in Taiz. We were aware of the political situation and the fighting, but the violence was mostly located in the North. It may as well have been in Sudan or Afghanistan. It didn't affect our lives or the lives of our Yemeni community. We weren't targets, shootings and bombings were aimed at military targets and were not random or haphazard. Attacks, like a bomb in 2006 killing two Yemenis and eight Spanish tourists, were as impossible to predict or build a life around as school shootings in the USA. We were able to

---

2. Ibid.

make reasonable choices about safety. Even once the Arab Spring exploded, the violence was never personal and I could work, travel, raise my family, and meet with believers in peace.

In January 2011, as the Arab Spring swept across North Africa and the Middle East, demonstrators began demanding President Salih resign. He had governed Yemen since 1978, thirty-three years was enough in demonstrators' opinions. Salih announced he would not seek reelection, but protests continued and turned violent.

In April, Salih refused to sign a deal handing over power, and fighting again erupted in Sana'a, a city the prophet Mohammad had once called "the paradise of earthly paradises."[3] In sad contrast, Sana'a, one of the world's oldest inhabited cities now erupted into flames, black curling smoke from burning tires rising above barriers across the city.

After months of clashes, in November, Salih finally agreed that his deputy Abd-Rabbu Mansur Hadi would take over and serve for two years. In August 2014, Hadi dissolved his government, and by September, the Houthis were in control of Sana'a. By February 2015, the Houthis had taken control of the government, and the country became embroiled in a bitter, seemingly endless, war.

Yemen has faced a multitude of conflicts throughout history and pinpointing responsibility or starting dates quickly grows fuzzy. The current fighting involves multiple nations with most of the bombing campaigns carried out by foreign entities. Peace talks currently being held are between the Houthis and Saudi Arabia.

Did the conflict, then, begin in September 2014, when the Houthis gained control of Sana'a or on March 26, 2015, when a Saudi-led intervention began in support of southern forces' battle to expel the Houthis from Yemen? Did it begin in 1994, when unification appeared to be failing? Maybe it began in 1990, when unification was forced on those who weren't ready or didn't want it. Or in 1967, when Britain fled, leaving behind an unstable and weakened government built on colonial arrogance and power. Did it begin long ago in localized tribal warfare?

Who is responsible? Guilt could lie with Britain or with the former Soviet Union. What about Iran and Saudi Arabia, using their neighbor

---

3. Johnson, *The Last Refuge*, 83.

in a proxy war? What role has the United States played? These questions were hotly debated during *qat* chewing sessions, though civilians, as those who suffer most during wartime, remained primarily concerned with survival. My concern, and the concern of Yemeni Christians, is not who started the fire or when, but how to survive, thrive, and care for one another while it burns.

Throughout the Arab Spring years, while Yemen's government focused on maintaining power, suppressing protests, and battling the Houthis, other influences infiltrated the country, including al-Qaeda and ISIS. ISIS pulled off suicide bomb attacks at mosques in Sana'a in the winter of 2015. The next ten years, up until this writing, saw Yemen descend into near anarchy. Violence, hunger, and poverty displaced millions. Diseases run rampant and unchecked, from cholera to Covid-19. As of 2025, according to the United Nations Office for Coordination of Humanitarian Affairs (UNOCHA), nearly 20 million Yemenis need humanitarian aid and protection. Children, especially, are suffering. Half of children under age five face "moderate to severe stunting."[4] Young teenage boys are conscripted into fighting, and girls and women are taken as forced brides.

I asked my security team if they thought future peace was possible in Yemen.

"It is foggy," one said. "I see no clear path forward for the country."

"Do you have any hope?" I asked.

"Christians are growing," he said. "They are more mature."

"Christian families are the ones serving Yemen now," another man said.

We were speaking over a meal shared with a Yemeni Christian woman, an American Christian woman, a Christian man from a Yemeni marginalized population, and these two Muslim security professionals. We tore chunks off the same loaves of bread, dipped our bread into the same bowl of *sahawiq*.[5]

---

4. "Yemen: Humanitarian Response Plan," *United Nations Office for the Coordination of Humanitarian Affairs (OCHA)*, January 1, 2025, https://www.unocha.org/publications/report/yemen/yemen-humanitarian-needs-and-response-plan-2025-january-2025.

5. A spicy and flavorful condiment made from a blend of fresh herbs, chili peppers, garlic, spices, and at times, cheese. It is widely used as a dip or sauce.

If we only looked at the war, or history, or poverty, or politics it would be almost impossible to feel hope. But when I think about that meal and the words of my Muslim friends as they spoke of their hope lying in the growth of the Yemeni Christians, hope shines. Only in Christ can barriers of such magnitude as Muslim-Christian, marginalized-elite, male-female, and Yemeni-Westerners be broken down.

Athir's imagery of Yemeni Christians as a strand of pearls pertains even here, after all of this violence and disruption. She said, in that conversation years ago, that the strand was broken by the war. But that is not the end of the story. Brokenness is never the end of the story.

"We had a leader," Athir continued, "who kept us connected. We couldn't live nearby or fellowship in large groups, but we were united." This leader checked in on people who had been displaced. He connected believers who fled to a new city with believers already in that city. He carefully shared phone numbers and prayer requests.

Pearl by pearl, believer by believer, the necklace came back together, stronger than ever.

20

PERSECUTING THE
PERSECUTED

The war has been especially cruel to already marginalized and impoverished populations like the Muhamasheen. Over 1500 years ago, the Muhamasheen in Arabia Felix were majority Christian, with unknown geographical origin. Some believe they are descended from enslaved Africans or Ethiopian soldiers who came to Yemen as far back as the sixth century. Others stress that the Muhamasheen have Yemeni roots.[1] Regardless of their origins, their plight today is one of the most extreme forms of social exclusion in Yemen.

Social custom has prevented the Muhamasheen from marrying outside their caste, freezing them out of Yemeni economic, tribal, and political structures. This has left them facing unique difficulties in escaping poverty and illiteracy in a society organized around the belief that a person's ancestry dictates the totality of their social and biological essence.

The name itself means "marginalized," and they are often called *akhdām*, or "servant." In 2013, the Yemeni government told the International Convention on the Elimination of Racial Discrimination

---

1. "Muhamisheen in Yemen," *Minority Rights Group International*, January 1, 2018, https://minorityrights.org/communities/muhamasheen/.

that "The vast majority of them are dark-skinned and live in social, economic, cultural, and political isolation." Relegated to the bottom of Yemen's social structure, the Muhamasheen are only offered low-paid, low-skilled work, such as street cleaning. Meanwhile, without rights to land ownership or tenure, the majority are forced to live on the edges of urban areas in makeshift accommodations constructed of cardboard, cloth, wood, and sheet metal. These dwellings are clustered into shanty towns, which lack sewage systems and have only sporadic electricity.

Over ninety percent of Muhamasheen are denied official identity papers, meaning they can't vote, travel, or attend school. From Night to Darker Night, an extensive report on discrimination and inequality in Yemen produced by the Equal Rights Trust in 2018, explained how prejudice prevents the Muhamasheen from accessing aid available to other Yemenis. One man quoted in the report said, "I was discriminated against by relief distributors who did not give me a share of the food aid … [They said] I would sell the food and that I am used to begging … However, they distributed the food baskets among those who belonged to tribes or those they had personal connections with. They gave the assistance to undeserving families. I could not cover my daily needs or the needs of my kids, who go to bed with empty stomachs."[2]

The conflict in Yemen worsened their plight. Reports indicate that armed groups exploit Muhamasheen men for frontline fighting, often with little compensation or recognition. Meanwhile, Muhamasheen women and girls face heightened risks of sexual violence and exploitation. According to a 2025 report by the Sana'a Center for Strategic Studies, many are forced into begging or street vending, exposing them to harassment and assault, often by armed groups or tribal figures who act with impunity.[3]

Waddah, a Muhamasheen Christian, described how conditions grew worse in his community during the war. "We feel death, a slow death.

---

2.   Luca Nevola, "Blood Doesn't Lie: Hierarchy and Inclusion/Exclusion in Contemporary Yemen," *IRIS*, January 1, 2015, https://boa.unimib.it/handle/10281/88750?mode=full.

3.   Mohammed al-Harbi, *Forgotten Victims of Yemen's War: The Plight of the Muhammashat* (Sana'a Center for Strategic Studies, January 20, 2025), https://sanaacenter.org/publications/24021.

Before the war, we ate food from barrels of trash. People started sleeping in the streets. Children had to beg and many of them were raped."

People built tent homes out of cloth materials and when neighbors burned them down because they didn't want to live near Muhamasheen, the outcasts moved into cemeteries or caves in the mountains. Some families sold their daughters as young as twelve to be married to men in their sixties. Other girls disappeared at the border, and when they reappeared, had either lost their minds or told stories of being used as sex slaves among the fighters.

One evening, Waddah was home with his wife and children. The kids were studying for their exams, and the family was about to eat dinner when someone pounded on the front door. Waddah stepped outside.

Two or three men yanked on his arms; Waddah couldn't tell how many there were. Their faces were covered, and before he could think, they started to beat him with their fists and rocks from the street. He cried out, and his wife came to the door just as Waddah was pushed into a police car and driven away.

At the prison, he was fingerprinted, and the interrogations began. For twenty-eight days men shouted at Waddah about being a Christian. They covered his eyes, pulled his legs apart, hung him from his arms, and beat him repeatedly. They demanded to know how he met Jesus, how he knew me, what were the names of other Christians, who gave him a Bible.

I have debriefed half a dozen Yemenis who were tortured and imprisoned for being a witness to Christ. During interrogation, they had also been questioned about my family and other expats in Yemen. This raises complicated questions about persecution, and again, the role of the foreigner. When another expatriate asked Yemeni brothers or sisters how they felt about me as a foreigner, their immediate responses were, "You are not foreign. You are one of us. We don't see Yemeni or foreign. We see brothers and sisters in Christ." Still, I had to face the reality of people being tortured, including tortured for information about me.

When is persecution Christian persecution? Often, it is defined as being persecuted for Jesus's sake and for bearing witness to what Jesus has done in one's life. Most often when Yemenis are persecuted and questioned for their faith, they are also questioned about foreigners they might know. So are they being persecuted for their faith or because they know foreigners? Does the distinction matter? Those who arrested them might assume they have joined a new political group or religious group for personal, nonreligious benefit. It is hard for the persecutors to come to terms with the fact that these Yemenis simply have chosen to follow Jesus, that they are often in relation with other disciples of Christ, whether Yemeni or foreign, and they have no desire to overthrow any government.

Often in cases of Christians persecuted in Yemen, the first assumption by outsiders, including high-profile organizations and authors, is that they suffered for Jesus's name. However, upon digging, sometimes these turn out to be situations of a land dispute in which someone tragically got shot. They didn't get shot because of Jesus but because of the land dispute. Or someone defied the government and pontificated on their political views on social media. If they lose their job or are arrested, that is not for Jesus's name, even if they are a Christian, but for political activism.

If a Christian is persecuted solely because of their relationship with a foreigner, that has nothing to do with faith in Christ, an employer for example, then the idea that they are not suffering for Jesus stands. But when Yemenis know and love a foreigner because of Jesus, and are in a relationship with them because of Jesus, I would categorize that as suffering for their faith.

If they are arrested for reading the Bible, participating in a church gathering, being baptized, and are questioned about the foreign Christians they know who are partnering with the church, that is suffering for Jesus. Yemeni Christians do not live within a Western dichotomy of a spiritual life and a physical life.

We need to mercilessly analyze what the foreign Christians are doing, whether they are behaving unwisely or not, and be willing to adjust as necessary for the sake of the local church and the gospel. How many Christian workers come to a place like Yemen and assume they should attend every meeting, every men's gathering, every women's Bible study? If foreigners did this in Yemen, we would interfere constantly, with dire implications on security and discipleship. If we ask Yemenis for permission to attend, of course they are going to say yes. Culturally, they can't refuse. Discerning when to participate and what activities to participate in is key when partnering with an existing church.

But this has not been the historical role of the foreigner in Yemen or around the world. Mission organizations have not been ready for the foreigner to take a backseat. This level of healthy partnership requires a high degree of spiritual maturity, discernment, humility, and trust.

We must be intentional about coming to learn, to sit quietly, to pray, to contribute when invited, to model raising children or holding a professional job or hosting a mixed-gender group for dinner as Christian families. It is important to allow Yemeni families to observe us, even when they see things they don't like, and they might call us out on our weaknesses. If we are not ready for that kind of reciprocal relationship, we are not ready to do the inverse in their lives.

When a foreign Christian disrupts the local community by over-attending, drawing attention to their gatherings and lacks cultural knowledge, and then that community is persecuted on account of the foreigner, it might be right that the foreigner has contributed to this suffering and should leave. But when the foreigner lives in a place, partners with the local church appropriately, and pursues their professional work faithfully, this can be an effective model of ministry. Discernment and humility are obligatory when partnering with the indigenous Church.

Waddah told his interrogators he loved them. One man in particular would beat Waddah terribly. The worse the beatings, the more Waddah proclaimed that he loved him.

"I love you *ghasban 'annak*," whether you like it or not. The more Waddah said this, the worse the man beat him. Over time, however, the man's heart softened, and when others beat Waddah, he would step in to defend the prisoner.

Waddah spent hours in his cell in prayer, reminding himself that

God was with him. It helped that he saw Jesus in the prison. The first time, it was around 7:30 at night. He looked across the prison yard and there was Jesus, standing on top of one of the buildings.

Is that really Jesus? he asked himself. *I wasn't expecting him to be here.* Then again, why wouldn't Jesus be with his people, especially in prison? The second time Waddah saw Jesus, Jesus was with two other men and Jesus said to him, "Do not be afraid." The third time, Jesus appeared in a dream and told Waddah someone would come and open the door for him soon.

"Your case is clean, the accusations against you are cleared."

After that, people from the neighborhood began showing up outside the prison. They sat and even slept on the ground—widows, the elderly, families, people Waddah had helped previously.

"We are Christians, like Waddah," they told the prison guards, unafraid.

Sometimes a few guards sat with those protesting Waddah's imprisonment, chewing *qat* and reading the Quran or listening to Bible stories. "We hope he gets out soon," they said.

There were three other men in prison with Waddah. One had been a driver for a famous, wealthy Yemeni. One was a police officer, and one had murdered a man. The only time they were allowed to be together was during lunch. Over the little food they were given, the men grew to know one another, and Waddah began to share about his faith in Jesus. The others were in prison for murder, for betrayal, for actual crimes. They expressed surprise at the torture Waddah was enduring simply for having different beliefs.

By the time the other men were released, each of them had accepted Waddah identifying as a Christian and no longer vehemently resisted. Waddah remained in prison but one of the men circulated a petition for his release. Muhamasheen men and women, Christian and Muslim alike, began coming to the prison to protest. Some even slept outside the prison walls on the ground. The petition garnered over four hundred signatures of people vouching for Waddah's good character and lack of criminality.

Eventually, the prison guards gave in to the community pressure and released him. No longer in jail, Waddah continued to struggle with nightmares and PTSD. He didn't allow his wife to lock any doors in the house and jumped at loud sounds, which were frequent during the war. In the early months after being released, he lived in fear of being rearrested and moved the family to a different part of Yemen. And yet, he held no resentment.

"I got to know Christ in prison," he told me. God appears during the hardest times of our lives. Christ gives us new life, and the church has treated me like a human, with love coming from their hearts."

"God is alive," Waddah continued. "God hears us and is with us. God sent the Spirit to fill us. We died, with all our sins, and now we live with Jesus and this is beautiful. God forgives us. I don't need to go on an airplane to find forgiveness. I don't need to shave my head or sacrifice animals. There is no money to buy it. God gives forgiveness to the good person, the bad person, everyone. There is something like a door to God. It isn't beautiful, there are no diamonds or gold. Maybe the doorway is painful, but on the other side is new life as God's child."

One of the most powerful moments I witnessed from Waddah came as he prayed among a group of Yemeni men. Holding hands with Hussein on one side, who had recently spent two years in prison, he wept and said, "I forgive the prison guards that tortured me."

21

TIME TO GO

Beginning in March 2015 the atmosphere in Yemen was tense. Not only was I still a target, but the indiscriminate airstrikes had increased, putting our home at serious risk of being completely obliterated. The house offered little protection from artillery rounds, shell fragments and mortar fire. We created what we intended to be an office space at home for me. In the end, I never actually used the room for work. It became our amateur bunker. Jamil and I had unintentionally built an amateur bunker, which gave my family more protection.

Our house already had an exterior wall surrounding our property, and the wall of the actual house, both made from cinderblock. The room Jamil and I built was another two layers of blocks. At two meters by three meters, it was just big enough for the six members of my family to sit in relative comfort, though we hoped to never need to hunker down for more than a few hours at a time. We built the room near a bathroom and added electricity using solar panels. We stocked water, snacks, toys, and homework. Lydia put headphones in the bunker so the kids could pop them on and listen to music or school lessons rather than to the rain of bullets and missiles outside.

Lydia and I didn't have long discussions about whether to stay or leave. She knew I wasn't going anywhere without God's direction. She expected God to be clear about when we were supposed to leave and waited for that to be revealed. As a couple, we rely more on prayerful discernment than discussion, and Lydia's steady faith and calm demeanor throughout our years in Yemen were instrumental in the healthy, even joyful thriving of our family.

Parents are the compass for our children. If my kids see me authentically love Muslims, they will love Muslims. If I model a savior complex, if I treat Muslims as projects or problems to be solved, my kids will follow that example. If they watch me partner on equal grounds with Yemeni Christians, they will not feel superior to Yemeni Christians. If they see Lydia and me embody peace through airstrikes, they will mimic that.

We never denied the struggles, that isn't healthy, either. The kids knew what happened to John and why, they heard the airstrikes and picked up pieces of shrapnel from the yard. But they didn't exhibit fear. For them, just like for every other Yemeni child, this was normal. They might be playing on their swing in the yard when a siren went off or gunfire exploded nearby. I didn't have to call them into the house each time, as they had already been trained to come inside until the bullets stopped flying.

To an American or Western audience, to those who have not lived in a conflict zone, this might sound radical, or insane and irresponsible. That judgment needs to be balanced with the truth that this is the reality of childhood for millions across the world, children who have no choice, no other option. Yes, we consciously chose to stay, with faith. Others chose to leave, with faith. It is not complicated. The choice did bond us with Yemenis and did increase our empathy for families in South Sudan, Sudan, Afghanistan, Iraq, Syria, Congo, Somalia, Ethiopia, Ukraine, and Palestine.

Saying that this is as simple as a choice doesn't mean everyone will survive or everyone's faith remains steady. Some children will not respond with faith or health, some may rebel or reject or experience trauma. A secondary message for parents, after being a compass for children, is to know your kids. God commanded David to know the condition of his flock, and parents need to understand the unique needs and personalities of their children, and faithfully steward the little ones God has given.

The makeshift office space that doubled as a bunker would protect us from indirect hits and debris, but if a missile struck us directly, we were toast. That, and the reality that the war had now become a war of indiscriminate attack rather than being limited to military targets, drastically increased the danger we were in and impacted our decision-making.

By late 2014, I went weeks without leaving the house. Looking back, I realize what allowed me to stay in the home for weeks (and Lydia for months) was purpose. We knew we were supposed to stay. I was helping build capacity in Yemenis so they would be ready to step in when I was gone. And my family had a community in the local church that visited us from time to time.

Even so, by spring of 2015, three things made me reconsider staying. First, our neighborhood emptied. Our Muslim neighbors, people who had lived their entire lives in homes their grandparents or great-grandparents built, people with cultural cover, were fleeing. They left behind houses filled with family heirlooms and memorabilia. We were one of two families left in our cul-de-sac. When local people determine a situation is too dangerous, it is time for foreigners to pay attention.

Second, the local church had formed a community and reached a place of maturity. Already, Yemenis were leading and multiplying their faith among families and friends. Already, Yemenis were leading Bible study, preparing worship services, baptizing each other, and performing other sacraments. There were still church issues and conflict at times. Find me a church without interpersonal or theological squabbles. But they were equipped to face the differences with grace and wisdom, grounded in scripture and prayer, and filled with the Spirit.

And third, my presence had increased the danger to our Yemeni community to the point that staying no longer made sense. I had become a liability. Our foreign family's presence on this street brought more danger. Our need for groceries put Zayn at too much risk. The shootings and bombings had become too unpredictable, too indiscriminate. Us staying was endangering local people. I was not in Yemen to be "Joan of Arc," a hero of sorts. It was time to move to a new city.

I didn't know all of that when we planned our next trip out of the country. We had been leaving for two weeks every few months, and our next trip was set for May 2015.

We packed clothes for two weeks. Lydia brought a few homeschool materials. One carry-on each. I told no one when or where we were going. I called our driver after dark one evening and asked him to pick us up. It would normally take ten minutes to get to the other side of town, where we would hit the open road and drive to Sana'a. From there, we would catch an International Organization for Migration flight out. IOM was the only airline still operational at that point in the war.

Because of snipers, we needed to drive without headlights, and without electricity, the city was pitch black. I also didn't want to alert any potential al-Qaeda operatives in our neighborhood. Lydia and I hustled the kids into the car, and we tried to leave.

Getting out was more complicated than I'd anticipated, far more complicated than when we had left only two months prior. Bombs and missiles had destroyed homes on every block and left certain parts of town inaccessible. Downed telephone poles, heaps of electrical wires, burned-out cars, and twisted rebar strewn across roads blocked our path. Fear of snipers kept people from collecting trash and mountains of garbage grew in every corner of the city. The stench was unbearable as we drove by half-burned heaps.

The driver would turn down an open road only to discover it was blockaded by a military or al-Qaeda checkpoint. We had no interest in risking additional al-Qaeda checkpoints. As soon as they saw my foreign face, we would have risked being on their next YouTube propaganda video. We passed through the first check, but as it was late, the guard looked in the small van at several covered women. I was in the back, a *mashadda* covering most of my face, pretending I was sleeping. The man let us pass. That was the first of many stops. Next came a military checkpoint.

"Where are you going?" a soldier asked our driver.

"To help a woman on the other side of town," he said.

The soldier glanced into the vehicle. Lydia, our Ethiopian housekeeper, and another American woman traveling with us, wore *lithmas*[1]. My kids sprawled on people's laps; their foreign faces covered. I sat in the shadows in the back of the van, with a *mashadda* still wrapped around my head. The soldier waved us through.

My phone rang. It was Sheikh Walid. "You are not going to get out of the city tonight," he said. "It's too dangerous right now."

As he spoke, the driver momentarily flicked the headlights on to see past a pile of cement blocks and wires stretching across a road, and within seconds, gunfire pinged around the car. We had already been driving for hours, through city streets that should have taken us mere minutes and had made almost no progress. Taiz was built in the foothills of mountains, the city a tangled maze of narrow alleyways and dead ends without the added complexity of snipers, checkpoints, cratered roads, and makeshift barriers.

"You could die tonight," Walid said. "Maybe a sniper. Maybe an RPG. You could die with your whole family. Or you can try again in the morning."

The morning was risky because of the light. People would know we left. We wouldn't be able to put hours between us and anyone who might pursue us. But he was right. Traveling in the dark had its advantages most days, but tonight it was too dangerous.

"Come to my house," Walid said.

We drove there and wearily climbed out of the van. Walid fed us and prepared a place for us to sleep, including the driver. I watched the kids stretch out on their blankets, tucked each one in, and whispered, "I love you, goodnight." As I lay down on my own makeshift bed, I thought about the Muslims sheltering my Christian, foreign family.

"The most dangerous thing in this season," Shihaab, a member of my security detail, once said, "is to be in a car with a foreigner. Especially a foreign Christian."

And yet, he drove in cars with me. Walid invited us under his roof. We didn't need to agree on religious matters. We agreed on the value of

---

1. Niqab (نقاب), lithma (لثمة), and burqa (برقع) are used interchangeably to refer to a face-covering worn by Yemeni women. However, there can be subtle distinctions in North Africa and the Middle East.

human life, the importance of freedom to choose who and how one worships, and the devastating effect of extremism on this country we loved. That night, Yemen didn't exude a sense of her native happiness, but we knew what was possible. We knew the jovial laughter and legendary hospitality, the warm welcomes, and the creative storytellers. We shared a yearning for the nation to once again embody her former moniker.

Shihaab described his work of promoting peace by protecting the Christian religious minority as, "a message from heaven. Christians are our brothers and sisters." He was weary of what he considered the brainwashing of his people by those who told lies about what Christians believe and how they behave. He wasn't alone. Yemeni Muslims had grown weary, too, of the violence perpetuated in the name of Islam. They wanted peace, they wanted food for their families, schools and hospitals, they wanted to work and to be paid for their work.

Walid, Shihaab, Zayn, and so many others also had legal precedent to undergird their protection of Christians. Christians had built a church building in Aden in 1864. In 1970, three years after the British left the country, the building was turned over to the community, which used it as a gymnasium and storage center. But, in 2007, the Grand Mufti of Yemen, His Excellency Zabarah, wrote a fatwa delivering the building back into the hands of Christians to be used as a church. He wrote,

In the name of Allah,

I hereby issue my formal religious rule stating
that there is no objection for the church in the city of Tawahi,
Aden, to continue conducting religious services,
and to allow it to be renovated. It is our duty to allow members
of the Christian community to exercise their religious rights,
and to worship in their churches, as it is the case in
our mosques and Islamic centres all over the United Kingdom
and the rest of the Christian world.[2]

---

2. Crooks, *Yemen: Heartbreak & Hope*, 46.

I fell asleep to the sounds of sporadic gunfire and my family's light breathing. I woke to the call to prayer, sounds of birds nearby, and beautiful Saber Mountain that I could see from the windows of the sheikh's home. There was war, gunfire, terror, devastation, and fear surrounding us. But in that house, that very night, we experienced peace.

In the morning, Walid fed us again, and then we slowly picked our way through the decimated city. Once we crossed from the al-Qaeda-controlled side to the Houthi-controlled side, I felt a tangible sense of relief. Praise God, we made it out of al-Qaeda territory. Sort of. I felt like we'd arrived at an oasis, the difference between the extremist zone and the rebel zone was so palpable.

We still weren't in the clear, though. If the Houthis stopped us, they would arrest me at least, if not the women as well. They weren't going to put us through a public mock trial and chop our heads off, but I'd be locked away in prison for years. The higher profile a prisoner was, the longer their sentence. Mine would have been interminable.

Once we made it out of Taiz, the rest of the drive to Sana'a was uneventful besides the dozens of checkpoints we had to pass.

"This will hopefully blow over in two, maybe three weeks," I said to Lydia.

We boarded the IOM flight and watched Yemen disappear beneath the clouds.

In Taiz, al-Qaeda visited our home the next day. The only people there were my security guards.

"Where is the man who lived here?" the operatives said.

"He's not here."

"Where did he go? How did he get out?"

"He left normally," one guard said. "In a car. With his family."

Al-Qaeda threw the guards in prison, but because I had told them nothing about when we were leaving, where we were going, or when we were coming back, it became evident that the guards didn't know anything. They were released after five days.

It would take me seven years to bring the whole family back to Yemen.

But it did not take seven years, not even seven months, for another murder to deal a blow to the Yemeni church.

22

SHARING BREAD IN A WAR ZONE

My family flew to Khartoum, then Cairo, then Cyprus. In Cyprus, we stayed in the empty house of friends who were on leave in Europe. It was a safe, but temporary, place to land. We intended to return to Yemen.

After several conversations with our security team and friends in Yemen between May and August that summer, it became clear that my foreign family could not return. I longed to. I hated the idea of being outside the country, especially with my firm conviction of staying to be present with the church. And yet, I also had a firm conviction about submitting to local leadership. Walid, as my head security advisor, and Jamil, as one of the church leaders, told me it was not advisable to return at that time, which translated to *don't come*. Sorrowfully, but with understanding, I agreed.

That didn't mean I would fully leave, though, either. Yemen couldn't get rid of me that easily. I wasn't about to resettle in the USA. It was impossible to picture Lydia and me in a suburban Florida home, sending our kids to American schools, and strolling down white sand beaches.

Where could we go regionally? I figured we needed two months, maybe three, for the situation to calm down in Taiz. That meant I needed a place where we could rent a furnished apartment and put our kids into school so they wouldn't fall behind while we waited. And I needed a place nearby so I could pop back into Yemen when the chance arrived.

We rented a furnished house in a regional country where a portion of the population hailed from Yemeni heritage and where the kids would be able to slide into the school system. The kids had grown used to our Bedouin lifestyle over the past few years of going in and out of Yemen. They didn't flinch when we made the move with our few suitcases in August 2015. They simply added daily prayers of moving back to Yemen to their routines and threw themselves into making new friends.

I wasn't ready to admit we couldn't return soon. I also understood a strange dynamic that expatriates experience in which a dangerous, volatile, or unstable situation looks worse from the outside. This is why people on the ground struggle with decisions made from a Colorado corner office or a London business suite or a South Korean pastor's office. When you are in the country, experiencing the situation, you understand that life goes on while bombs fall on the other side of town. You know the power of sharing the gospel through the literal sharing of bread[1] and suffering alongside people you love. You can receive intelligence reports in real time and react to them in real time. I needed to go back and make a fresh assessment.

Three of us entered Yemen through the Sana'a airport that August, and immediately upon landing, the other man in our group was arrested and thrown into prison. He was held for twenty-one days. Houthis were in charge of the airport, and they confiscated my passport and the passport of an American woman traveling with us, refusing to return them and refusing to let me out of the airport. They threatened to deport us, to send us back on the flight we had just arrived on. I didn't want that

---

1. In the Yemeni context, "bread and salt" (*'aysh wa-milḥ*) is a traditional concept symbolizing hospitality, trust, and reconciliation. Sharing bread and salt signifies a binding social covenant that fosters loyalty and mutual respect, often invoked in tribal customs to establish or restore relationships. Betrayal after partaking in bread and salt is seen as dishonorable, reinforcing its role in conflict resolution and communal harmony.

on my travel record, it risked hindering any chance of returning to Yemen in the future.

Members of my security team met us at the airport and tried to delay the deportation process by negotiating and pleading.

"Let them stay overnight. They can always leave on the first flight out in the morning."

The stalling worked, and the plane took off without us. Immigration security let us out of the airport. That night, we stayed in accommodations arranged by the security team, and in the morning, we drove to Ibb. Then Taiz. Then Hudeidah. We drove to the coast and into southern Yemen. Everywhere we went, when possible, we stopped to visit believers and to hear their stories of the past few months of war. And, everywhere we went, the situation was intense. If I describe a situation as intense, after taking my family out of Yemen under gunfire, know that it was extreme.

The Houthis had marched south since March and tried to take control of Aden. The government fought back and by July had won full control of the city, but tension remained high and memories of Aden as a war zone lingered. Al-Qaeda and extremist groups had aligned themselves against their common enemy, the Houthis, and various parties patrolled different sections of town. One block had an al-Qaeda checkpoint. The next might have a southern movement checkpoint. Men in black ski masks with AK-47s patrolled the next block.

Internally Displaced People flooded into Aden from all over the South. They sought refuge in hotels, and hotel owners were forced to give every room to housing IDPs. By the time we got to Aden, hoping to fly out of the airport there rather than risk returning to Sana'a, there were no available rooms. Even if we managed to find one, they might not want to fill it with high-risk foreigners.

We stopped at a checkpoint guarded by an extremist group. They demanded ID cards, and my driver began to show his. If I showed my American passport, we would likely be arrested and possibly sold to another extremist group. I slowly reached for my passport, trying to think of a plan. Right before I passed it through the window, I recognized a young man nearby.

I had met him a few years earlier when I visited Aden every other month to spend time with believers. We swam in the Gulf of Aden and studied the scriptures together. I caught the man's eye, and he recognized me as the friendly foreigner who used to drink tea with him.

He wasn't an extremist, but this was his neighborhood, and the group was using him to screen cars. He signaled to those checking the vehicles to wave us through as if to say, "I know them and I vouch for them."

If not for him, if not for God placing him there at that moment, I might have been the next gruesome show on social media. Clearly, Yemen lacked basic infrastructure. We could barely make it to the airport. And, equally clearly, my presence as a foreigner only increased the dangers for believers. It wasn't time to come back.

I managed to fly out of Aden unhindered. We shared wonderful fellowship with believers throughout the country. However, Walid's and Jamil's counsel proved wise. I didn't know it at the time, still didn't want to believe it, but as my plane took off and I watched war-torn Aden disappear beneath me, I sensed that I wouldn't be returning to Yemen for a long time.

Life in the city we'd left behind had been known for generations by its friendly people who enjoyed safe streets and frequent social gatherings. Now, hunger, thirst, and bloodshed stood in sharp contrast to the city's historic reputation for moderation. Now, the streets were lifeless. No fuel. No transportation. No one moved about. "Here, you live waiting for the moment of your death," one woman told me.

And yet, I wanted to be there. The best thing I could do from outside, besides pray, was to support Yemenis' response to the developing humanitarian crisis. I thought of the disciples in Acts 11:27-30. "Agabus stood up and through the Spirit predicted that a severe famine would spread over the entire Roman world ... The disciples, as each was able, decided to provide help for the brothers and sisters living in Judea."

Collectively, the believers turned to Acts 6 and apostolic letters from Paul for guidance in responding to the humanitarian crisis. Leaders wanted to ensure help went where it was most needed, indiscriminately, to a Muslim, Christian, Jew, or atheist. One family might have two bags of rice, so they shared it with their neighbor who had empty cupboards. People with water tanks collected rain and shared it with the thirsty. They never attached a Bible study or a religious tract to the aid. If a Christian needs to write, "Jesus loves you," on a bag of food, they should wonder if they are failing to embody the love of Jesus relationally.

The work of sharing a loaf of bread or helping a child attend school might not seem spiritual, but Yemenis believe that the "religion that God our Father accepts as pure and faultless is this: to look after orphans and widows in their distress."[2] They show their faith by their deeds.

Eating and drinking in community led Yemeni Christians to consider how they could apply principles of practically loving their neighbor to their ministries. We studied non-faith-based organizations' grant-writing procedures and policies and learned how to measure outcomes, outputs, and accountability. We learned how to track measurable goals, monitoring, and evaluation, and studied tools for needs assessments. In this way, even the project cycle became a tool we could apply to church life and witness, reminding us that every task—whether practical or pastoral—belongs to the Lord.

Too many foreign Christian workers step into a city or a village and assume they have the answers to what they perceive as problems. The first wrong assumption is that they have arrived to lead, implement, and decide. The second wrong assumption is that they understand what the problem is and what solution is necessary. But they have not done a needs assessment. They have not evaluated available resources. They have no plan for monitoring or evaluating. They have not had dialogue with local leaders. How will they know if they have been successful or not? Studying the project cycle ought to be an integral part of any church planting vision.

Some Christian workers are quick to denigrate secular humanitarians for everything from wasted funds to lack of knowledge of local customs. These aren't always off-base, and secular organizations could

2. James 1:27

learn from Christians' commitment to relationships, longevity, and use of resources. Humanitarians are often quick to criticize Christians' failure to develop systems, lack of monitoring, ineffective programs, and using work as a "platform" rather than doing it professionally. Christians need to learn analysis and methodology from these organizations.

In Yemen, we developed a program cycle approach to our dual ambition of blessing the nation physically and blessing the nation spiritually. The cycle begins with a needs assessment and analysis. Next comes strategic planning. Then resource mobilization, implementation, and monitoring, and finally operational peer review and evaluation.[3]

This is not about spreadsheets and documentation only. One Yemeni said, "It is a balance between grace and being intentional and proactive. Accountability and intentionality are keys to consistent reproduction and consistent growth in the church."

In Matthew 28:16-20, Jesus said, "Go and teach them everything I have commanded you." This "everything" can be summed up in Jesus's answer to an expert in the law. He tested Jesus with a question about the greatest commandment. Jesus said one should love God and love one's neighbor. Jesus's life demonstrated what that love looks like. He did not drop down to earth one day and die. He lived thirty-three years, pursuing justice, healing the sick, raising the dead, feeding the hungry, engaging in economics, and developing meaningful relationships.

Sharing bread is Great Commandment living with Great Commission vision.

∽

Jamil called me a few days after my short trip in August.

"Rauf's dead," Jamil said.

---

3. *Humanitarian Programme Cycle (HPC)*, OCHA oPt, https://www.ochaopt.org/coordination/hpc.

✤ III ✤

LISTENING
THE WISDOM OF SHEBA

Now when the queen of Sheba heard of the fame of Solomon concerning the name of the Lord, she came to test him with hard questions. She came to Jerusalem...with camels bearing spices and very much gold and precious stones. And when she came to Solomon, she told him all that was on her mind. And Solomon answered all her questions; there was nothing hidden from the king that he could not explain to her. And when the queen of Sheba had seen all the wisdom of Solomon...and his burnt offerings that he offered at the house of the Lord, there was no more breath in her. And she said to the king, "The report was true that I heard in my own land of your words and of your wisdom, but I did not believe the reports until I came and my own eyes had seen it. And behold, the half was not told me. Your wisdom and prosperity surpass the report that I heard. Happy are your men! Happy are your servants, who continually stand before you and hear your wisdom! Blessed be the Lord your God, who has delighted in you and set you on the throne of Israel! Because the Lord loved Israel forever, he has made you king, that you may execute justice and righteousness."

1 Kings 10:1–9

23

A SECOND NATIONAL DAY OF PRAYER

Danger didn't come only from war and destruction raining down from the skies. Violence could be personal too. Threats by al-Qaeda against Rauf continued throughout the summer and early fall of 2015 but did little to deter him from sharing his faith. Rauf spoke so often and with such affection about Jesus that some of his Muslim friends accepted his faith, not that they all became Christians, but some took less issue with him being a Christian. Still, the threats from strangers convinced Rauf was an apostate grew so persistent that Rauf decided to have a candid conversation with his wife, Maha.

"If anything happens to me," he told Maha, "you will have to be father and mother to our children. Teach them about Jesus, and about what our Lord said. That those who follow Jesus will be persecuted and killed because of his name."

Maha didn't like to think about the implications of what he was saying, but neither could she imagine urging him to stop talking about Jesus. She had not been a Christian when they got married during Ramadan in 2005, and only learned about her husband's faith after their marriage when she saw him reading a Bible. As she observed his life and the way he loved and respected people, she became attracted to the teachings of Jesus, especially the call to peace, not violence or terrorism.

When Maha met other Christians, both local and foreign, she felt love and peace overflow. She stopped warning Rauf that he would go to hell for reading the Bible and stopped insulting him for avoiding prayer times at the mosque. She remained unconvinced of Christianity's truth, though, and needed to study for herself. Maha didn't want to follow any religion simply because her husband told her to. She wanted to understand it and believe it for herself.

Six years after they got married, Maha committed to following Jesus. And now, post-revolution, in the middle of a war, and with the crumbling of Yemeni society all around them, her husband was asking her to consider the reality of becoming a widowed mother of four young children.

Christians of these early generations in Yemen didn't fear their own death. Their greatest concern was dying before they had a chance to pass on their faith to their children. Could Maha raise their children in the Lord without her husband at her side?

The answer was that she wouldn't be alone. In the years since the Jibla shooting and John's assassination, through political turmoil and religious persecution, Yemeni believers had committed to one another in unshakeable ways. If someone were arrested or if someone were murdered, their loved ones would not be left to fend for themselves. Other believers would rally around them. There is a difference between a Christian who wants to participate in Bible study and a Christian who is ready to answer the phone at 3:00 a.m. and respond to an emergency. Yemeni Christian leaders grew into those who answered the phone in the middle of the night and were willing to visit each other's families when someone was imprisoned because of their faith.

If extraction had been the main response to the earlier persecution and hardship, who would now be taking care of Christians in Yemen? Who would answer the call in the night or sell their gold to feed a prisoner? Who would have a voice able to speak authoritatively in situations like that of Rauf and Maha? An expatriate who left Yemen too soon, relying on the power of their passport nation to provide refuge wouldn't hold much sway. A Yemeni who left wouldn't hold much sway. A Yemeni believer who moved to Europe, attended an expatriate church, and sent his children to a private Christian school told me, "I can never tell Yemenis to stay in Yemen. I have no authority to say such a thing." As difficult as that is to hear, he is right. Believers inside Yemen struggle to trust those who have left, who have not lived through the crucible with them.

Yemeni Christians consider diaspora Yemenis their brothers and sisters, and believe they have an important role to play, but they also say clearly that those who left cannot be leaders of the church inside Yemen.

One Yemeni Christian said, "We trust those who have been with us in the hardest times inside Yemen more than those who show up at conferences abroad." Yemeni diaspora Christians are more known and are often showered with praise, positions, and money by churches, mission organizations, and donors abroad, with very little accountability. But in my mind, the leaders of the Yemeni church are those serving on the front lines *inside* Yemen.

Foreign organizations and groups seeking to serve the Yemeni church often talk about "exceptions" to this belief that people should be encouraged to stay in their home country. They may argue that a case is unique or especially severe. It is worth examining carefully, however, whether extraction truly remains an exception or whether, over time, it has quietly become the default, the go-to response whenever persecution comes. Too often, when many are relocated, the local church is left with less mature leadership. Family units that might have reproduced and discipled others are no longer present. Those who remain inside the country can feel less supported. The result is a slowing of church growth, with few visible models of leadership willing to bear the cost.

I have seen Christians imprisoned for their faith, killed for their faith, and endure all manner of attack for their faith. I have never seen a situation in which the Yemeni churches I associate with said someone would be justified in leaving Yemen. The local church does believe God has placed some Yemenis abroad for a reason. But those should be the exception, and extraction must not be the norm.

If there is no way to stay where one is, if that rare exception becomes a reality, what about moving to a nearby city? Even in Yemen, there is always a last refuge, a place where it is still safe. If the situation in Sana'a becomes too intense, move to Hudeidah. If Aden is untenable, disappear to Al-Ghaydah or even Socotra. This is what Jesus did in Judea, he moved from town to town. It is what Paul did when he faced persecution. It is what the believers in Acts did. If we truly want to see the gospel spread through an entire nation in our lifetime, we must encourage and model remaining in that nation.

Now, I *did* leave for a season! I am probably among the top three most wanted people by extremist groups in Yemen. I left under the guidance and direction of local church leaders who told me the time had come to step out for a season. Submission to local leadership is crucial for foreigners in these types of decisions.

Rauf and Maha may not have articulated it this way, or so clearly, but neither of them exhibited any intention of leaving. They knew they had the presence of the Holy Spirit filling them, the support of other believers, and their conviction of the truth and beauty of what they believed, and that was enough to hold them in place. It would need to be enough.

~

One day, Rauf and Maha went to the market to buy vegetables for lunch. Rauf hadn't eaten much and was weary after the long work week. When they came home, he took a shower to refresh himself. He had invited a friend to share their meal and wanted to be energized when the friend arrived. Maha and her mother, who was staying with them, prepared the food and waited for Rauf's friend, who was late.

"Rauf!" a man's voice called from outside the house.

"That must be him," Rauf said. He walked to the front door.

He opened the door, and Maha did not hear the usual flurry of warm greetings. Instead, she heard a barrage of gunfire. As soon as the gunfire stopped, she and her mother sprinted outside.

Two men with their faces covered stood beside a black car. Five more men sat inside the truck. The two men held AK-47s. Rauf lay face down on the ground, his body filled with bullets.

Maha couldn't believe what was happening. Later, she said it was like a movie, not real life. Armed, masked men, coming to murder her husband. This wasn't happening. Except, it was happening. Right at her door, in front of her children. Her husband's blood spilled onto the tile at her feet.

In shock, she screamed at the men, "Why? Why? What did he do to you?"

One of them pointed his rifle at her, but the others shouted at him, "Let's go! We have to get out of here!" He lowered the gun and climbed into the truck.

Maha fell to her knees beside Rauf. Surely, there would be a miracle. Something could be done. Someone would come and gently place his brain matter back inside his skull. Someone would come and patch up the holes in his chest. Someone would breathe the breath of life back into his lungs. She knew he was dead but refused to accept it. *Wake up, Rauf. Wake up!* Maha began to process that her children had come out of the house now and surrounded their father. The youngest sat at his head, crying, "Baba, wake up."

She rolled his body over and knelt on the ground, weeping and yelling. She saw that his ear had been cut off, as though it weren't enough to steal his life, the assassins wanted to steal his dignity too.

Two women from the next-door building came to Maha's side. No one knew what to do. Suddenly, the street filled with people. And still, no one knew what to do. There was nothing to do. Rauf was gone.

It was September 4th, 2015, the second annual day of prayer for the Yemeni church.

If anyone's situation qualified as a reason to seek religiously persecuted refugee status and residency in a new country, Maha's qualified. And yet, she chose to stay in Yemen. The believers surrounded her with social, spiritual, and economic support. She and the children moved to a new city, where people provided her with a small house. Eventually, she returned to school so she could find more secure work in the future. Someone else provided money for her children to attend school.

Rauf's murder cut through the Yemeni church community. John's death had been a shock, and they had responded with grief and prayer and determination to stand strong in courage and faith. But Rauf was Yemeni. Now, Yemenis were being targeted.

Jamil took Rauf's murder hard. Rauf had given him his first Bible. They shared a baptismal birthday. Rauf had encouraged him throughout the years, even from a distance, saying Jamil was one of the elders Yemenis needed. Rauf's faith strengthened Jamil's own, and their brotherhood ran in his bones. Now, Jamil knew in a more profound way than ever how much he needed the community of believers. He had nothing outside of Christ and the church. Other Christians sensed this, too, and in their shock and grief, the church grew stronger.

Jamil also realized he was on a hit list too. Probably even higher up, a more prominent target than Rauf had been. He'd known this, but death has a way of reinforcing unwelcome truth. Like Maha, Jamil had good reason in the eyes of the world, and of many in the global church, to flee Yemen. He could call on Western organizations and be plucked out within weeks, with ample evidence to support his case.

Instead, Jamil followed the path of believers in Acts 8 and moved to a new city. He moved where there was no established church. Jamil wasn't sure if any believers were present in the new city, but the gospel moved with him.

As believers relocated for various reasons within Yemen, they had an advantage over first-century disciples: telephones and the internet. They managed to stay in contact, carefully and cautiously updating one another on their location, praying for each other, and offering support when possible. Even as they scattered, they remained one body.

𝕾 24 𝕾

WITH JESUS IN PRISON

Believers in Yemen were still reeling from Rauf's murder when another blow struck. On Christmas Eve 2015 the Houthis raided Hussein's home. He lived in a rural area with little access to the internet or electricity, but Hussein had a modem that he would place near a window and the neighbors could see this strange device. He had solar panels, laptops, and a backup battery system. This concerned fellow villagers. Maybe he was a spy. Maybe he was an infiltrator. What they didn't know was that he also had Bibles. Lots of Bibles.

The Houthis confiscated everything: the Bibles, the electronic equipment, the laptops. Then they arrested Hussein. When I heard about his arrest, my heart fell. Houthis were known for holding people for years at a time. There seemed little hope that Hussein would be released any time soon.

Hussein had been corresponding with a woman named Salaam and had started discussing marriage. How would she handle his imprisonment? Counting the cost is not a hypothetical what-if game for Christians in Yemen. Counting the cost means weighing the decision to marry a man or not while that man is in prison for his faith. Men need to consider the possibility of a future wife being arrested or killed too. There needs to be consideration of children being raised without a mother and the weight of wondering what might be happening to her inside. When will the prisoner be released? What suffering will they have endured while inside? Will their mind or body be broken beyond repair? Will they lose faith, or grow in intimacy with Jesus? If released, will they live in fear of being rearrested? Will that fear be realized one day? Or will they hold fast to trust in God through every circumstance?

And yet, building a marriage on the foundation of a shared faith and a shared commitment to following Jesus no matter the cost was an opportunity to build a marriage on a foundation far stronger than most. Many marriages were for convenience, tribal alliances, or motivated by financial desperation. Some were between cousins and intended to keep families bound together. These marriages were fine, sometimes happy. But Christian marriages could hold all those factors along with a mutual love for and faith in Jesus that could uniquely sustain a couple through tribulation.

Salaam wasn't naïve about marrying Hussein, but she was optimistic. Idealism is natural at the start of a marriage. We all hope trouble won't come, or that when it does, it won't *really* be that bad.

No life is without hardship or pain. Thankfully, most of the time, God doesn't tell us exactly what we will endure. 2 Timothy 3:12 promises there will be suffering as believers follow Jesus. But other than Paul or Peter, we don't know how much suffering, or what kind will come our way, so we choose love and commitment. It isn't naïve or thoughtless but hopeful and idealistic.

As a young woman, Salaam had been devoted to Islam. She covered her ears when music played in the street to keep herself from being corrupted. Her family restricted her movement outside the home and determined who she could interact with. But her devotion centered on rule-following and no matter how well she kept in line, she never felt loved by or close to God because she was a woman. She heard Islamic teachings that convinced her God preferred men to women, teachings that seemed to hold women in contempt as though they weren't also made by the hand of God.

Salaam worked as a teacher, and one day as she was searching online for children's stories to share in class, she came across a song with the lyrics, "Jesus loves me. Whether I am good or bad, he loves me."

Whether I am good or bad? Now *that* was a radical notion. How bold for someone to declare, *Jesus loves me*! She turned these thoughts over and over but didn't discuss them. Later, she took a new job with a foreign humanitarian organization. There, she was fascinated by the patience and kindness one of the Arab trainers showed to misbehaving students. She knew that one of the trainers was a Christian, so she asked him for a Bible, but he refused. Undeterred, she later asked her brother to bring her a Bible from abroad. However, he suggested she read it online instead. As a result, her first Bible was a PDF she found online. After becoming a believer, she received her first physical Bible from the same Arab Christian who had initially refused her request.

Hussein and Salaam met online in 2012. She, like so many new believers, thought she was the only Christian in Yemen, and when she found other Christians online she threw herself into the opportunity to study and fellowship. Hussein was impressed with her eagerness and quick intellect. He had been praying for a Christian wife for more than two years, and the discovery that they were from the same region felt like a special nudge from God to pursue engagement, which was easily accepted by her family because of their shared heritage.

Before Hussein could propose, he was arrested.

In the first week of his imprisonment, guards took Hussein into the prison yard and told him he was about to be executed. Twice, they held guns to his head and vowed to shoot. Twice, they held back and threw Hussein back into his cell.

One of Hussein's relatives was a local judge, and when he learned Hussein, a *Sayyid*,[1] was in prison, he was furious. In an indignant rage, he ordered the guards to come before him. But by that time, the guards who had participated weren't able to comply. They were dead, killed in a missile attack.

Hussein knew when he was arrested and all his files were confiscated

---

1. A Sayyid refers to a person who is considered a direct descendant of the prophet Muhammad, often holding a respected status in Islamic societies, particularly in Yemen.

that other believers were at risk because of the documentation the Houthis now had in their possession. He prayed throughout his two months in prison that the files would be destroyed. The missile attack that struck his tormentors also destroyed all the files they had taken.

Despite his suffering, Hussein was encouraged by this destruction of his property. God was not oblivious to the suffering of the people in Yemen. Hussein was surprised by how much the Houthis already knew, including details and names. Under duress, he had confirmed some of the information the Houthis demanded. But now the men who knew this information were dead, and the evidence corroborating his words was destroyed in flames.

Two and a half months after being arrested, far sooner than anyone expected, Hussein was released. His relative, the judge, made the prison guards apologize for keeping him. Hussein left in honor, with his head held high, accepting their apologies, and rode home in the police chief's car.

Hussein was free, albeit a tentative freedom, as he could be re-arrested any day. He wondered if he should propose now to Salaam. But who would want to marry an ex-prisoner? A man who would likely spend more time behind bars? He hesitated, and eventually, it was Salaam who proposed to Hussein.

"Are you going to propose to me," Salaam said to Hussein, doing the opposite of Yemeni tradition, "or should I send my mother to arrange our engagement?"

One month later, Hussein and Salaam got married. Yemeni believers raised money to help fund their wedding and marriage: the rings, the dowry, the gift to Salaam's family, and a few small household items.

The early weeks of marriage introduced what life would be like for the newlyweds. Hussein couldn't stand locking any of the doors in the house. He battled night terrors. He woke up screaming, and Salaam would hold him and cry and pray. He wasn't alone in these reactions. Others talk about not being able to be in bright rooms or keeping their phones on silent so they won't be startled by an unexpected noise. They insist on the end seats in auditoriums or a chair near an exit at a restaurant. They don't take phone calls from strange numbers or without preestablished appointments. These are safety precautions and trauma responses and, when handled with faith and supportive counseling, don't hinder full life. Hussein and Salaam found healing in those early days, but every prison experience would carry additional trauma into the next one, and the church needed to grow in preparedness for trauma and for healing.

There would be many of those future prison experiences, but prison wasn't the defining characteristic of Hussein and Salaam's marriage. Together, they focused on their love for one another, their faith, and the fellowship they found with other Yemeni Christians. They shared how God met them through the prison trials, and their testimonies encouraged others that God would be with them, too, when persecution came. Like Peter, in Acts 12:17, who "described to them how the Lord had brought him out of the prison. And he said, 'Tell these things to James and to the brothers.'"

Hussein reminded people that they could keep themselves free from persecution. All they had to do was disobey the mandate of the Great Commission. No one would harm or imprison them if they kept quiet. However, their lives as believers were meant to be witnesses.

Both Hussein and Salaam felt marriage made them more effective in ministry. Before marriage, Hussein had struggled to connect with families. He saw men being trained and noticed that women didn't have the same access to training. This was often due to the fact that single women didn't have an excuse to leave their homes; therefore, she had little opportunity to access training. What if there were well-trained women who could go to those restricted to their homes?

Along with praying for a wife, Hussein had prayed for women believers to be well-taught and not excluded. With Salaam by his side, they could serve whole families. After they got married, Hussein baptized Salaam, and then she baptized other women. For Salaam, being married brought her out from the surveillance of her family and freed her to visit other women and families where she studied the Bible and shared her faith.

Their marriage itself became a testimony. Salaam's sisters and friends saw a husband who treated his wife with respect, who valued her input, who refused to take another wife, even though they had no children.

They saw a wife who partnered with her husband and supported him joyfully.

~

The stories of men and women like Hussein and Salaam weren't stories in *Foxe's Book of Martyrs*, and they weren't stories from centuries ago or from across the planet. These are Yemenis in 2015 or 2020 or 2025. As seekers and new believers observed the response of the Christian community when persecution came, the new generation found hope in the support and faithfulness they saw rather than the fear and division experienced in earlier years of the church's development.

Yemeni discipleship came to include what to expect in prison, how to sustain faith while inside or while waiting for the release of a loved one, how to heal, how to support each other, how to reintegrate after release, and how to deal with the guilt and shame that someone may feel regarding their actions in response to pressure and torture in prison.

Believers recognized that it was okay for people to respond in a variety of ways after someone was arrested. Some might pull back for a time. Some might get involved. Some might help hire lawyers or care for children, while others might relocate inside the country. Every situation and person was different.

Christians learned that release didn't end the suffering. People experienced nightmares and panic behind locked doors or in the dark. Some suffered from debilitating chronic pain. Others bore psychological wounds, faced financial repercussions, strained marriages or frightened children. There was also the risk that the released person had been turned and was now an informant for the government. These were all realities the church was learning to address, maturing in its ability to teach and model a biblical response. In the first generation, there were disciples facing the lingering fear of rearrest and many lacked a community to help them overcome post-imprisonment challenges. It was important to embrace the brother or sister with wisdom and give the person time to rest and recover in community. When people came out of prison, the church asked them to refrain from ministry for six months, at minimum. This was to give them time to rest, recover, and be with their families. It also gave them time to discern if this person had grown proud and would exploit their prison testimony in search of money or access to the West.

Shaadi and Jamila, who had once been afraid to reveal their names or to invite Yemeni Christians to their home, demonstrated remarkable courage. They publicly identified themselves with Hussein and Salaam. During one of his imprisonments, in 2015, Jamila made trouble with the guards and sold her gold jewelry to try to help release Hussein. Shaadi visited the prison, risking his own life, to ask about Hussein's welfare.

In 2021, during another of his imprisonments and while in solitary confinement, Hussein learned that the man imprisoned next to him belonged to al-Qaeda. They spoke when the guards were far away, and Hussein began to tell him about Jesus, about God's mercy and compassion, about love and forgiveness. By the time the other man was released, he had abandoned extremist ideas and began to pursue peace rather than violence.

It was hard enough for some Yemenis to believe that another Yemeni would choose to follow Jesus, but a Sayyid? That felt impossible. Hussein's interrogators couldn't fathom that a man, and his wife, from such an esteemed and knowledgeable line could be a Christian. Often, their shock led to them demanding that he explain more about Christianity, as though testing his sincerity. Sometimes, after the interrogations ended, they would sit with him and ask more questions about Christian faith and doctrine. They eventually admitted they had held a mistaken and incorrect view of Christians.

Everyone knew that prisoners would talk. No one can withstand prolonged torture and remain silent. Prison is not a movie, and prisoners are not Navy Seals with elite SERE training.[2] The reality of talking is something all Yemeni believers prepare for early in their discipleship training. They are taught to trust in God and not to worry about what to say when they are brought before their interrogator

---

2. Survival, Evasion, Resistance, and Escape training. It is designed to prepare military personnel to survive and evade capture, resist interrogation, and escape if captured.

because the Holy Spirit will teach them what to say in that very hour.[3] Believers needed to understand that there was no shame or guilt in revealing information, even partial information. Hussein didn't hold back. By his second, third, and fourth arrest, he didn't even wait for the questions or the beatings. Most of the time, interrogators already had the information they wanted anyway. Sometimes he would pretend to forget a particular name and the interrogator would fill it in for him.

Often, interrogators wanted information about me. Some groups in Yemen considered me the most dangerous person in Yemen. They couldn't imagine why an American would come to Yemen because of his faith in Jesus motivated by love, surely there was another reason. From their perspective, I had to have a more nefarious motive. Who would face possible kidnapping, assassination, or prison in a foreign country only to share the good news of Jesus Christ?

Hussein would say he *wished* he could bring me to them so they could see what a simple man I was. That I was not impressive in stature or rhetoric. But I had grown larger than life in Houthi intelligence, and men I cared about suffered. I hated this. Like the priest in Shusaku Endo's novel, *Silence*, there could be the sense among prisoners like Hussein that, "Behind the depressing silence of the sea, the silence of God ... the feeling that while men raise their voices in anguish God remains with folded arms, silent." And yet, no one expressed that to me. Instead, they spoke about Jesus filling prison cells with light, about missile strikes in answer to their prayers to destroy documents, about the body of believers exhibiting faith-inspired courage, and about God's presence with them in their pain.

Still, I wondered, would they resent me or others who were not in prison but who were used as pawns for torture? Would Hussein grow bitter? Would we be able to enjoy fellowship in the future, him knowing he had endured pain because of our connection?

A foreign Christian asked Hussein about this a few months after he was released from his fourth arrest, when he had spent two full years behind bars.

He laughed at her question. "Oh no, Sister," he said. "I do not

---

3. Luke 12:11-12

resent him. This is not about him, but about Jesus. When I became a believer, I counted the cost. We know being a Christian in Yemen is not a game. It might cost you your life, your family, at the very least your freedoms. Anything that happens because of our faith, we are willing to pay that price—beginning not when we are taken to prison, but from the moment we come to faith."

Hussein had told Salaam, during their engagement period, "I might not come back to you, or I might come back to you in a body bag. Maybe we will go to prison together. Are you ready to take those risks? Are you ready to be under attack because you are with me? To lose me at any time?"

"Yes, I am ready," Salaam said.

Not the most romantic proposal in the world, but a true Yemeni Christian one. Another person might promise their future wife a bounty of wonderful things they will do for her. Yemeni Christian men tell their fiancés, "You're going to lose your life if you marry me."

Interrogators used other believers, like myself, to inflict more pain. They also used family.

"We know your wife is a Christian," one said. "We have many pictures. We can even show you the picture of her baptism. If you don't tell us about her, we will bring her here and force her to talk."

Hussein started to shake and cry, the first time he had broken down. Her family didn't know Salaam was a believer. The news would be dangerous for her if it got out. When the guards saw his tears, they realized how much he loved his wife.

"She isn't a real Christian," he told them. "I made her do those things. I forced her."

"We know she was a Christian before you married her, we have her Facebook information."

"No, no," Hussein said. "I made that up and put her name on it."

As soon as Hussein spoke the lie, he regretted it. The words didn't honor his wife and certainly didn't honor God. A conviction was planted in him to always tell the truth and that seed grew. Later, after his release, Hussein developed a teaching of thirteen essential principles for living as a faithful Christian in a Yemeni prison. One of these is to speak honestly. Not that prisoners need to pour out everything they know, but if asked, answer truthfully. God will honor your truth-telling, and if God wants you in prison, you'll stay. If God wants you out, you'll get out. Your responsibility as a prisoner and Christian is to be faithful to the end.

His teachings are a gold mine for other believers. They are specific to the Yemen context, produced by a man who speaks from experience, an elder in the faith, someone who could leave but has consciously chosen to stay in the country, and who is transparent and vulnerable about the challenges. After his release, he sought support from a trauma therapist, openly acknowledging the need for healing.

Lying to the guards about his wife's faith didn't help Hussein's situation anyway; they didn't believe him and began to use her against him.

"Maybe we should throw her in prison," they said. "We know she is a respectable woman. What if she comes to visit and we take her into the interrogation room?"

They didn't arrest her, but sometimes when she visited, the guards refused to let her see Hussein. Sometimes for weeks at a time. When Hussein was able to see Salaam, she kept smiling but he could see the growing weariness and grief in her eyes. What he didn't see or know at the time was how much she was suffering alone on the outside. He suspected it, the loneliness, the anxiety, and fear. But he didn't know that her brother died, and then his brother also died. She didn't tell Hussein but bore the pain alone. Her family didn't know Hussein was even in prison, and she maintained a stream of stories to keep them from pressing into the reasons for his prolonged absence, including their demanding questions at the two brothers' funerals. *What kind of husband wouldn't come to such an event?*

Jamila, Jamil and his wife, and other faithful and courageous women checked in on Salaam often, but she bore the brunt of the stress alone. Some sent her recordings of scripture and the names of people all around the world who were praying for Hussein's release. She listened to the recordings over and over and ran her finger down the list of names. Women made her heaps of food to carry to the prison for Hussein to pass around. Sometimes the guards allowed her to distribute the food, other times they refused.

Hussein knew his wife was suffering. And yet, sometimes when she visited, he yelled at her. This was the source of his deepest shame, and he cried as he told me, with Salaam's hands holding his and her eyes brimming with tears too. If he had endured a beating the day before and his body was in agony, all the tension would explode toward Salaam. After she put up with the long bus ride, the weary walk, the harassment from the guards, the burden of carrying food, her husband yelled at her.

"Why did you come?" Hussein shouted. "You shouldn't be here! I should kick you out of here!" Or Hussein would demand a specific item or food dish, something he knew she hadn't brought or couldn't afford.

The anger and pain in her face was clear, and Hussein felt his heart break. The shame, guilt, and fear created a tumultuous tension he couldn't bear. What kind of man was he? Certainly not a man of God! Certainly not a man worthy of a woman like Salaam! Shame flooded him when he reflected on his behavior and abuse toward his beloved wife. After he yelled at her, Salaam would skip her next visits, something they both laughed about after his release, even while they cried together.

When Hussein was eventually released, there was no grand celebration, no public rejoicing. Salaam described the fear that filled her when he came home. Why did they let him go? What else would be demanded? When would he be taken again? Who was he now?

Along with relearning how to be married and under the same roof, there was also the slow, staggered process of reengaging with the church community. Some believers expected to jump straight back into their previous roles of leading or teaching, but Hussein and Salaam accepted the six-month time of restoration as a much-needed gift.

"One reason I was put in prison," Hussein said, "was to learn the value of my wife. To learn how wonderful she is and how to treat her well."

Hussein's release from prison would be just the first step toward healing himself and healing their relationship. With the help of the Spirit, the support of the community, a trained trauma counselor, and through remaining in their beloved homeland of Yemen, they are finding wholeness and reconciliation.

25

WHOLE FAMILIES

Jaad wanted a Bible so badly, he attacked his friend to get one.

He had lost interest in the Quran long ago, as a young child. He had too many questions that went unanswered by teachers and by his own readings. His uncle had a bookshelf filled with books, and one looked like a religious text but Jaad didn't understand it. He pulled it off the shelf when his family visited his uncle's home and would copy out passages into a notebook. Later, he read and reread the passages. They talked about Jesus and only brought him more questions.

When Jaad went to university in Dhamar, he made friends with a Yemeni student who was a believer. This friend had a Bible in his possession and Jaad wanted it, but his friend refused to give it to him. He wouldn't even let Jaad see it or touch it. Maybe he didn't trust Jaad enough and was afraid of being caught with a Bible. Jaad pleaded with him but the friend never acquiesced. Sometimes, he promised to give Jaad the Bible but he never did.

One day, Jaad saw the Bible sticking out of the back of his friend's pants pocket. Desire swept over him and he lunged at his friend.

"Wait, wait!" the friend shouted, but Jaad tackled him to the ground, wrestling to get his hands on the book.

Once it was in his hands, Jaad said, "Thank you for giving me the most wonderful gift."

Apparently, for some people hungry for God, seeking, asking, and knocking are not sufficient. Maybe Jesus should have said something about tackling and wrestling. In fact, Jesus did say that "forceful men take hold of the kingdom" in Matthew 11:12. Jaad is one of those forceful men, and once he grabbed hold of the kingdom of Jesus, he never let go.

Once he became a believer, the next strong desire to fill Jaad's heart was to find a wife. He longed to marry a Christian Yemeni woman, someone willing to stay in the country he loved, someone able to teach others, someone to partner with him in the complicated treasure-filled life of following Jesus in Yemen. Where would he find such a woman?

Healthy families are the foundation of healthy churches, and healthy marriages are the foundation of healthy families. In the early years of the church's development, many of the new believers were single men. Although some single women were present, they were often harder to meet—even for couples—because they had fewer opportunities to leave their homes. Even when a Yemeni woman disciple-maker was available to visit single women, it often didn't work, as the new believers couldn't honestly explain how they had met this new Yemeni friend. Their fathers, uncles, and brothers closely monitored their movements. Naturally, these single male believers desired to marry and build families. Others were already married to Muslim women, and in a few cases had multiple wives from before they came to faith. Concepts of a wife as partner rather than possession, or of resolving conflict within the marriage relationship and without violence weren't widespread in Yemen. Discipleship needed to address issues of marriage for the building up of the body and for developing a visible witness.

When Jaad tells the story of how he got married, he makes it sound like he picked Athir up like a sack of potatoes from the store—no problems, no questions. Just, *that's the one I like, and done.* Athir remembers it differently.

Jaad approached me. He had met Athir at a church event and was interested in pursuing her. I tucked those words into the back of my mind, along with the ones Athir had told me about marrying a believer and then about never getting married.

Eventually, I told her, "There is someone in the church who wants to get to know you."

"*La,*" Athir said. No.

"He's a good man," I said. "He's been a believer for a couple of years. Pray about it."

"No. I don't know him. I've never seen him."

"I've been studying him, to make sure he is the right person," I said.

"If there is any trouble, you will be responsible," Athir said. I agreed.

There was no love in Athir's heart, but she prayed and decided her Muslim father would never accept this mysterious man's proposal. He was strict and had high expectations of what kind of man could marry his daughter. There would be no harm in agreeing to allow this man to approach her father, so she agreed to a meeting.

A meeting was arranged with a nephew of Athir's father, her father, and Jaad. They met three times, each time Athir was convinced that when Jaad broached the subject of marriage, her father would refuse. She didn't know that her father had been researching Jaad. He had interviewed neighbors from Jaad's home village and spoken with men who knew him well.

To her great shock and dismay, when Jaad finally asked her father about marrying Athir, her father agreed. She felt no love, no joy, no feeling. Only surprise. But she had been praying and decided to trust her father's instincts, my insight, and God's guidance.

Jaad and Athir's marriage in October 2014, like Hussein and Salaam's, became a testimony to their families, communities, and the church. Their love is not based on romantic gestures or feelings of attraction only, but on mutual respect, humility, cooperation, and their relationship with Jesus. Christian marriages in Yemen vary as much as Christian marriages anywhere in the world. Likewise, both Yemeni Christian and

Muslim marriages experience brokenness, just as anywhere else, while there are also couples from both faiths who genuinely serve one another in love.

Athir and Jaad's marriage stood out because of the way they loved and served one another, in contrast to some of their extended family members, where relational struggles were common, and where men treated their wives as less than equals. Athir's experience with her husband caused her family and friends to take notice, wondering what was different about their marriage.

At the same time, Christian marriages in Yemen often reflect values that distinguish them within their cultural context. Husbands see their wives as partners rather than subordinates, actively participating in raising their children even as they grow older. Women refrain from publicly criticizing their husbands to family and friends. Couples seek to resolve disagreements without shouting, resorting to violence, or fleeing to their parents' homes. Above all, they share a deep spiritual life, which shapes their approach to love, respect, and mutual service.

As the church grows, Christian marriages will become more commonplace. Often, though, people come to faith after they are already married. One spouse is a believer, and the other is Muslim. When men come to faith who are already married, the church is direct with them. They cannot now divorce their Muslim wife and get a new, Christian one. They are responsible for their wife, and this is an opportunity to humbly love and serve her, whether she becomes a believer or not. Some, like Jamil, prayed and shared and loved for eight years or more until their wives accepted Jesus. If a man has multiple wives before he decides to follow Christ, this church community has the conviction that they should not divorce them. That man was responsible for all these women and remains responsible for them.

If a Christian man is married to a Muslim woman, his treatment of her will be a powerful witness. Helping with the children or the cooking, respecting her ideas and having meaningful conversations together, speaking kindly and making requests rather than demands, and not speaking badly about her behind her back testify to a changed man. For Christian women married to Muslim men, the situation can be more complicated. Her service to and respect for him are expected. If she obeys his commands and responds to his demands, she is simply behaving as a Yemeni woman "should." In her case, one strategy to show her husband the love of Jesus is to develop a friendship with a believing couple. In this way, her husband can observe how a Christian man lovingly serves and honors his wife, which may challenge his assumptions about marriage. At the same time, it creates an opportunity for the Christian husband to build a natural relationship with him, allowing both words and actions to testify to the hope of the gospel.

Jaad was a man of high character, evidenced in that when the president of his company stepped out of his role, the entirely Muslim board voted unanimously to hire Jaad as his replacement. Jaad is one of a few Christians in the organization. Athir, though, as his wife, had a clearer view of his faults.

Ten years into their marriage, Athir called me one day with a massive complaint against Jaad.

"He said he would take out the trash and he didn't do it!" she exclaimed. I burst out laughing.

"If that was the biggest complaint my wife had about me, we would be in paradise!" I said.

A few years earlier, her major complaint was that when she asked Jaad to bring something from the store, sometimes he forgot the specific item. I laughed just as hard then.

Yemenis were drawn to marriages like Jaad and Athir's. Arranged, yes. Complicated by the reality of two human beings making a life together, of course. But they were happy, and their home was full of mutual enjoyment and respect and a shared vision for life and work.

As Christians build families together, they naturally wrestle with how to raise children in a Christian Yemeni home when there are few models to look to for inspiration. One of the first issues they face is recognizing that a child born to Christian parents is not a Christian by default. Muslims call someone who becomes Muslim a "revert," not a convert. They believe everyone is born Muslim, so if a person lives for a while as a Hindu or a Christian and then becomes Muslim, they have not converted but reverted back to their original created identity. Christian parents must shed the assumption of belonging to a religious system by birth and faithfully nurture their children to make their own commitments to following Jesus.

This is a great challenge to Yemeni Christians when it comes to raising children in the faith. Second-generation Yemeni Christians, or Yemeni Christians from a Christian background, can develop a lackadaisical attitude toward faith. Christian parents in every country must recognize that their children are also born into a broken world where sin touches every life, like my mother had done in the Canary Islands. They need to pray their children would have their own experiences with the God of the universe and intentionally evangelize and disciple them.

That Yemeni Christians are even talking about how to raise second and third generations boggles the mind. Those I learned from in my early years could hardly have imagined such a beautiful discipleship challenge. And that challenge extends beyond children into the broader church community as they wrestle with what it means to be one family in Christ.

The Yemeni church takes the family of God so seriously that as men and women mature in their faith, physical evidence of this doctrine abounds. They learn to treat each other as brothers and sisters and reconcile when there is brokenness in the family. Rather than reverting to secrecy or avoidance if someone is arrested, they move toward the imprisoned brother or sister and their family. They celebrate each other and place kinship in Christ over other allegiances.

This risky love is even more impressive considering tribal and regional differences. The Yemeni church is not homogeneous. People come from Hajjah or Hadhramaut, where women don't go outside after dark alone. They come from Aden or Taiz, the comparatively liberal "NYC" or "London" of Yemen. They come from Dhamar and Shabwa, staunchly tribal and conservative regions.

It is like building a church from Mennonites, Pentecostals, and Southern Baptists. Regional and cultural differences matter because it affects how women feel about wearing or removing their face veil, it impacts customs around childbirth and parenting. There can be linguistic misunderstandings or ancient feuds broiling beneath the surface. To the outsider, these are not evident areas of growth or discipleship, they are not obvious points of contention or disunity. But in a country as diverse as Yemen, and at war, it is a miracle that northerners and southerners and people from Amran and Lahij gather and don't kill each other.

Raising children in the faith and building a diverse community of faith have parallel lessons and require similar character qualities: faith, patience, intentionality, gentleness, and vision, among many others. Growth in the church in one area impacts the other, meaning that as children see diverse Yemenis love one another in the name of Jesus, they are encouraged in faith. As diverse Yemenis observe parents raising children with grace through all the challenges parents around the world face, they are observing a model of leadership and purpose.

26

THE INCENSE OF WISDOM

When she was twenty years old, Wa'ad's father changed her name. He went to the government office and made her a new certificate, gave it to her, and said, "Now you are Bilquis."

He refused her confused protest. "No, you are Bilquis."

Wa'ad couldn't understand what made him change her name. She thought maybe he liked the meaning of the name Bilquis, but no one in the family knew what it meant. Scholars aren't even sure what the name means. It has been related with wisdom and leadership and nobility, as Bilquis is the name Islamic tradition has given to the Queen of Sheba. Yemen has a long history of wise, benevolent, powerful, and creative female leaders, Bilquis being one of the earliest.

One of the most powerful royal women in Yemeni history was Queen Arwa, also known as the "little Queen of Sheba." Arwa bint Ahmad al-Sulayhiyya lived in the eleventh century, an Isma'ili Yemeni woman. She ruled for fifty-five years and was a master of religious jurisprudence, grounding her fatwas in four different schools.[1]

Arwa observed the geographical and economic strengths of the

---

1. Samer Traboulsi, "The Queen Was Actually a Man: Arwā Bint Aḥmad and the Politics of Religion," *Arabica* 50, no. 1 (2003): 96–108.

people and saw that when people from Sana'a came to visit her, they brought weapons. When people from Jibla visited, they brought farming tools or sheep or butter. Based on this, she convinced her husband to move Yemen's capital from Sana'a to Jibla, the more fertile region. She said, "Here, Jibla the bread, and there, Sana'a the army."[2]

She was given the rank of *hagga*, the highest rank in the Yemeni religious hierarchy, and eventually gained the status of being the spiritual authority people were expected to follow. Her reign was largely peaceful and prosperous and her tomb in Jibla continues to be a site of pilgrimage, as is the mosque named after her.

Bilquis, the original queen of Sheba, laid the groundwork for women like Arwa and Wa'ad centuries earlier. Isaiah 60 sings the powerful promise of the glory of the Lord rising:

Arise, shine, for your light has come,
and the glory of the Lord rises upon you.
See, darkness covers the earth
and thick darkness is over the peoples,
but the Lord rises upon you
and his glory appears over you.
Nations will come to your light,
and kings to the brightness of your dawn...
...herds of camels will cover your land,
young camels of Midian and Epha,
and all from **Sheba** *will come,*
bearing gold and incense
and proclaiming the praise of the Lord.

How did the message of the glory of the Lord reach the people of Sheba? Presumably through their ancient queen, Bilquis. Yemen is one of a few nations that appears in both the Bible and the Quran. One contains a story of punishment for disobedience, the other a story of inquisitive faith.

---

2. Farea al-Muslimi, "Geography of War and Agriculture in Yemen," *Sana'a Center for Strategic Studies*, September 21, 2021, https://sanaacenter.org/publications/analysis/33.

Yemen appears in the Quran in Sura Saba 34:15-17 with the collapse of the ancient Marib Dam. The city of Saba' (950-115 BCE) was known as the "Paris of the ancient world," a vibrant oasis irrigated by the waters of the dam.[3] The dam was a wonder of ancient engineering at 1,800 feet long and watering more than 4,000 acres of land. It sustained structural breaks in the fifth and sixth centuries and was ultimately destroyed in the seventh century by either an earthquake, a flood, an act of God, or all three. According to the Quran, the dam was destroyed and the city flooded because the people rebelled against the word of God. A new dam was built in the 1980s and continues to irrigate Yemen's governorate of Marib. UNESCO declared the ancient dam site and surrounding ruins a World Heritage Site in 2023.

The Bible doesn't mention Yemen by name explicitly, though many scholars believe the nation-state contained within Yemen's borders today includes the location of the ancient kingdom of Sheba. Debate swirls around the geographical origins of the queen, oscillating between arguments for Somalia, Ethiopia, or Yemen, but average Yemenis aren't concerned with scholarship. For them, the debate is settled.

Yemeni legend claims that three thousand years ago parts of present-day Yemen were ruled by Bilquis. The ruins of a temple in the province of Marib, near the ancient dam, mark what was the political center of her kingdom, which stretched from there to Ethiopia. Yemeni Bedouins still guard the ruins of this ancient temple today.

In 1 Kings 10, the Queen of Sheba heard about King Solomon's wealth and wisdom. She left her country and arrived in Jerusalem to test Solomon with hard questions, bringing with her a "great caravan—with camels carrying spices, large quantities of gold, and precious stones."

The Queen and Solomon discussed all she had on her mind, and he answered every question. By the time the Queen left, she was overwhelmed and said, "Praise be to the Lord your God, who has delighted in you and placed you on the throne of Israel. Because of the Lord's eternal love for Israel, he has made you king to maintain justice and righteousness." She gave King Solomon even more gold, precious stones,

3. The Editors of *Encyclopaedia Britannica*, "Ma'rib," *Encyclopaedia Britannica*, May 29, 2024, https://www.britannica.com/place/Marib.

and spices as she left Jerusalem. Generations later, her people were still praising the Lord in the vision of Isaiah 60.

~

When Wa'ad was seven, before she became Bilquis, she grabbed a knife and sliced her sister's eye. "I want to see you cry blood," she said to four-year-old Iman. Another time, Iman ignored Wa'ad, so Wa'ad grabbed her sister's leg and burned it with a hot iron.

Wa'ad's parents beat her as punishment, but rather than restraining her, the beatings fueled her rage and violent behavior. She tried to run away before second grade but was caught, brought home, and beaten. At school, children stole her shoes and cut her hair in class, and she responded with fury. In high school, a teacher irritated her, so that afternoon, she and a few friends tied the teacher to a chair and shoved a cotton bud into his ear.

Wa'ad eventually stopped acting out violently but kept her fiery spirit. She directed it at her two sisters who, to her shame and horror, had both become Christians. Wa'ad reported Iman to the government, and when Iman decided to leave the country, Wa'ad tried to stop her at the airport. When she failed and Iman left anyway, Wa'ad ordered her parents to cut them off.

"They are no longer our family," she said. "You can't talk to them or talk about them."

"*Khalas*," her mother said. "I have lost my two daughters. I need to go to my family." She left her husband, abandoned Wa'ad, and moved to Kuwait, where she lived with her sisters.

Wa'ad's father developed a brain tumor, and he forced her to quit her job to care for him. Life had slammed to a halt and it was all because of Christ.

Six months later, still sick, her father decided to travel to get medical treatment and to reconcile with his wife and so he moved to Kuwait. Wa'ad was furious. Her mother had abandoned them, her sisters were persona non-grata, and now her ill father, whom she had given up her education and job to care for, was returning to his wife! It was too much to bear due to the shame that the society would have brought upon her, and Wa'ad fled abroad, as far away from painful memories of Yemen as she could get.

Prior to her sisters coming to faith, Wa'ad lived a beautiful life. She had a job, was in school, she had friends, and she had positive relationships with her neighbors. She had stability and her family was well-respected. Now that her sisters decided to become Christians, her entire life was overturned. The situation, beyond her control, was infuriating. She was angry at her sisters, and she felt too embarrassed by her family's shame of having two Christians to deal with relationships in the community.

Amal and Iman, living abroad, were also in pain during the season when their parents, sister, and friends no longer spoke to them. The tentacles of pain spread far and wide when someone decides to follow Jesus.

Amal, one of Wa'ad's sisters, had gotten her address from their mom and mailed Wa'ad a Bible with a hand-written note. *God promised me that you and all our family will come to faith.*

Wa'ad was furious. But she didn't tear up the note and she didn't burn the Bible. She didn't read it, either.

Five months later, in the summer of 2016, a rickshaw struck Wa'ad as she rode her bike to school while studying abroad. She broke both legs and fell unconscious. While knocked out, she had a vision of Jesus. He said, "You will not die. You will have new life." Wa'ad woke up in a hospital with no idea who had brought her or how she got there, both legs encased in plaster casts. She wanted to talk to her sister and got her number from their mom.

Wa'ad called her sister and told her about the accident, about the dream.

"Have you accepted Jesus?" Amal asked directly.

"Yes," Wa'ad said, shocking herself. But she realized even as she said it that it was true. "Teach me to pray!"

"When you get out of the hospital, I will teach you, but right now you have a lot of anger to deal with first," Amal said.

Wa'ad thought of the anger she carried. She still blamed her sisters for ruining her life when they started following Jesus. Amal was right about that rage too.

"You need to deal with that anger so you can have full peace," Amal said.

Amal arranged for someone to teach Wa'ad the Bible online, an Arab living in central Africa. They studied for two hours every evening. He taught her inner healing practices, and she inched toward forgiving herself and her family.

"Are you ready to forgive your sisters?" the man asked after a year of studying.

"Yes."

"Do you think you could talk to your sisters?"

"Yes."

"Good," he said. "Because Iman is sitting here next to me."

To Wa'ad's surprised delight, the man who had been discipling her for over a year was the brother-in-law she had never met. Iman lived and worked abroad, and the couple had decided it was a good time to reveal his identity to Wa'ad.

Wa'ad was thrilled. Not only was she growing in her own faith, but God was faithfully and tenderly caring for her once-shattered heart. The faith that had previously bitterly divided her from her sisters now had brought them back together. She was happy for her sister to have found a wonderful Christian man, and happy for herself to be welcomed into this fellowship of family and Christian kinship. She could easily picture the rest of her life abroad, part of a church, communicating with her reconciled family around the world, and praying for her parents together with her sisters.

And then, based on Iman's recommendation, I called her regarding Yemen.

Wa'ad loved her life abroad, and it was easy to be a Christian on her own there. Just her and God. Or just her and God and her sisters on the telephone. She didn't want to move back to Yemen. Her primary concern was that the conservative society, compared with her current life, would feel like a prison. She had no idea that a more significant trial would come from the iron-on-iron sharpening effect of dealing with other Christians.

Wa'ad prayed and asked God to tell her she was not supposed to return to Yemen. Instead, God brought her back. She is a strong woman, and the Yemeni church needed women like her. Able to teach, able to inspire, ready to challenge and push. The church needed her, and God brought her back.

In 2021, while Covid-19 had restricted travel around the world, Yemenis were struggling to survive a war that had escalated across more than fifty frontlines and was now in its seventh year. Covid was just one more thing to add to a growing list they could do nothing about. The Iranian-backed Houthis attempted to retake Marib, a strategic oil and governmental resource location. Massive internal displacement continued and the humanitarian crisis deepened, inching toward famine. The USA signaled a shift of policy in removing the Houthis from their list of terrorist organizations[4] and the UN approved sanctions in Yemen. The country was reeling as much as ever when Wa'ad landed at the airport to move home.

All she could think was, *this is crazy. What am I going to do here?*

I had plenty of work for her at the company, and Wa'ad threw herself into learning the programs and systems we had in place. She also began to meet other Christians. Jamil and Athir had been at her baptism, but they were the only Yemeni Christians Wa'ad knew inside Yemen. As a single woman returning from abroad, Yemeni but unknown to most of the believers, Wa'ad had to labor to earn trust.

The first meeting in Yemen in which Wa'ad participated was a leadership, nonchurch affiliated meeting, which included Christian men and women, followed by a church training made up of all men and herself.

Afterward, she called me to express her frustration. "Why was I the only woman in the afternoon church training?" she asked. "Why aren't there more opportunities for women to be trained?" she asked.

---

4. As of 2025, U.S. President Donald Trump had once again designated Yemen's Houthis as a "Foreign Terrorist Organization" due to their attacks on Red Sea shipping and their involvement in actions linked to the Gaza war and Israel.

The women had attended the morning sessions along with Wa'ad but she was hungry for more—both for herself and others. However, the discipleship training among women in that city was still in its early stages. Women were not yet meeting for spiritual growth on a consistent basis due to various challenges that the community was working through.

Since the days of Shaadi and Jamila, every opportunity available for women to be discipled had been pursued, but Wa'ad had recently arrived in a different Yemeni city, where the work among women was just beginning. There were still obstacles to overcome, some of which were not immediately visible to a newcomer.

"Start something," I said. "Be part of training the women." I made sure she knew that the other women involved in ministry, the men, and I would support her.

Although women had played an active role in the Yemeni church throughout history, it was encouraging to see Wa'ad long for even more opportunities—not just in this training but across the country. More importantly, she was willing to put in the hard work to make it happen. Too often, I have seen well-intentioned people desire change but lack the initiative to lead and champion the effort or even be a part of the effort. This was not the case with Wa'ad.

The church had a ministry segment they called *integrated discipleship,* which included the training of women in everything from Bible study to money management and project leadership. Women had been part of leadership historically and had taken active roles for years. But what Wa'ad was picking up on in this particular city was that there weren't many women receiving effective discipleship and that most of the gatherings and trainings were composed of men. There was an imbalance in who was receiving discipleship. Illiteracy was one issue, as was the reality that women were consumed with household management responsibilities and childcare.

If Yemeni Christians wanted to see whole families come to Christ and whole families grow in faith and whole families impact their neigh-borhoods, women needed to become more integrated and better equipped. The church needed to offer literacy training and adapt its sessions to accommodate illiterate women, even though literacy is not essential for leadership or spiritual influence.

Women's involvement required tangible support from men. Fathers would care for children while women attended meetings, taking on a radically counter-cultural responsibility. Traditionally, women are not accepted as publicly influential, and their voices are ignored. Society expects women to only sit and listen, tending solely to children or staying occupied in the kitchen. That husbands and fathers stepping into childcare and household work is one of the most shocking things newcomers notice about the believing community, and one of the most appealing.

Yemen had changed since Wa'ad left almost two decades earlier. They had been through the Arab Spring and now were still in the middle of a war, Covid and natural disasters, displacement, and financial challenges. Wa'ad stepped into a leadership position in the business but didn't share that painful history with her coworkers. There was tension in the early days. She also sensed a lack of clarity about her role.

"I can't believe you made me come back to Yemen!" Wa'ad said to me.

"I didn't make you do anything," I said. "God called you."

"No, that's you," she said. "God called *you*. I can't work with these people."

"You can do this well."

"They don't like me."

"They don't know you, so they are still learning to trust you."

"I don't know what I'm supposed to be doing."

Wa'ad's job description for the business was clear, but she wanted to do more. First, though, she had to build solid relationships and would have to watch, listen, and learn. Like a foreigner, as a returning expatriate, Wa'ad did not have the freedom to determine her role alone, but together with the community and the support of the leadership, they would discern where she could thrive. The church did not have the freedom to refuse partnership with her, either. Grafting in new leaders and new members of the body is a mutually refining process that takes time, discernment, and humility.

~

Yemeni women built on the legacy of leading, powerful women like Bilquis and Arwa to secure their democratic rights. After throwing off the yoke of colonial rule, southern Yemeni women gained the right to vote in the People's Democratic Republic of Yemen (PDRY) in 1967. Northern Yemeni women in the Yemen Arab Republic (YAR) followed suit just three years later in 1970, in the wake of a popular revolt against a theocratic autocracy.[5]

By 2013, Yemeni women had managed to negotiate a thirty percent quota in elected bodies and governmental institutions at the National Dialogue Conference (NDC) that followed Yemen's Arab Spring revolution. Now, however, nearly a decade of conflict has largely wiped out their hard-won gains, and women are virtually nonexistent in Yemen's governing bodies.

Like so many Yemeni women before her, Wa'ad has learned that true strength is not limited to appropriate force or resistance but also found in wisdom, resilience, and gentleness. She came to see that balancing these qualities—knowing when to stand firm and when to respond with grace—was both her greatest strength and one of her greatest challenges.

Western expatriates must not rely on their experiences and vocabulary definitions when looking at the lives of Yemeni women. It is too easy for an outsider to equate a black face veil with oppression or to overlook the creative and culturally persuasive ways women have been involved in politics, religion, and family life.

While those systems have restricted women from public leadership roles, they have also historically provided women with access and influence in dispute resolution processes—ranging from female-led tribal mediations to the important role that most women play in influencing

5. "Women's Voices in Yemen's Peace Process: Priorities, Recommendations, and Mechanisms for Effective Inclusion," *Sana'a Center for Strategic Studies*, December 2022, https://sanaacenter.org/publications/main-publications/19400.

community dispute processes through lobbying male family members at home or in private.

According to the research of Nahj Consulting, in Yemen's tribal areas there have historically been four ways for a woman to resolve or stop a conflict: (1) cutting her hair; (2) taking off her veil and replacing it with the opponents; (3) taking weapons away to stop the fighting; and (4) invoking *tadreek* (suspension of hostilities)—a temporary measure to stop fighting to seek a third party to arbitrate—or by going to the opposing tribe to ask for *tahkeem* (arbitration).

During Yemen's Arab Spring protests, women in Sana'a drew on similar tribal traditions when they burned their face veils. This was not a statement about the veil or a feminist and Westernized act of "freedom" but was a culturally appropriate impassioned plea for justice and peace. It was the women's very embrace and value of veiling that made the gesture meaningful.

Throughout Scripture, women navigated the cultures of their time to pursue justice, peace, life, and faith—sometimes by influencing the men around them and other times by leading outright. Abigail saved her family from being massacred by four hundred hungry and armed soldiers led by David, who was bent on bloodshed. How did she accomplish this? Through wisdom and decisive action, providing food and diplomacy to de-escalate the conflict. The Hebrew midwives, Shiphrah and Puah, defied Pharaoh's genocidal decree, saving Israelite baby boys from slaughter. They acted with boldness and cunning, using Pharaoh's own sexism and racism against him to ensure the survival of a generation. Tamar, the only woman explicitly declared righteous in all of Scripture, used her courage and strategic thinking to secure justice from her father-in-law, Judah.

But beyond influencing men, Scripture also highlights women who took full leadership roles in God's redemptive story. Deborah, a prophetess and judge, led Israel in both spiritual and military matters, guiding the nation with wisdom and strength (Judges 4-5). Huldah, another prophetess, was sought out by King Josiah's men for divine guidance, and her words led to national revival (2 Kings 22:14-20). Esther did not merely influence King Xerxes—she strategically orchestrated the salvation of her people, risking her life and making critical decisions that turned the fate of Israel (Esther 4-7). And Mary Magdalene, entrusted by Jesus Himself, became the first witness of the resurrection, declaring the Good News to the apostles at a time when women's testimony was often disregarded (John 20:17-18).

Women in Scripture acted both within and beyond the social structures of their time—sometimes influencing men, sometimes taking charge themselves, always playing a vital role in advancing God's kingdom.

According to the Yemen Policy Center, many international organizations and activists adopt a narrative grounded in an oversimplified understanding of Yemeni women's lives that centers on rescuing them from their patriarchal societal structures and customs that seem misogynistic to Westerners. Such approaches risk eroding valuable roles women have played within those structures.[6]

Whether they are working toward political peace, addressing marital conflict, or striving toward food security and quality healthcare, Yemeni women are an integral part of the nation's flourishing. Whether they are creating literacy programs, resolving conflict between believers, or preaching and teaching the next generation, Yemeni women are an integral part of the church's flourishing. They are rising up as queens, proclaiming the praise of the Lord.

---

6. H. Tabbara and G. Rubin, *Women on the Frontlines of Conflict Resolution and Negotiation: Community Voices from Syria, Iraq and Yemen – A Discussion Paper* (UN Women, 2018).

27

MIRACLES AND DREAMS

"I have to leave my wife!" the man sounded panicked and kept repeating the phrase over the phone.

Tariq struggled to reason with him. He knew this believer loved his wife, but terror seemed to be consuming him. "What happened, brother?"

"I have to leave her. She found my Bible."

Tariq had answered the phone in the middle of a Bible study with other church leaders. He put the phone on speaker.

"Calm down," he said. "We are listening together. Is she upset?"

"I don't know. But she will tell her father or my father and then what? What do I do?"

"Take her out for a walk," Tariq said.

"I have to leave her. I can't take her out."

"Go and buy her flowers. Take her to dinner."

The other men in the study nodded, but the man on the phone was barely listening, blinded by fear.

"Have a conversation and explain yourself over a nice meal," Tariq said.

"That will never work, and I don't have money anyway."

Tariq turned to the others and motioned for them to open their pockets. Without hesitation, the men made a pile of coins and paper bills in the middle of the *maglis*.

"We have money for you," Tariq said. "Come and get it and take your wife on a date."

Slowly, the man calmed down. He followed Tariq's suggestion. His wife did not cause her husband any problems, and within two years, she became a Christian. The worry over how their spouses will react is very real for Yemeni Christians, but it is also the case that the worry is often misplaced. It isn't that wives or husbands want their now-Christian spouse to suffer, or that they want a divorce. They are usually sincerely concerned about the condition of their loved one's soul and are surprised when the extended family reacts harshly. More often than not, if a wife tells her father about her husband's Christian faith, she is hoping her father will bring her husband back from what she considers to be the wrong path. Navigating the space between worry, fear, and wisdom is challenging, and the more elder believers are in proximity and in healthy relationships, the more they are able to positively contribute to this conundrum.

Tariq laughed with joy at the memory. "This is the new generation of believers," he said. "They still have anxiety and troubles, but they are not alone anymore."

Tariq understood this man's trepidation. His wife, Buthaina, was not a Christian when they got married over twenty years earlier. Because he had a large family and their home was in the village, even as newly-weds, people were constantly in their house, congratulating him at all hours of the day. Tariq rarely had time alone with his wife.

"We never had that honeymoon month," Tariq said, remembering the chaos. One night, the house was finally empty and the couple sat together in the *maglis*. Without quite realizing what he was doing, Tariq said, "Please bring me the *Kitaab Al Muqadis*" (the Bible).

"What?" Buthaina was perplexed. "Where is it?"

"Behind the blankets on the far side of the room, there is a box and in it there is a Bible, a book. Bring it."

Buthaina looked but couldn't find it. "Do you mean you want the Quran from the other room? Is the *Kitaab Al Muqadis* the Quran?"

Tariq's heart thumped. Had he just ruined his marriage in the first month? She didn't even know what the Bible *was*. What should he say? They both came from a close minded tribal society, and Tariq was uncertain what would happen.

"The Quran is *tamam*," he said, fumbling for how to describe the Bible, "but the Bible is *tamam tamam!*" As if to say the Quran is ok, but the Bible is very, very good! "Keep digging beneath those blankets, maybe it fell down farther."

Buthaina rummaged some more and eventually emerged with the book in her hand.

Suddenly, Tariq felt strangely nervous. "Can you go lock the door?"

She looked at him quizzically.

"Make sure no one is coming and then lock it tight."

Buthaina checked the alleyway outside, locked the door, and then sat beside Tariq, the Bible in hand.

"Don't you want to go and relax?" he said. He wasn't planning to share about his faith that day, but she wouldn't leave.

"Let's read it together," she said.

"Sure, sure," Tariq said. "Another day."

"No, it's ok. I want to listen."

Tariq had been reading in John, but he wasn't sure it would be wise to start with Jesus. Maybe it would be better to begin with common ground, stories Muslims also knew. He flipped to the beginning of the Bible and began to read from Genesis, about creation.

She listened and commented that yes that was good. "This makes sense."

"If there is something you don't understand," Tariq said, "you can ask about it."

"But if this is the word of God we shouldn't question it."

"No, no. It is good to ask questions. God wants us to understand."

From that evening on, every night Tariq read a chapter or two out loud from the Bible. Buthaina noticed that Tariq didn't go to the mosque on Fridays, and if he was with people when the call to prayer sounded, he removed himself from the group until they finished the *salat*.[1] Slowly, slowly, she began to understand that her new husband

---

1. Salat – Islamic ritual prayer performed five times daily

was following a different religious path than what she had assumed.

His deepest longing was that his wife would come to love Jesus and that he could have security in his home. One of the hardest things for believers was if their spouse did not accept Jesus. There were people he knew who had broken relationships with their wives and situations where the wife rejected Christ, involved the family, marriages ended up in divorce and often problems with custody over their children. He had a good relationship with his wife and didn't want to lose her or cause trouble with their families, including her brother who was a fundamentalist.

"I need you to know that I will never force you to believe a certain way," he said. "I don't want to have conflict with our families. We will live in the traditions of our tribe and culture."

He wanted her to discover and learn who Jesus was in her own time and not just follow Jesus because her husband followed Jesus. Tariq understood that if his family heard he was a Christian with no explanation, they could misunderstand and think he had joined a Western political movement or man-made religion. Tariq wanted to be able to explain to his entire family who Jesus was and what he had done in his own time, rather than having them hear it from his wife.

They read together over four weeks, and Buthaina began to see the character of Jesus in Scripture. She also discovered more about her husband and encouraged him to open up even more.

"You know the Naṣārā are better than the Muslims in many areas," she said, poking at him.

Tariq wondered if he should be more transparent or if she was trying to trick him. He hesitated and finally said, "I believe like the people called the Naṣārā."

"Do you have friends who believe like you?"

"Yes."

"Foreign or Yemeni?"

"Both."

Two months after the two started reading the Bible together, I visited their city to meet with believers, including Tariq. He told me about Buthaina and how God had worked on her heart. He described how she used to comment that she didn't understand why Muslims took issue with the things she learned about Jesus.

When Tariq and Buthaina tell the story now, they glance at each other with a sparkle in their eyes, and say, "Of course love also had a role in it all!"

"She and God have a unique relationship," Tariq says. "Even more than me. God has given her a special experience."

One Friday afternoon, a dispute erupted in the wadi near Tariq and Buthaina's home. Nearly thirty people swarmed around. Some held rifles, some waved jambiyas. Some threatened to shoot into the air, or even into the gathering crowd. Tempers flared and tension was high. Ever since he worked to bring peace between expat and local Christians when I first met him, Tariq had been recognized as a peacemaker. He called the people into his home to try and mediate. Twenty-five men stood inside and poured out the front door, each shouting and waving their arms. The scene was chaotic and explosive.

Suddenly, one sound rose above all. A high-pitched wailing came from the kitchen.

Tariq knew it immediately. It was his baby girl, Nadia. She was barely one year old and still crawling. The wailing was followed by Tariq's wife's voice screaming his name.

The shouting stopped, the chaos ended abruptly. The men shifted from arguing to offering assistance, no matter what had happened. Tariq assured them if he needed anything, he would reach out, and the men went home, leaving the heated discussion for another day.

Buthaina sprinted out of the kitchen holding Nadia in her arms.

"Hospital, Tariq. We need to go to the hospital."

Tariq barely glanced at his daughter, but he knew. The skin on the upper half of the left side of her body, from her face down her arm, was bubbling and blistering. She must have pulled over the pot of boiling water for tea.

They rushed to the hospital, where a friend of Tariq's saw Nadia immediately. His diagnosis was grim.

"This is serious. You need to bring her to the hospital in the city. All I can do here is lessen her pain."

At the larger, better-equipped hospital in the city, the doctors didn't have much encouragement to offer, either.

"She will keep her face," one said. "But she will need many surgeries."

Tariq and Buthaina were in shock. Their precious firstborn baby girl, with her face, shoulder, and arm destroyed. They couldn't afford multiple surgeries, and even if they could, the prognosis was that she would remain scarred. They returned home devastated. Maybe they could raise money from their family. Maybe Tariq could find more work.

Bandages covered the burned parts of Nadia's body and despite the pain medication, she was in agony. Her cries filled the house at all hours of the night and day. Buthaina added her tears to the sound, and Tariq's heart broke at the grief and pain that had invaded his home. He couldn't bear to look at Nadia and refused to see her. He didn't go into her room. Didn't help change bandages. Couldn't bring himself to look at her melted skin.

For five days all Tariq could do was pray and plan a way to get her to Sana'a where there may be more help.

The sixth day after the accident, Tariq and Buthaina hosted a group of visiting doctors. They came from a Christian community in Germany and the Netherlands. He wasn't sure how he could host them well with a broken heart, but Yemeni hospitality won out, and Tariq opened the doors of his home to these foreign strangers.

While they sat in his *maglis*, Tariq showed them photos from the hospital of Nadia's face, photos he hadn't been able to fully look at yet himself. The doctors cried when they saw how bad the burns were.

On the seventh day, Buthaina called Tariq to come into the baby's room.

He opened the door but kept his gaze on the floor.

"You need to look at her, Tariq," Buthaina said.

"I can't." Tears filled his eyes. "I don't want to remember her like this."

"Look at her." Buthaina put her hand gently under his chin and she lifted his face. "Look at her."

Buthaina wiped away the tears and opened his eyes. Buthaina cradled Nadia in her arms. The baby was finally quiet, soothed momentarily, her body wrapped in a blanket.

"You see?"

"That is her healthy side," Tariq said.

"No, Tariq. This is the burned side."

Tariq glanced at his wife. She was somber but glowing. She tilted the baby over and he saw both sides of her face.

They were exactly the same.

"What . . .? Where . . .?"

"There are no burns on her face."

"No burns," he whispered.

Buthaina held something in one hand, and she lifted it to Tariq's eyes. "When I lifted her bandage this morning, this came off with it." Tariq flinched. It was dead skin tissue. "Underneath there is nothing, no scars, no blisters."

Tariq felt his knees go weak and he leaned against the wall for support.

"Last night," Buthaina said, "I had a dream."

They were sleeping in bed with Nadia between them. A large man entered. He wore white and was so bright, his light filled every space of the room. He had long hair and was massive, taller than the room, and yet he fit inside it. She reminded Tariq of a saying from her region of Yemen, "All the prophets have large legs." She asked the shining man, "Are you Jesus, the Messiah?" The man didn't answer but reached down to touch the baby. He brushed his hand down the side of her face, only her face. Not her shoulder or arm. Buthaina saw the burned skin fall to the ground, and the fresh baby skin beneath, like new. The man stood up, and Buthaina moved to hug him, but he disappeared.

"I woke up and came to change the bandage and this is what I found."

Tariq felt like shouting and dancing for joy. He hugged his wife, and they burst from the room, carrying the baby and laughing with tears streaming down their cheeks. He showed his baby to the doctors who were moved to tears themselves by the miracle.

Tariq and Buthaina believed Jesus left the scar tissue on Nadia's arm as a reminder. It was impossible to deny what she had been healed of. They also kept the scrap of tissue that fell from Nadia's face.

Buthaina committed her life to following Jesus and has become a key leader in the community. She is a voice of wisdom and discernment and God uses her when difficult topics in the church are discussed. She uses healthy tribal customs and Biblical principles to offer solutions to challenges at hand.

Yemenis are not surprised by or uncomfortable talking about the supernatural: miracles, dreams, visions, or miraculous feats performed by holy men.

The Well of Barhut or "Yemen's Well of Hell" is a hotbed of such tales known even to the prophet Mohammad. A hadith quotes him saying, "The worst water on the face of the earth is the water at Wadi Barhut in Hadramawt, which is like locusts in comparison with other pests. It gushes in the morning and is dry by the evening."[2] In early usage, "Hadramawt" sometimes referred broadly to the eastern deserts of Yemen, which likely explains the wording. Today, the well is known to be located in Al-Mahra Governorate, near the Omani border. The perfectly round black hole—ninety-eight feet in diameter and 367 feet deep—in the far eastern part of Yemen is a naturally formed well. Until 2021, no one had descended to the bottom amid rumors held that any who did would have their head cut off.

The legends claimed that talking about the well would bring bad luck, that the stench emanating from it would stop people from breathing, that it was haunted by wild animals, and that strange voices and screaming came from inside. The hadith also likely contributed to the

2. Sarah Durn, "The History and Mystery of Yemen's 'Well of Hell,'" *Atlas Obscura*, October 20, 2021, https://www.atlasobscura.com/articles/yemen-well-of-hell-cave-explored.

idea that the well was a portal into hell and the souls of the damned wound up here.

When St. Bartholomew visited Aden on his way to India, legend said he exorcised a devil from Sirah Island. The devil had been bothering the people nearby for centuries by "belching fire and bad-egg smells at them when they came to draw water" from the well. Another prophet expelled a ten-headed beast from Aden. Yet another saint rescued a sinking ship by "going into a trance and flinging his tooth-cleaning stick at the peak of a mountain, which flew off and blocked the hole in the ship's hull."[3]

Of course, these folk stories are laughable. The stinky demon burping fire was likely a geyser. The men who explored the depths of the Well of Hell returned to the surface with their heads still attached. I never saw the ten-headed beast and will let you resolve the mountain-top-plugging-the-ship's-hole story. I have, however, seen my hands and Lydia's hands healed of warts. I have seen the flawless skin on Nadia's face and the burn on her arm.

Some Christians don't believe God speaks this way any longer, or that God doesn't do miracles in the modern era. That is fine as a personal conviction but it should not be imposed on others. What is the value of insisting God doesn't move in these ways now? What good would come from discrediting what some consider evidence that God loves them?

Foreign Christians need to come to a place like Yemen with a blank canvas, willing to let God paint as God sees fit to paint. Do not bring qualifications for how God can or can't work. Don't suggest parenthetical limitations. Don't require dreams and visions and miracles, either. They are not a strategy. Do expect God to work and to reach people uniquely, creatively. Do test whatever happens and make sure it does not contradict the word of God or common sense, that it builds up the body of believers. Wait and see what happens.

Acts 2:42-47 shows the utopian experience of the early church. No church, not even the early church, remained so tidy for long. Only two chapters later, Ananias and Saphira are struck down dead at the apostles'

---

3. Mackintosh-Smith, *Yemen: The Unknown Arabia*, 138.

feet. But this first picture in Acts 2 is of believers sharing all things in common, breaking bread together, listening to the apostles' teaching, and "everyone was filled with awe at the many wonders and signs performed by the apostles." This was a church open to anything God might do. They had no experience, and they had few guardrails. They used all the tools available to them so that the spread of the gospel would not end in their generation.

This is what the church in Yemen, and other places around the world, needs. We need every possible method available. It is hard enough to see a movement spread in Yemen, in Syria, or in Afghanistan. How much harder if we place theological limitations on what God might be pleased to do. The small tools theological restrictions leave us with are not working. Church planters and local church leaders need to be open to everything, and if something produces good fruit, bless it.

According to Job 33:14-18, "God does speak—now one way, now another—though no one perceives it. In a dream, in a vision of the night, when deep sleep falls on people as they slumber in their beds, he may speak in their ears and terrify them with warnings, to turn them from wrongdoing and keep them from pride, to preserve them from the pit, their lives from perishing by the sword."

Saif continued to pursue marriage to Amira. He had been talking to her about Jesus for months, but confusion plagued her; she couldn't organize her thoughts about God, Jesus, the Bible, or Islam.

"How can I know what you are saying is true?" Amira asked.

"Pray about it," Saif said. "Ask God to guide you to the true path."

That night Amira prayed before she fell asleep that God would answer all the prayers she had offered, asking God to show her the straight path.

Amira was walking on a path, but it was the wrong path. She didn't know how she knew it, but clearly, she was going in the wrong direction, on the wrong road. She tried to turn around, but suddenly she died. She didn't know how she knew she died, but again, she knew it. A voice came to her and repeatedly said, "You are on the wrong path. You are on the wrong path."

She woke up. She pinched herself to make sure she was still alive. Eventually, she fell back to sleep.

After this dream, Saif taught her the Lord's prayer. The day after she memorized it, the same dream came, and this time, demons filled the room.

In the dream, Amira crouched in a corner, trying to hide, hoping the demons wouldn't see her. She started to recite the prayer Saif taught her:

Our Father in heaven,
hallowed be your name,
your kingdom come,
your will be done,
on earth as it is in heaven.
Give us today our daily bread.
And forgive us our debts,
as we also have forgiven our debtors.
And lead us not into temptation,
but deliver us from the evil one.

The demons disappeared.

Amira woke up again. She tucked the two dreams into the back of her mind and tried to sleep. Tomorrow, she would talk to Saif about them.

～

Nearly every Yemeni person featured in this book has had dreams and visions. Many have experienced miraculous, unexplainable events. Many have suffered and others have died without being miraculously rescued. Dreams, visions, and miracles are given, often to one person, but they are to be shared with the body of believers for testing and for the building up of the community.

In the Bible, God speaks through dreams to King Abimelech and

King Nebuchadnezzar, to Daniel and Jacob and both Josephs, to Sarah and Pontus Pilate's wife.

Amira had no hesitation about how to respond to her dreams. She described them to Saif, joyfully exclaiming that her confusion had been cleared. She confessed faith in Jesus and a desire to commit her life to following Jesus's teachings. She was baptized three months later, and a day after, she and Saif were married.

Yemeni church leadership asked that couples getting married in the church choose an elder couple as "sponsors," someone to be the official witnesses of the marriage. At the ceremony, this couple prays a blessing over the newlyweds. Saif and Amira asked Shaadi and Jamila to serve in this capacity for them. At first, their choice surprised people because Shaadi and Jamila lived farther away. They didn't have as frequent contact or interactions with the young couple as other leaders did. But when Saif articulated their decision, a beautiful and honoring tribute to the elder couple, he powerfully demonstrated the gift of what it means to have Christians stay, long-term, and through many trials and tribulations, in their home country.

Shaadi and Jamila, Saif reflected, had proven themselves faithful from the late 1990s, from years when there were almost no known believers to now walking into Christian gatherings filled with whole families worshipping together. Shaadi and Jamila knew what it was to have loved ones killed because of their faith, and they did not abandon Jesus.

A story believers love to tell, which demonstrates his growing courage, is about the time Shaadi gave a man a ride on his motorcycle for two days. He drove from the village to the hospital where the man worked. Shaadi's rider started to talk about a friend he made at a training center.

"He gave me a valuable gift."

"Was it a watch?" Shaadi asked.

"No. More valuable."

"A computer?"

"More valuable."

"A car?"

"More valuable."

"What can be more valuable than a watch, a computer, or a car?"

"A book."

A week later, Shaadi brought his son to the hospital and saw the same man working there. He waved Shaadi into his office. There, he pulled out a book wrapped in a cloth.

"This is the book."

It was a New Testament.

Shaadi said he, too, was a Christian. The two men started meeting together to read and study. Their wives met. They began socializing together in ways that made their spiritual connection blend into community life and minimized suspicion, and the man and his wife became believers.

Shaadi and Jamila's lives demonstrated the power of the gospel to transform believers from fear to courage, isolation to community, dread to hope. Shaadi and Jamila, by their humble love and faithfulness, had a marriage Saif and Amira wanted to emulate, of holding on to faith and to one another, and of coming out at the elder end of life with wisdom and joy.

From my days in Peru until now, I have still not seen a dead person raised to life. But I have seen dead souls raised to new life. I have seen new creations of healed bodies and healed marriages and healed lives. I have seen the miraculous activity of God being close to the broken-hearted and saving those who are crushed in spirit.[4] These are miracle stories.

Nadia's miraculous healing of her burns and Amira's dream of the healer surprised no one. Saif didn't question Amira's dreams. Shaadi and Jamila have been transformed by the power of God. The Yemeni church is growing. God is still speaking now in one way, now in another. In a dream, in a vision of the night.

Do we not perceive it?

---

4. Psalm 34:18

❧ 28 ❧

SALT AND LIGHT IN YEMEN

"I have the perfect solution," Saif told me. "It will solve all the persecution problems."

"Oh?" I braced myself to not laugh out loud. Saif was a fearless evangelist, and I wondered what he had come up with this time.

Amira had gotten into trouble with neighbors who noticed her wearing a cross necklace. It slipped out from her abaya when she walked outside, and they were offended by the visible Christian symbol. She and Saif decided they would need to move but first came to me for advice.

"Are you going to stop wearing the cross necklace?" I asked.

"No," Amira said.

"Then why move? The new neighbors will have the same issue with you. Are they causing trouble because you are a Christian? Because of how well you love and serve them?"

"No. They just don't like the cross." Maybe they felt it was an affront to their faith. Maybe they didn't understand it and the confusion bothered them. Maybe they didn't like that Amira advertised her different beliefs publicly.

That was when Saif came up with his solution.

"We could make a Christian community," he said. "A physical place where we all live together. Maybe society will accept us if we bunch up together, show them we aren't the only ones."

Now, I started to laugh. "Great idea! It will be so easy for extremist groups to find us and kill us all at one time too! They can get us in one swoop."

Saif's face fell.

"Anyway, how would you share the gospel if you aren't part of the outside community?"

He acquiesced, though later Saif told me he fostered that idea for three years, determined to find a way to make it work. He only gave it up when a church elder convinced him that the best, most effective way to witness as a Christian was to share the gospel in an appealing, gentle way, to model the sacrificial love of Jesus through doing good to those who persecuted him, and to demonstrably love his wife the way Christ loved the church.

When I was young, someone told me, "Evangelism will solve eighty percent of your problems." I don't remember who said it, but the line has remained with me. One could plausibly argue that in Yemen, evangelism will *cause* eighty percent of your problems, depending on how you do it. Many zealous Yemeni Christians who came to faith without wise shepherds burned bridges with their families by sharing too harshly and not being compelled by love. Hussein is one who admits to this and continues to deal with the ramifications. Saif too. In his early years as a Christian, he caused such offense that some family members still want to kill him. However, as he learned from church elders, and after years of praying and serving, many of his family members became Christians, and others stopped causing him trouble.

There is validity to the argument for evangelism solving eighty percent of the church's problems. If Christians focus on evangelism, there is no time for petty disputes over dunking versus sprinkling or which songs to sing or how to structure a worship service. If the church is focused on evangelism there will, Lord willing, be so many new believers that leaders will be too busy training and discipling to argue amongst themselves or to be jealous of someone else's fruit-bearing.

The church can't grow complacent, thinking that because entire families are responding to Jesus, the work of spreading the love of God can slow. But the church must also be wise, not out of fear of persecution, that will come. But wise to not be the very stumbling block that stops someone hungering for more. This means being sensitive to cultural norms and religious values. It means respecting the Muslim prophet, their holy book, and the traditions and celebrations of Muslims.

It means understanding the pain points, the questions, and the hunger of the people they love and want to share Jesus with. It means "engaging others at the heart level in a much kinder, humble, and more loving, empathetic manner."[1] This runs deeper than engaging on an intellectual or doctrinal level and moves into the realm of emotion, what theologians call orthopathy. It asks Christians to be "open to the feelings of religious others."[2] And it means paying attention to what the receiver is hearing when a Christian presents the gospel. Are they hearing something that is good news?

There is not one way of sharing the gospel in Yemen. As everywhere, it depends on to whom one is speaking and the context of the conversation. If a Muslim brings up a belief or concept from Islam, Yemeni Christians respond with respect and love with the goal of moving the conversation back to Jesus. The Jesus-centered gospel message shared by Yemeni Christians has a notable impact.

"I don't start with the cross. We can come back to the cross, which is offensive to Muslims, that a prophet would die such a shameful death," one Christian said. "Yemenis don't think in a linear way. Logic can be circular and cyclical, and I don't need to present things chronologically."

This evangelist starts with the resurrection, that Jesus is alive and

---

1. Jose Abraham, "A Pneumatological Theology of Religion: Amos Yong's Approach," *Global Missiology English* 20, no. 1 (January 9, 2023): 42, http://ojs.globalmissiology.org/index.php/english/article/view/2723.

2. Ibid., 43.

present through the Holy Spirit, and eventually comes around to talking about the cross. It may sound strange to a Western Christian as we are often taught to make sure people understand the concept of sin before offering a solution. This man starts with what he considers a gap, what Muslims don't experience, which is the true love and the presence of God. The point is not to present a one-size-fits-all on how the gospel is presented in Yemen, but to say that God doesn't need Western techniques or specific sets of arguments. Yemenis are coming to faith weekly in 2025, and while the foundation of the gospel message does not change, the details of the presentation adapt to the person sharing and the person hearing.

Some Christians start with the love of God and the life of Jesus through stories they memorized from the gospels. Others start with their own experience of life in the Christian community. Many Yemenis are weary of violence, exhausted by fundamentalism, and disillusioned by how life has turned out: painful marriages, wayward children, sickness, financial insecurity. Knowing Christ doesn't make these struggles instantly disappear, but it offers the presence of a faithful God and the comfort of a loving community who will walk through them together.

But even before Christians speak of Jesus, they show him. Collecting rainwater and sharing food with neighbors has brought people into relational proximity. Hussein loves to share meals, and said, "Before we started this, some people knew we were Christians, and they stayed away from us. Now, with the war and hunger, when we give them food, the relationship changes. We are no longer strangers from two different belief systems but have a relationship of Yemeni brotherly love as we endure hardship together."

Actively living out their faith opens opportunities for conversations with Muslims and it helps Christians and seekers find each other. One man approached Jaad and showed him a notebook of one hundred pages of notes he had scribbled, documenting his search for faith.

"I sensed you might be a Christian," the man said. "You behave like someone who follows the Bible's teachings." He had been praying to find other Christians, hoping he wasn't the only one.

The work that Yemeni Christians do throughout the country in their various professions isn't a platform, and they don't view it as a distraction from evangelism. Jesus told his disciples that "the harvest is plentiful, but the workers are few." These words come immediately after Jesus walked through towns and villages teaching, proclaiming the good news of the kingdom, and healing every disease and sickness. The work the disciples were sent into the field to accomplish was the same: teaching, proclaiming good news, and performing acts of mercy and compassion. The Yemeni church my family fellowships with doesn't pay Christians to pastor, preach, or share the gospel. Believers are encouraged to have jobs and provide for their families and within those jobs and families, they serve as sent ones, proclaiming good news and performing acts of mercy and compassion.

A comfort and draw for Saif when he first encountered Jesus, as for many newer Yemeni Christians, was seeing whole families worshipping together as part of the church. He had assumed it would be impossible to live in Yemen as a Christian. He didn't want to leave his beloved homeland. He wanted to stay, to get married, to enjoy following Jesus in Yemen. When Saif saw the trust between believers, the peace they had together, and the way they cared for one another, he felt secure to become a disciple of Jesus. He could stay and he wouldn't stand alone. If there was a marriage or parenting struggle or a sickness, if he or Amira went to prison, they and their children would be cared for. They belonged to a body, and they were also charged with caring for others. The mutuality bonded them.

Since the Reformation, and especially since the Enlightenment period, individualism has invaded the Western church. Individual salvation, a personal relationship with Jesus, an isolated "quiet time," a lonely pursuit of holiness and sanctification, and one-on-one discipleship became the focus. Alex G. Smith argues that this represents a theological shift from the early church's family-based approach. "The move from biblical theology to systematic theology helped advocate this ignoring of family evangelistic approaches, too. Calvin's *Institutes*, as well as synthesized or summarized creeds, or shortened theological tenets like the Westminster Catechism, tended to focus on the individual growth and not on evangelizing and discipling whole families and their entire extended families."[3]

God is not limited by this individualistic approach, and often the Spirit "overruled in his harvest and spontaneously gathered whole family networks, tribes, and people groups into the church, especially in the non-Western world."[4]

But, it is time for Western expatriates to recognize what God is doing among family networks and to join in. Reaching families the way Yemenis are doing it is not only an evangelism strategy or church-planting method. This is what it looks like to live as a Christian in relationships, what it looks like to be a blessing and bear fruit that lasts.

Evangelism in Yemen is not limited to a Bridge Illustration or a compilation of spiritual laws. It doesn't merely walk people down the Romans Road. Instead of a fifteen-second or even a three-minute testimony, it is all day, every day, living as the salt of the earth in community, growing organically. It is based on a theology of suffering and a theology of living the life of Christ. Evangelism is whole-bodied, holistic, and relational. That said, it is not without theological grounding or conviction.

The Yemeni church is in the process of creating their own statement of faith, and the process is slow and deliberate, as they wrestle, study, and reflect. In the meantime, to demonstrate their identity as members of the global body of Christ, they ascribe to the World Evangelical Alliance's Statement of Faith. They know that comprehending these doctrines, or any human-made statement in its entirety, is not a prerequisite for saving faith. The gospel message for Yemeni Christians is simple, "that Christ died for our sins in accordance with the Scriptures, that he was buried, that he was raised on the third day in accordance with the Scriptures."[5] They invite others to put their faith in Jesus

---

3. Alex G. Smith, "Evangelizing Whole Families," in *Understanding Insider Movements: Disciples of Jesus within Diverse Religious Communities*, ed. Harley Talman (Pasadena, CA: William Carey Library, 2015).
4. Ibid.
5. 1 Corinthians 15:3-4

Christ, the Messiah, our Lord and Savior. The message begins with Jesus and ends with Jesus.

Believers dream of a day when Yemenis will remember their ancient connection to Christians in Najrān and to the Queen of Sheba. Their spiritual roots connect them to a Middle Eastern man, Jesus, who was born in Bethlehem of Judea, and who demonstrated God's power to heal, who elevated women and compassionately touched lepers, who drew divided people into relationships, and who modeled the love of God through life, death, resurrection, and ascension. This is the good news Yemeni Christians find compelling.

MULTIGENERATIONAL
LEADERSHIP

I would love to tell a story of a thriving church community with no conflict but that is not this story. That is no church's story this side of paradise. What I *can* tell is a story about growth and learning. As the Yemeni church grows in numbers, all of us also grow in wisdom, especially in learning to lead ourselves first and then to lead together.

Recently, I was back in Yemen and preparing to head into a meeting I knew would be heated. Strong opinions on all sides, high stakes, past hurts, and passionate people were about to crash in the *maglis*.

I called my father, now eighty years old.

"Come to the meeting," I said.

"Why?" he said. "What will I do there?"

"Don't do anything, just come."

He hesitated.

"Sit in the corner, pray and smile at everyone," I said. "Greet them, listen to them, and don't do or say anything else."

He agreed.

The meeting went off without a problem. Despite the high emotions, everyone behaved, and we came to a productive yet tentative solution. Why? Because no one was about to act foolishly in front of an elder. Especially not a humble elder. By virtue of his age, in Yemen, my father was easily the most powerful person in that room, though he didn't contribute one word to the discussion.

Elders, those over sixty, seventy, eighty years old, are the keepers of tradition, the guardians of the stories, the fountains of wisdom unsearchable on Google. In the church, they are the ones who hold the history, who remember before women were involved as teachers, and who remember when there were no families or no married couples. The elders are the ones who laid foundations on which future generations will build. They are not shuttled off to the side, they are active members of the church community.

Any young person, when in a room with an elder, should aim to leave that room with at least one piece of wisdom or one life lesson gleaned from that elder. Part of discipleship is training people to steward the wisdom available to them. Even if there is disagreement, or someone practices a method you wouldn't use, there is always at least one thing to gain.

Respect for elders and gleaning wisdom from elders is just one tribal value in Yemen that the church is learning to incorporate.

I know my father's name and his father's name and that's it. Three generations, including myself. That doesn't even reach back to before World War I. When I asked Wa'ad about her family, she listed off fifteen generations without taking a breath. Conservatively, that takes her back over five hundred years. And she could have gone further if I'd given her the chance.

Not many Westerners can list off more than three or four generations of their family. Not many Yemenis can rattle off fewer than fifteen.

This, a culture steeped in a multigenerational mindset with roots running back to the Middle Ages and tendrils reaching out toward the next thousand years. Ignoring this in building the church is to hinder sustainability and growth. Our vision for Yemen is not for a rash of people coming to faith and fizzling out after twenty years of a "golden era." We long for a story that reaches forward eight, nine, ten generations and continues. We trust in a God who is "the faithful God, keeping his covenant of love to a thousand generations of those who love him and keep his commandments."[1] To accomplish that means preparing for fruit beyond a single generation.

A multigenerational mindset impacts every aspect of growth: leadership, church planting, decision-making, program implementation, activities, outreach, discipleship, everything. A multigenerational mindset is not the same as a communal mindset. Westerners are often trained to think of the individualistic versus communal orientation of people outside the West. This is valuable, and part of the Yemeni church's emphasis on reaching whole families stems from their value of community. However, a multigenerational mindset is different. It means tapping into the wisdom of elders. It means planning for the next generation to thrive and laying a foundation they can rely on and expand on.

Across Yemen, houses appear unfinished to a Western eye. The first floor will be complete—windows, door frames, paint, décor, solid brickwork. But the second or third levels are half-built rooms, four walls without a roof, no window frames, and they lack the finishing touches, with exposed rebar and iron bars or piles of stones heaped in a corner.

This is because the owner of the home, the patriarch, is planning for the next generations of family to live in the same building. He knows his son will marry and move his new wife to the second floor. He knows this couple will want shelter but will want the freedom to create their own home to their tastes. What looks like an unfinished home to a foreigner is a home built with dreams to a local. More than one or two stories, these Yemeni dream homes of the wealthy tower three, four, even five stories tall. The comfort and safety of the top floors depend on the structural soundness of the bottom floors.

This is the necessary mindset for long-term, healthy growth in the church, and any expatriate involved in setting a vision or building a leadership team must understand this. Intentionality is vital; study the local culture and see what is being done well and what can be incorporated. Be wary of people adopting Western patterns because they are considered "Christian" when what is local works.

Estimates on the number of tribes in Yemen range from two

---

1. Deuteronomy 7:9

hundred to four hundred and defining tribes for the Yemeni nation doesn't do much to reduce the complexity. Tribe "can refer to a simple grouping of families that inhabit a specific geographical location, or a union of branches of tribes that share a common tribal name. "Tribe" can thus denote kinship or a political or economic relationship. Tribal structures are not based on a single clan or tribe, but rather include multiple kinship and spatial tribal divisions linked to each other by distinct relationships. These complex networks of families or clans are intertwined together through common lineages, customs and alliances. Families and clans belonging to a particular tribe are also bound by the common traditions that regulate relations within and between tribes."[2]

Along with a multigenerational mindset and respect for the wisdom of elders, the tribe offers lessons in mediation, conflict resolution, reconciliation, and in pursuing consensus. Leading toward consensus requires an immense amount of patience and self-control, both fundamental in the fruit of the spirit. Mediation, conflict resolution, and reconciliation are vital for peacebuilding, a core element in Jesus's beatitudes. *Blessed are the peacemakers for they shall be called sons of God.*[3] As the church grows in training leaders and maintaining indigenous qualities, they must learn from what Yemeni culture has to offer.

Consensus leadership means listening and waiting while decisions are debated so that everyone involved can say their piece. In Yemen's tribal system, consensus is built on the key traditions of "transparency, accountability, solidarity, collective responsibility, the protection of public interests and the weak, prioritizing community interests over those of the individual, empathy, and forgiveness."[4] Dialogue and apology are also part of the system.

Tariq is a tribal leader and still holds that role in society. During church leadership discussions, he sits back and listens. He waits. People

---

2. Rim Mugahed, "Tribes and the State in Yemen," *Sana'a Center for Strategic Studies*, January 21, 2022, https://sanaacenter.org/publications/main-publications/16156#Tribes_as_Mediators_and_Resolvers_of_Conflict.

3. Matthew 5:9

4. Nadwa Al-Dawsari, "Tribal Governance and Stability in Yemen," *Carnegie Endowment for International Peace*, April 24, 2012, https://carnegieendowment.org/research/2012/04/tribal-governance-and-stability-in-yemen?lang=en.

say ridiculous things or voice foolish opinions, and he allows it, encourages it sometimes, to ensure every angle has been considered and every person feels heard. People make wise and insightful comments, and he considers them as he formulates his own contribution. He often doesn't insert his opinion until the end of the discussion, and even then, will occasionally demure until coerced to express himself.

The patience, humility, and self-control necessary for consensus-based leadership are ongoing areas of growth for me, and I am constantly learning from Tariq's example. Consensus is not instinctual for most Westerners, where self-control is more centered on not eating too much chocolate or limiting screen time. Wise leaders from the Global South have modeled consensus well. Nelson Mandela wrote about learning patience from his guardian, Chief Rolihlahla Jongintaba. The chief presided over tribal meetings in which he seated all the elders in a circle with no one, not even himself, set apart. The meetings lasted for days, and the chief did not say a word until everyone had spoken their piece. When he did speak, it was not to share his own opinion but to foster consensus. Mandela concluded that a leader "does not impose a decision but molds one."[5]

Tribal culture contains a wealth of wisdom earned over centuries of tension and dialogue when it comes to the kind of peacebuilding that leads to true reconciliation. One of the global church's greatest weaknesses, and one of her greatest needs, is reconciliation. Ironically, this is the very ministry we are given by God, who "reconciled us to himself through Christ and gave us the ministry of reconciliation: that God was reconciling the world to himself in Christ, not counting people's sins against them. And he has committed to us the message of reconciliation."[6]

Reconciliation in Paul's second letter to the church at Corinth does not mean only reconciliation between humans and God. It means reconciliation between humans. I Corinthians contains one of Paul's harshest rebukes. In Chapter 5, he addresses an issue of sexual

---

5. Richard Stengel, "Nelson Mandela: The Making of a Leader," *Time*, May 9, 1994, https://time.com/archive/6725274/nelson-mandela-the-making-of-a-leader/.
6. 2 Corinthians 5:18-19

immorality among the believers and instructs them to remove the man from fellowship. Yet even this act of discipline is framed with the hope of eventual restoration and salvation. The letter also contains challenges on how to deal with lawsuits among believers, marriage, divisions based on who people followed, how to deal with food sacrificed to idols, propriety in worship, and several other contentious issues. The second letter is a follow-up. Paul knew his letter grieved the Christians in Corinth and 2 Corinthians reminded them that they are called to one body, one faith, and that in their weakness, God proves strong. It is a letter of reconciliation.

Today, though, it is the rare group or church that goes through a divisive conflict and can reconcile to the point of continuing to worship and partner together. Too often, reconciliation stops at forgiveness or the cessation of anger, but there is a lack of rebuilt trust. It is a truncated, feeble reconciliation that won't last through fiery trials.

What can Yemeni tribal custom offer the church to help her develop deeper, more lasting practices of conflict resolution and reconciliation?

Consider the conflict resolution built into the Mahri region's tribes' code of conduct. Five main traditions govern multiple tribes. First, solidarity is supratribal, not limited to only one's immediate tribe but to the broader Mahri cohort. Second, violence between Mahris is highly discouraged, "taboo." Third, "bearing arms does not necessarily mean using them."[7] A tribe's display of weaponry is intended to reduce violence. Fourth, should armed conflict occur, the winner does not take all. Instead, the victor is expected to compensate the loser for its losses. And fifth, intratribal mediation is effective in limiting violence as tribal leaders work to ease tension before it explodes.

These principles can be translated to conflict between believers and can be utilized by believers who are tribal leaders, like Tariq, in their Muslim communities, infused with the power of the Holy Spirit and the love of Christ.

---

7. Ahmed N. Al-Dawsari, "Eastern Yemen's Tribal Model for Containing Conflict," *Carnegie Endowment for International Peace*, March 31, 2020, https://carnegieendowment.org/research/2020/03/eastern-yemens-tribal-model-for-containing-conflict?lang=en.

Christians belong to more than their immediate church or family community. They are part of the whole church in Yemen and the global church. This suprachurch allegiance can inspire them to be quick to bless another believer, for example, even if they have a different theology regarding women teachers or infant baptism. The Bible teaches the importance of doing good to all, especially those who belong to the household of believers.[8] Leaders can recognize that though they have a position of authority, this is not to be wielded harshly. There should not be an attitude of competition or oppression among believers. And church leaders from other regions may be useful in mediating a conflict according to biblical principles.

The reconciliation that rebuilds trust is vital in times of conflict, but it must be built on an already firm foundation of trust and quality leadership.

In 2019, Jamil and his family fled fighting in the North and tried to settle as IDPs in the South. The war followed them south as secessionists, the Southern Transitional Council (STC), evicted the internationally recognized government. The government fought back, and conflict erupted in the South, with Saudi Arabia and the United Arab Emirates supporting opposite sides of the fighting.

Southerners raged against northerners and violence broke out among civilians in the streets. Northern IDPs, already vulnerable, were kicked out of their homes, evicted from their shops, beaten, and ordered to go back to the North. Jamil feared for his life, more than at any previous time during Yemen's long conflict. His family sheltered with a Muslim family, hoping to ride out the current violence. The men would be easily recognized in the streets as northern, so only the women could go out for food and supplies, hidden behind their scarves and veils.

In August of 2019, the pressure grew, and threats of violence became so intense, Jamil decided the only thing he could do was flee.

---

8. Galatians 6:10

Perhaps the time had finally come for them to leave Yemen. He contacted Yemeni church leaders.

"I have to leave," Jamil said. "We need to evacuate, or we might die. I can get to Cairo, or somewhere else nearby."

The elders discussed the situation and responded by asking Jamil to go to a hotel for a week.

"Take your family, bring the other family with you too," they said. "Go stay at a hotel. Leave your house and go to an area where people don't know you are from the North. After a week, if the situation is still this bad, let's talk about where else you could go in Yemen."

Stressed and shaken, Jamil reluctantly accepted their counsel.

The church sent money to pay for the hotel and food for his family and the Muslim family. They would give it seven days. They moved in and waited.

Miraculously, as though Jesus waved his hand over the nation like he did with the raging storm on the Sea of Galilee, within one day, the southern regions calmed down. Government policy toward northerners became more flexible and took the stance of welcoming those from the North as brothers and sisters rather than enemies. Within two days animosity toward northern Yemenis was quelched by the government's new instructions that there should be no divide between northerners or southerners. Shootings ended. Looting and beatings stopped. The families were able to move about the streets safely and without fear.

"I might have ended up in Egypt," Jamil said. "But I trusted and respected the words of my brothers and sisters. Oh, I disagreed with them! I wanted to run away. But I also trusted them."

These are the marks of the leadership qualities that can carry the Yemeni church through generations. Faithfulness to stay and to support those who stay. Humility to seek counsel, and willingness to submit to trusted leaders even in disagreement. Generosity to stand together with Yemeni Christians and Muslims. This is not a leadership imposed on anyone or that is top-down and hierarchical. It flows from within; it is leadership and authority believers grant to one another as they grow in unity.

~

One of the ongoing focuses of the Yemeni church is identifying, training, and equipping these key leaders. This process never ends, though there is a stable leadership team—the one Jamil is part of and had reached out to. It takes time for people to mature and show evidence of their faithfulness and character. Some people don't want or can't take the pressure of leadership. Some are too fresh out of prison and need to experience trauma healing before taking on responsibility again. Family or political unrest or external struggles may hinder someone's development as a leader.

Leaders may come from surprising places. Foreign Christian leaders would do well to recognize this too. God has spread his gifts throughout organizations and churches and people on purpose.

The church has learned that leadership needs to be localized, meaning each region is represented and has a real voice in making decisions and casting vision, and that no region feels it is being governed by another. This could either lead to competition and envy or to complacency and dependency. At the same time, the regions interact in supportive ways, as in mediation of conflicts, sharing of resources, and standing with one another during times of persecution.

Leadership qualities begin with the qualifications in 1 Timothy 3:1-13 and Titus 1-2. The way couples like Jaad and Athir, Tariq and Buthaina, and Jamil and Hiba manage their families is countercultural. Their families become witnesses of the gospel outside the church and a mode of discipleship inside it. Three other leadership qualities the Yemeni church looks for are faithfulness, humility, and the willingness to accept accountability, as Jamil did when he considered fleeing.

Faithfulness does not mean a person is full of faith or has a more powerful or deeper faith than normal. It means have they exhibited steadiness in life and relationships. Maybe a woman works as a nurse, and she showed up to her job every day for months, even without a salary during the war. She refused to abandon her fellow Yemenis, and that demonstrates a character of faithfulness which she will likely also bring to the church. Tariq and Buthaina are examples of such faithfulness. They visit other families in which the wife may not yet be a believer, and work as a team together. If a husband or wife was imprisoned for several years, Tariq and Buthaina faithfully made sure the family's needs were taken care of the entire time, even at the risk of their own lives.

Salaam could have left Hussein while he was imprisoned—the first time, the second time, the third time, the time he remained behind bars for more than two years. Women all over the world do leave their husbands while they are locked up, or threaten to, or leave and return multiple times. Salaam faced incredible pressure to abandon Hussein during his prolonged imprisonment, yet she remained faithful.

Humility is easily the most important character quality a leader needs. In Matthew 11:29, Jesus says, "Take my yoke upon you, and learn from me, for I am gentle and humble in heart, and you will find rest for your souls." This is the only time in the Bible that Jesus shows the nature of his heart so explicitly. Out of all the traits Jesus could have chosen, he highlighted the importance of a gentle and humble heart. Leadership modeled after Jesus's example exudes gentleness and humility. If you don't have it, find someone who does, and get your people in rooms and conversations and relationships with that humble person. I know this by experience; I am not naturally that person. I can be cocky and competitive and my striving to excel spills over in negative ways at times, especially in my younger days. With men and especially with Yemeni men who will work in partnerships with women, humility is vital.

Saif and Amira are young and newly married but are more effective in evangelism than many of those who lead them. It could be tempting for them to look at what they accomplish and become proud, boastful, or disdaining toward their elders. Instead of insisting, however, that they have a better way of doing things. They are quick to be in accountable relationships and to maintain humility. They are learning even from the mistakes and failures of others, gleaning wisdom to become more effective and to guard against premature persecution.

Accountability means being willing to accept and submit to input from others, particularly other locals. Some might be quick to submit to the input, accountability challenges, and leadership of a foreigner, but will they listen to a Yemeni? With Yemeni women, this sometimes needs to be turned upside down. Can a woman speak her mind openly and honestly, even in a room full of men? Can she speak in a way that is honoring while confidently disagreeing so that her contribution is authentic and well-received?

Jamil did not immediately turn to a Western resource when he considered fleeing Yemen. Instead, he sought the wisdom of Yemeni leaders. He knew and trusted them. He knew they loved him and his family. He accepted their insight, even though it was painful and frightening at the time. These are the kinds of men and women who are leading the Yemeni church into a hopeful, flourishing future.

Yemeni church leaders have not developed their vision or strategy in a vacuum. While in prison, they pray about discipleship plans to help new believers remain faithful in prison. When they are displaced by fighting or persecution, they rely on a trustworthy network of fellow leaders. If someone is hungry or stranded with a Muslim family in a warzone, they model sharing all things in common. They come from families, tribes, and an ancient nation from which they glean leadership principles.

Outside the church, conflict continues to rage across Yemen. But Christians are growing, and the church is spreading. The true religion of caring for the widow and the orphan is tangible. Welcoming a foreigner, or someone from an opposing region, and praying for enemies is practical. Christians' hunger and thirst for justice, and for playing their part in it, grows as suffering increases.

In a time of desperation, the prophet Mohammad urged his followers to seek refuge in Yemen. Fourteen hundred years later, a group that would coalesce into al-Qaeda in the Arab Peninsula sought refuge in Yemen. By God's grace, may this fledgling body of Yemeni disciples of Christ become a refuge in Yemen. A refuge to the weary and sick, the hungry and thirsty, the peacemakers and the wounded. And may all Yemenis taste and see that the Lord is good; blessed is the one who takes refuge in him.[9]

---

9. Psalm 34:8

EPILOGUE

NOW

The book of Acts is often referred to as the story of the "early church." It is also the story of the *beginning* church. How did eleven men and an unspecified number of women transition from following the flesh and blood Jesus to establishing a community to launching a global movement? In writing Acts, Luke made no attempt to gloss over the mess or to downplay the highlights. The book opens with Jesus's followers continuing to fundamentally misunderstand his work. They ask, "Are you going to restore the kingdom to Israel now?" After all that dying and rising from the dead, isn't *now* maybe a good time to give us our political power back?

Instead, Jesus tells them they will suffer, they will be his *martyrs*, witnesses, starting in their hometown and spreading into all the world. Then, Jesus disappears, and they stare after the empty space he left until two angels challenge them: What are y'all standing around for?

The next thing this group does, the first major decision they make as a unit without Jesus, is to face the devastating reality that one of their own had betrayed Jesus and then died by his own hand. They cast lots and replaced Judas. It sounds quick and tidy, but one can easily imagine the grief, confusion, anger, and hurt the disciples likely felt.

This is not a happy starting point. These people are wounded and

stunned. They have been party to the most incredible and most terrifying event in history. They are excited and wary. United and uncertain.
Full of ideas and riddled with questions. They are like all Christians
throughout time. Human, bumbling around to find hope, aligning
themselves with the impossibly risen-from-the-dead Christ, longing for
all things to be made new in the full and glorious coming of the
kingdom of God.

The rest of Acts and the rest of the New Testament are about establishing this motley crew into a flourishing, spreading community. They
learn how to talk about who Jesus was and what he had accomplished.
They learn how to serve both Jews and Gentiles, how to worship
together, how to be peacemakers, and how to address serious sin. They
learn how to establish leaders and what Christian marriages and
parenting and professionals look like. They create meaningful rituals
and write their own music. They fight and disagree and design and
redesign and re-redesign worship gatherings. They also sought reconciliation through dialogue, humility, and the Holy Spirit's guidance. They
discover the power of the Holy Spirit and the unique ways the Spirit
manifests in individuals. They realize that they, the church, are now the
incarnation of the body of Christ on earth.

It is messy and painful, funny and compelling. And when I read
Acts and the letters, I see the Yemeni church's experience: messy,
painful, funny, compelling, and so beautiful.

My role in the church continues to adapt as we discern together. I am
learning to balance empowering locals to lead, while being available to
serve as a consultant, sounding board, and strategic advisor as the
church enters new stages of growth. Nearly every tension faced by the
apostles in the years of the beginning church is mirrored in the modern-
day Yemeni context.

The church is devoted to teaching, fellowship, breaking bread, and
prayer. We have seen signs and wonders, like Tariq's daughter's healing,
like the man whose son was raised from the dead in the hospital, like
families surviving gunfire. Believers have sold their possessions to give to

those who had need, like when Jamila sold her gold to benefit Hussein in prison. Believers gather together in homes and in public spaces where they break bread and eat with glad and sincere hearts, praising God and enjoying the favor of all the people. Well, maybe not *all* the people. But many. And the Lord may not be adding to their number *daily* those who are being saved, but nearly.[1]

There have been arrests,[2] internal strife and betrayal,[3] leaders chosen to serve the needy,[4] martyrs,[5] a scattered church bringing the gospel with them,[6] people abusing the power of the gospel for their own advantage,[7] and on and on it goes as Christians faithfully incarnate the love and presence of God in their communities.

And we long for more.

In the summer of 2024, the church held six family trainings, one men's training, and one women's training. Eight Bible trainings in eight weeks. In this particular network of churches alone, two hundred men, women, and children have come to faith in 2024. What an incredible work of God!

But.

There are approximately forty million Yemenis. That means in the past year, only two hundred of them entered the kingdom of God. Even if we multiply that number by one hundred, and there are twenty thousand new disciples of Christ, that is still not a drop in the bucket. If I lived one hundred years, and each year twenty thousand people came to faith, that would still leave thirty-eight million people who have not experienced the love of God through Jesus.

We are waiting for the explosion.

If I compare the growth of the Yemeni church to Somalia or Bahrain or Qatar, Yemen looks pretty good—pretty successful. But comparison is meaningless because the ambition isn't to be a little bigger than the

---

1. Acts 2:42-47
2. Acts 4
3. Acts 5
4. Acts 6
5. Acts 7
6. Acts 8
7. Acts 9

country nearby or to grow a little faster than the country across the Gulf. We are not satisfied. The vision is to spread the gospel and teachings of Jesus Christ to every family and tribe in Yemen. The DNA of Yemeni Christians is to reach all of Yemen. Strategies that accompany such an audacious goal must reach beyond two hundred people a year, combining human endeavor and faith that all growth ultimately comes from God.

Twenty years ago, if I heard twenty believers met together twice and didn't end in division or jealousy, I would have rejoiced at such a miracle. But always burning in my heart is that there must be more. God made us for more than this. More than twenty believers gathered in peace. More than two hundred new believers. More than eight training sessions in eight weeks.

So, while we celebrate the unprecedented growth, we cannot rest. My roles now include honoring, championing, and being part of envisioning the next strategic move. We honor the people who have come before. This current growth is not built on sand, and we are reaping a harvest from seed sown in blood and tears. We regularly reconnect with foreigners who spent years investing in Yemen and share with them stories of what God is doing. They were clearing out stones and some never met a Yemeni Christian. We look back and honor them.

I champion new visionaries who are thinking to the third and fourth generations, who dream and push forward, who are never satisfied, and who ram through brick walls and over the stony ground.

And I push for a new, creative, and innovative vision. Even when we stop to celebrate, we must remain open to new things God is doing. "See, I am doing a new thing! Now it springs up; do you not perceive it? I am making a way in the wilderness and streams in the wasteland."[8]

None of the church leaders want a movement in Yemen that fizzles out in twenty years because there are weak roots, absent elders, and a reliance on foreign money or leadership. We don't want to see a church built on the hay and straw promises of Western visas, financial stability, or a persecution-free life. We long to see God establish God's church on a solid foundation with Jesus Christ alone as the cornerstone. Not a

---

8. Isaiah 43:19

certain style of worship or a charismatic preacher. I can spout off all the principles we've learned and the methods we've implemented, but none of that matters if Jesus is not the center.

"If I speak in the tongues of men or of angels but do not have love, I am only a resounding gong and a clashing cymbal. If I have the gift of prophecy and can fathom all mysteries and all knowledge, and if I have a faith that can move mountains, but do not have love, I am nothing. If I give all I possess to the poor and give over my body to hardship that I may boast, but do not have love, I gain nothing.

Love is patient, love is kind. It does not envy, it does not boast, it is not proud. It does not dishonor others, it is not self-seeking, it is not easily angered, it keeps no record of wrongs. Love does not delight in evil but rejoices with the truth. It always protects, always trusts, always hopes, always perseveres.

Love never fails."[9]

There is no one who embodies love perfectly, other than Jesus Christ, the Word of God made flesh who dwelled among us. This Jesus is the center, the cornerstone, the rock on which the Yemeni church is built, and the gates of hell will not overcome it.

Yemen, redolent with frankincense and myrrh, home to wisdom seekers like the Queen of Sheba, land of ancient dams and modern tensions, rich with vibrant hospitality, where men sing praises to Jesus while gripping medieval-looking curved daggers and women ululate in celebration at seaside baptisms, Yemen's people captured my heart. They invaded my ideas of security and comfort and demonstrated that living a faithful life with God will never be easy but will always be deeply good. Walking with Jesus alongside Yemenis has upended my concepts of what church is, of what faith can expect, and has proven the beauty of the gospel. I am converted daily into loving Jesus more, through the gift of being part of the church in Yemen.

In *Arabs in the Shadow of Israel*, Tony Malouf writes, "it was an established fact in the ancient world that all of Arabia spread a very delicious fragrance, and that South Arabia in particular was the aromatic

---

9. 1 Corinthians 13:1-4

country 'par excellence.'"[10] He is referring to the incense trade Arabia Felix was famous for throughout history.

Yemeni Christians have inherited this fragrant legacy, and they are carrying it forward in their own bodies. *For we are to God the aroma of Christ among those who are being saved and those who are perishing. To the one we are the smell of death; to the other, the fragrance of life.*[11] May they be the fragrance of life to millions, and may other Yemenis, Arabs, and people around the world look at Yemeni Christians and say, like the magi, probably Yemeni wise men, in Matthew 2, "We have seen the star of the one born king and have come to worship him."

---

10. Tony Maalouf, *Arabs in the Shadow of Israel: The Unfolding of God's Prophetic Plan for Ishmael's Line* (Grand Rapids, MI: Kregel Publications, 2003), 209.
11. 2 Corinthians 2:15

APPENDIX A: GLOSSARY OF ARABIC TERMS

Alhamdulillāh – Praise be to God.
al-Masīḥ - The Messiah; Christ.
Akhdām - Marginalized Yemeni caste, literally servant
Bandora – Tomatoes (Levantine dialect).
Balṭo – Black floor-length robe
Bint al-Ṣaḥn - Buttery layered bread drizzled with honey
Bukhur – A general term for incense, especially blended incense
Dhimmi- A non-Muslim living under Islamic rule who was granted protection and religious freedom in return for paying the jizya tax.
Dhuhr - Noon
Eid – Holiday
Fool – Strings of jasmine
Gamarias - Intricately latticed windows
Injil – Gospels, also New Testament
Insha'Allah - If God wills
Janbiyya - A traditional curved dagger worn at the waist by Yemeni men as a symbol of cultural pride and social status.
Jinn – Supernatural beings in Islamic belief
Jizya- A tax historically paid by non-Muslims living under Islamic rule in exchange for protection and exemption from military service.

Kafan - A simple white shroud used to wrap the body in Islamic funerals.

Kanisa – Church

Khalas – Finished

Lithma – A face-covering worn by Yemeni women

Luban – A type of raw incense (frankincense).

Maʿawaz - Yemeni men's wrap skirt.

Maqluba - Upside-down rice dish.

Mashaddah - Yemeni headwrap or turban.

Masīḥī – Christian, believer

Mawlid - celebration of the prophet Muhammad's birthday.

Maglis – A Middle Eastern, Arab-style sitting room

Mukassar – Broken or shattered

Muta'wa'a – Fundamentalist or strict moral enforcer.

Naṣrānī - Another word for Christian, often derogatory.

Qadr Allah – God predestined it

Qahwa - Coffee

Qat - A leafy amphetamine commonly chewed by men and women in Yemen and the Horn of Africa.

Rashūsh - A soft, round, often slightly leavened bread, traditionally cooked on a griddle or clay stove.

Salat - Islamic ritual prayer performed five times daily

Sahawaq - A spicy and flavorful condiment made from a blend of fresh herbs, chili peppers, garlic, spices, and at times, cheese. It is widely used as a dip or sauce.

Sayyid - A person who is considered a direct descendant of the prophet Muhammad, often holding a respected status in Islamic societies, particularly in Yemen.

Sfiha – A kind of Arab pizza, Arab meat pie or flatbread.

Sheikh - Religious leader, also tribal leader

Shukran – Thank you

Shab – Young man

Takfīrī - One who declares others unbelievers.

'uṣūl - Family background or noble origin

Wadi - Valley

Yalla – Let's go, hurry up

Za'tar - Herb blend made from dried thyme, sumac, sesame seeds, and sometimes other herbs like oregano or marjoram.

STAY CONNECTED

To learn more about specific initiatives or to learn how you can support Yemeni Christians, please email:

info@danielalyamini.com

To continue engaging with the Yemeni Christian community, access resources, or stay updated on new stories and developments, please visit:

www.danielalyamini.com

Follow on social media for stories, updates, and behind-the-scenes insights:

Instagram: @danielalyamini

X: @danielalyamini

We invite you to explore, pray, connect, and share as the story of God's work in Yemen continues to unfold.

ABOUT THE AUTHOR

Daniel al-Yamini has lived and worked in the Middle East with his family since 2003. With a deep love for the people, language, and culture of Arabia, his life and calling have been shaped by the faithfulness of the Yemeni Church and the resilience of its believers.

Daniel is a storyteller, mentor, and disciple maker. His work includes training emerging leaders and supporting multigenerational church planting movements in complex and often difficult contexts.

An Aroma of Life is the fruit of years spent walking with Yemeni Christians—learning from their legacy and listening to the Spirit of God moving in their midst.